A World of
Prose
Third Edition

A World of
Prose
Third Edition

Edited by
Hazel Simmons-McDonald
Mark McWatt

HODDER
EDUCATION
AN HACHETTE UK COMPANY

Hachette UK's policy is to use papers that are natural, renewable and recyclable products and made from wood grown in sustainable forests. The logging and manufacturing processes are expected to conform to the environmental regulations of the country of origin.

Orders: please contact Bookpoint Ltd, 130 Park Drive, Milton Park, Abingdon, Oxon OX14 4SE. Telephone: (44) 01235 827720. Fax: (44) 01235 400454. Email education@bookpoint.co.uk Lines are open from 9 a.m. to 5 p.m., Monday to Saturday, with a 24-hour message answering service. You can also order through our website: www.hoddereducation.com

ISBN 9781510414327

© Hodder & Stoughton Ltd 2017

The CXC logo® and CSEC® are registered trademarks of the Caribbean Examinations Council (CXC).

First edition published 1994
Second edition published 2005 by Pearson Education Ltd, published from 2015 by Hodder Education
This edition published 2017 by Hodder Education

An Hachette UK Company
Carmelite House
50 Victoria Embankment
London EC4Y 0DZ
www.hoddereducation.com

Impression number   10 9 8 7 6 5 4 3 2 1

Year   2021 2020 2019 2018 2017

Typeset by Integra Software Services Pvt. Ltd., Pondicherry, India

Cover illustration by Mehrdokht Amini

Printed and bound by CPI Group (UK) Ltd, Croydon, CR0 4YY

A catalogue record for this title is available from the British Library.

Contents

Preface to students   vii

Raymond's Run   *Toni Cade Bambara*   1

Blackout   *Roger Mais*   8

Shabine   *Hazel Simmons-McDonald*   12

Blood Brothers   *John Wickham*   16

Buried with Science   *John T. Gilmore*   20

Emma   *Carolyn Cole*   27

Two Boys Named Basil   *Mark McWatt*   38

Victory and the Blight   *Earl Lovelace*   53

Child of Darkening Humour   *Noel D. Williams*   61

The Man of the House   *Frank O'Connor*   71

The Day the World Almost Came to an End   *Pearl Crayton*   80

It's Cherry Pink and Apple Blossom White   *Barbara Jenkins*   86

The Boy Who Loved Ice Cream   *Olive Senior*   93

Uncle Umberto's Slippers   *Mark McWatt*   105

The Creek   *Subraj Singh*   117

Georgia and Them There United States   *Velma Pollard*   122

Shoes for the Dead   *Kei Miller*   127

The Girl Who Can   *Ama Ata Aidoo*   133

The Pain Tree   *Olive Senior*   138

Mint Tea   *Christine Craig*   147

To Da-Duh, in Memoriam   *Paule Marshall*   156

Savi's Trial   *Hazel Simmons-McDonald*   166

Mom Luby and the Social Worker   *Kristin Hunter*   177

Berry   *Langston Hughes*   182

The Two Grandmothers   *Olive Senior*   189

What is a short story?   199

Notes and questions   206

Glossary of terms   218

Acknowledgements   222

The following icon is used in this book:

 This indicates the page number of the notes and questions which accompany the story or vice versa.

Preface to students

Dear students,

In this third edition of *A World of Prose* we have increased the number of stories to 25 and we have replaced seven of the stories from the earlier edition. The selections we have added include some stories from recent publications by Caribbean authors. The stories in this anthology are all good examples of the short-story genre* and they reflect the cultural diversity of the countries from which the writers come. This contributes to the overall richness of the collection. Each story is well crafted, and the events are narrated with economy and subtlety of language. In many instances the main characters of the stories are young people who have arrived at an important moment of their lives. You will find that you can empathise and perhaps even identify with some of them.

As with the second edition, we have included a higher proportion of West Indian stories. Those we have chosen use a variety of styles and, in all cases, the subject matter is interesting and not difficult to understand. However, the material is challenging enough to generate serious discussion and it provides scope for the kinds of analysis that CXC requires you to do.

We have not organised the stories around a single unifying theme, and we have not imposed a rigid format on the sequencing of the stories. However, in our selection we have tried to indicate the range of tone and nuance that exemplifies a good narrative style. We hope that the information on each short story that is included at the back of the book will help you to become more familiar with the short-story form, and will be useful to you as you try to interpret and analyse the stories. The section 'What is a short story?' explores the different components or building blocks of this literary form, while the 'Glossary of terms' provides useful explanations of difficult words and phrases associated with it.

In addition, we have included brief notes and questions on each story. The notes provide you with biographical information about the authors. The questions are not exhaustive and do not cover all aspects of the stories that deserve comment and discussion. We have deliberately refrained from providing a long list of questions because we do not want to suggest that only the points we have raised are the ones worthy of discussion. Our questions focus on areas that will, through discussion with your teachers and classmates, help you to begin your exploration of the deeper levels of meaning in the stories. Once started on this process of discovery, you will, no doubt, have questions of your own that you will want to discuss.

* For definitions of words used in this anthology, see the 'Glossary of terms' on page 218.

We hope you will experience many hours of enjoyment from reading these stories we have chosen for you.

Hazel Simmons-McDonald and Mark McWatt

Raymond's Run

Toni Cade Bambara

p.206 I don't have much work to do around the house like some girls. My mother does that. And I don't have to earn my pocket money by hustling; George runs errands for the big boys and sells Christmas cards. And anything else that's got to get done, my father does. All I have to do in life is mind my brother Raymond, which is enough.

Sometimes I slip and say my little brother Raymond. But as any fool can see he's much bigger and he's older too. But a lot of people call him my little brother cause he needs looking after cause he's not quite right. And a lot of smart mouths got lots to say about that too, especially when George was minding him. But now, if anybody has anything to say to Raymond, anything to say about his big head, they have to come by me. And I don't play the dozens or believe in standing around with somebody in my face doing a lot of talking. I much rather just knock you down and take my chances even if I am a little girl with skinny arms and a squeaky voice, which is how I got the name Squeaky. And if things get too rough, I run. And as anybody can tell you, I'm the fastest thing on two feet.

There is no track meet that I don't win the first place medal. I used to win the twenty-yard dash when I was a little kid in kindergarten. Nowadays, it's the fifty-yard dash. And tomorrow I'm subject to run the quarter-meter relay all by myself and come in first, second, and third. The big kids call me Mercury cause I'm the swiftest thing in the neighbourhood. Everybody knows that – except two people who know better, my father and me. He can beat me to Amsterdam Avenue with me having a two fire-hydrant headstart and him running with his hands in his pockets and whistling. But that's private information. Cause can you imagine some thirty-five-year-old man stuffing himself into PAL shorts to race little kids? So as far as everyone's concerned, I'm the fastest and that goes for Gretchen, too, who has put out the tale that she is going to win the first-place medal this year. Ridiculous. In the second place, she's got short legs. In the third place, she's got freckles. In the first place, no one can beat me and that's all there is to it.

I'm standing on the corner admiring the weather and about to take a stroll down Broadway so I can practice my breathing exercises, and I've got Raymond walking on the inside close to the buildings, cause he's subject to fits of fantasy and starts thinking he's a circus performer and that the curb is a tightrope strung high in the air. And sometimes after a rain he likes to step down off his tightrope

1

right into the gutter and slosh around getting his shoes and cuffs wet. Then I get hit when I get home. Or sometimes if you don't watch him he'll dash across traffic to the island in the middle of Broadway and give the pigeons a fit. Then I have to go behind him apologizing to all the old people sitting around trying to get some sun and getting all upset with the pigeons fluttering around them, scattering their newspapers and upsetting the waxpaper lunches in their laps. So I keep Raymond on the inside of me, and he plays like he's driving a stage coach which is OK by me so long as he doesn't run me over or interrupt my breathing exercises, which I have to do on account of I'm serious about my running, and I don't care who knows it.

Now some people like to act like things come easy to them, won't let on that they practice. Not me. I'll high-prance down 34th Street like a rodeo pony to keep my knees strong even if it does get my mother uptight so that she walks ahead like she's not with me, don't know me, is all by herself on a shopping trip, and I am somebody else's crazy child. Now you take Cynthia Procter for instance. She's just the opposite. If there's a test tomorrow, she'll say something like, 'Oh, I guess I'll play handball this afternoon and watch television tonight,' just to let you know she ain't thinking about the test. Or like last week when she won the spelling bee for the millionth time, 'A good thing you got "receive", Squeaky, cause I would have got it wrong. I completely forgot about the spelling bee.' And she'll clutch the lace on her blouse like it was a narrow escape. Oh, brother. But of course when I pass her house on my early morning trots around the block, she is practicing the scales on the piano over and over and over and over. Then in music class she always lets herself get bumped around so she falls accidentally on purpose onto the piano stool and is so surprised to find herself sitting there that she decides just for fun to try out the ole keys. And what do you know – Chopin's waltzes just spring out of her fingertips and she's the most surprised thing in the world. A regular prodigy. I could kill people like that. I stay up all night studying the words for the spelling bee. And you can see me any time of day practicing running. I never walk if I can trot, and shame on Raymond if he can't keep up. But of course he does, cause if he hangs back someone's liable to walk up to him and get smart, or take his allowance from him, or ask him where he got that great big pumpkin head. People are so stupid sometimes.

So I'm strolling down Broadway breathing out and breathing in on counts of seven, which is my lucky number, and here comes Gretchen and her sidekicks: Mary Louise, who used to be a friend of mine when she first moved to Harlem from Baltimore and got beat up by everybody till I took up for her on account of her mother and my mother used to sing in the same choir when they were young girls, but people ain't grateful, so now she hangs out with the new girl Gretchen and talks about me like a dog; and Rosie, who is as fat as I am skinny and has a big mouth where Raymond is concerned and is too stupid to know that there is not a big deal of difference between herself and Raymond and that she can't afford to throw stones. So they are steady coming up Broadway and I see right away that it's going to be one of those Dodge City scenes cause the street ain't that big and they're close to the buildings just as we are. First I think I'll step into the candy store and look over the new comics and let them pass. But that's chicken and I've got a reputation to consider. So then I think I'll just walk straight on through them or even over them if necessary. But as they get to me, they slow down. I'm ready to fight, cause like I said I don't feature a whole lot of chit-chat, I much prefer to just knock you down right from the jump and save everybody a lotta precious time.

'You signing up for the May Day races?' smiles Mary Louise, only it's not a smile at all. A dumb question like that doesn't deserve an answer. Besides, there's just me and Gretchen standing there really, so no use wasting my breath talking to shadows.

'I don't think you're going to win this time,' says Rosie, trying to signify with her hands on her hips all salty, completely forgetting that I have whupped her behind many times for less salt than that.

'I always win cause I'm the best,' I say straight at Gretchen who is, as far as I'm concerned, the only one talking in this ventriloquist-dummy routine. Gretchen smiles, but it's not a smile, and I'm thinking that girls never really smile at each other because they don't know how and don't want to know how and there's probably no one to teach us how, cause grown-up girls don't know either. Then they all look at Raymond who has just brought his mule team to a standstill. And they're about to see what trouble they can get into through him.

'What grade you in now, Raymond?'

'You got anything to say to my brother, you say it to me, Mary Louise Williams of Raggedy Town, Baltimore.'

'What are you, his mother?' sasses Rosie.

'That's right, Fatso. And the next word out of anybody and I'll be *their* mother too.' So they just stand there and Gretchen shifts from one leg to the other and so do they. Then Gretchen puts her hands on her hips and is about to say something with her freckle-face self but doesn't. Then she walks around me looking me up and down but keeps walking up Broadway, and her sidekicks follow her. So me and Raymond smile at each other and he says, 'Gidyap' to his team and I continue with my breathing exercises, strolling down Broadway towards the ice man on 145th with not a care in the world cause I am Miss Quicksilver herself.

I take my time getting to the park on May Day because the track meet is the last thing on the programme. The biggest thing on the programme is the May Pole dancing, which I can do without, thank you, even if my mother thinks it's a shame I don't take part and act like a girl for a change. You'd think my mother'd be grateful not to have to make me a white organdy dress with a big satin sash and buy me new white baby-doll shoes that can't be taken out of the box till the big day. You'd think she'd be glad her daughter ain't out there prancing around a May Pole getting the new clothes all dirty and sweaty and trying to act like a fairy or a flower or whatever you're supposed to be when you should be trying to be yourself, whatever that is, which is, as far as I'm concerned, a poor black girl who really can't afford to buy shoes and a new dress you only wear once a lifetime cause it won't fit next year.

I was once a strawberry in a Hansel and Gretel pageant when I was in nursery school and didn't have no better sense than to dance on tiptoe with my arms in a circle over my head doing umbrella steps and being a perfect fool just so my mother and father could come dressed up and clap. You'd think they'd know better than to encourage that kind of nonsense. I am not a strawberry. I do not dance on my toes, I run. That is what I am all about. So I always come late to the May Day programme, just in time to get my number pinned on and lay in the grass till they announce the fifty-yard dash.

I put Raymond in the little swings, which is a tight squeeze this year and will be impossible next year. Then I look around for Mr Pearson, who pins the numbers on. I'm really looking for Gretchen if you want to know the truth, but she's not around. The park is jam-packed. Parents in hats and corsages and breast-pocket handkerchiefs peeking up. Kids in white dresses and light-blue suits. The parkees unfolding chairs and chasing the rowdy kids from Lenox as if they had no right to be there. The big guys with their caps on backwards, leaning against the fence swirling the basketballs on the tips of their fingers, waiting for all these crazy people to clear out the park so they can play. Most of the kids in my class are carrying bass drums and glockenspiels and flutes. You'd think they'd put in a few bongos or something for real like that.

Then here comes Mr Pearson with his clipboard and his cards and pencils and whistles and safety pins and fifty million other things he's always dropping all over the place with his clumsy self. He sticks out in a crowd because he's on stilts. We used to call him Jack and the Beanstalk to get him mad. But I'm the only one that can outrun him and get away, and I'm too grown for that silliness now.

'Well, Squeaky,' he says, checking my name off the list and handing me number seven and two pins. And I'm thinking he's got no right to call me Squeaky, if I can't call him Beanstalk.

'Hazel Elizabeth Deborah Parker,' I correct him and tell him to write it down on his board.

'Well, Hazel Elizabeth Deborah Parker, going to give someone else a break this year?' I squint at him real hard to see if he is seriously thinking I should lose the race on purpose just to give someone else a break. 'Only six girls running this time,' he continues, shaking his head sadly like it's my fault all of New York didn't turn out in sneakers. 'That new girl should give you a run for your money.' He looks around the park for Gretchen like a periscope in a submarine movie. 'Wouldn't it be a nice gesture if you were … to ahhh …'

I give him such a look he couldn't finish putting that idea into words. Grown-ups got a lot of nerve sometimes. I pin number seven to myself and stomp away. I'm so burnt. And I go straight for the track and stretch out on the grass while the band winds up with 'Oh, the Monkey Wrapped His Tail Around the Flag Pole,' which my teacher calls by some other name. The man on the loudspeaker is calling everyone over to the track and I'm on my back looking at the sky, trying to pretend I'm in the country, but I can't, because even grass in the city feels hard as sidewalk, and there's just no pretending you are anywhere but in a 'concrete jungle' as my grandfather says.

The twenty-yard dash takes all of two minutes cause most of the little kids don't know no better than to run off the track or run the wrong way or run smack into the fence and fall down and cry. One little kid, though, has got the good sense to run straight for the white ribbon up ahead so he wins. Then the second-graders line up for the thirty-yard dash and I don't even bother to turn my head to watch cause Raphael Perez always wins. He wins before he even begins by psyching the runners, telling them they're going to trip on their shoelaces and fall on their faces or lose their shorts or something, which he doesn't really have to do since he is very fast, almost as fast as I am. After that is the forty-yard dash which I used to run when I was in first grade. Raymond is hollering from the swings cause he knows I'm about to do my thing cause the man on the loudspeaker has just announced the fifty-yard dash, although he might just as well be giving a recipe for angel food cake cause you can hardly make out what he's sayin for the static. I get up and slip off my sweat pants and then I see Gretchen standing at the starting line, kicking her legs out like a pro. Then as I get into place I see that ole Raymond is on line on the other side of the fence, bending down with his fingers on the ground just like he knew what he was doing. I was going to yell at him but then I didn't. It burns up your energy to holler.

Every time, just before I take off in a race, I always feel like I'm in a dream, the kind of dream you have when you're sick with fever and feel all hot and weightless. I dream I'm flying over a sandy beach in the early morning sun, kissing the leaves of the trees as I fly by. And there's always the smell of apples, just like in the country when I was little and used to think I was a choo-choo train, running through the fields of corn and chugging up the hill to the orchard. And all the time I'm dreaming this, I get lighter and lighter until I'm flying over the beach again, getting blown through the sky like a feather that weighs nothing at all. But once I spread my fingers in the dirt and crouch over the Get on Your Mark, the dream goes and I am solid again and am telling myself, Squeaky you must win, you must win, you are the fastest thing in the world, you can beat your father up Amsterdam if you really try. And then I feel my weight coming back just behind my knees then down to my feet then into the earth and the pistol shot explodes in my blood and I am off and weightless again, flying past the other runners, my arms pumping up and down and the whole world is quiet except for the crunch as I zoom over the gravel in the track. I glance to my left and there is no one. To the right, a blurred Gretchen, who's got her chin jutting out as if it would win the race all by itself. And on the other side of the fence is Raymond with his arms down to his side and the palms tucked up behind him, running in his very own style, and it's the first time I ever saw that and I almost stop to watch my brother Raymond on his first run. But the white ribbon is bouncing towards me and I tear past it, racing into the distance till my feet with a mind of their own start digging up footfuls of dirt and brake me short. Then all the kids standing on the side pile on me, banging me on the back and slapping my head with their May Day programmes, for I have won again and everybody on 151st Street can walk tall for another year.

'In first place …' the man on the loudspeaker is clear as a bell now. But then he pauses and the loudspeaker starts to whine. Then static. And I lean down to catch my breath and here comes Gretchen walking back, for she's overshot the finish line too, huffing and puffing with her hands on her hips taking it slow, breathing in steady time like a real pro and I sort of like her a little for the first time. 'In first place …' and then three or four voices get all mixed up on the loudspeaker and I dig my sneaker into the grass and stare at Gretchen who's staring back, we both wondering just who did win. I can hear old Beanstalk arguing with the man on the loudspeaker and then a few others running their mouths about what the stopwatches say. Then I hear Raymond yanking at the fence to call me and I wave to shush him, but he keeps rattling the fence like a gorilla in a cage like in them gorilla movies, but then like a dancer or something he starts climbing up nice and easy but very fast. And it occurs to me, watching how smoothly he climbs hand over hand and remembering how he looked running with his arms down to his side and with the wind pulling his mouth back and his teeth showing and all, it occurred to me that Raymond would make a very fine runner. Doesn't he always keep up with me on my trots? And he surely knows how to breathe in counts of seven cause he's always doing it at the dinner table, which drives my brother George up the wall. And I'm smiling to beat the band cause if I've lost this race, or if me and Gretchen tied, or even if I've won, I can always retire as a runner and begin a whole new career as a coach with Raymond as my champion. After all, with a little more study I can beat Cynthia and her phony self at the spelling bee. And if I bugged my mother, I could get piano lessons and become a star. And I have a big rep as the baddest thing around. And I've got a roomful of ribbons and medals and awards. But what has Raymond got to call his own?

So I stand there with my new plans, laughing out loud by this time as Raymond jumps down from the fence and runs over with his teeth showing and his arms down to the side, which no one before him has quite mastered as a running style. And by the time he comes over I'm jumping up and down so glad to see him – my brother Raymond, a great runner in the family tradition. But of course everyone thinks I'm jumping up and down because the men on the loudspeaker have finally gotten themselves together and compared notes and are announcing 'In first place – Miss Hazel Elizabeth Deborah Parker.' (Dig that.) 'In second place – Miss Gretchen P Lewis.' And I look over at Gretchen wondering what the 'P' stands for. And I smile. Cause she's good, no doubt about it. Maybe she'd like to help me coach Raymond; she obviously is serious about running, as any fool can see. And she nods to congratulate me and then she smiles. And I smile. We stand there with this big smile of respect between us. It's about as real a smile as girls can do for each other, considering we don't practice real smiling every day, you know, cause maybe we too busy being flowers or fairies or strawberries instead of something honest and worthy of respect … you know … like being people.

Blackout

Roger Mais

p.206
The city was in partial blackout, the street lights had not been turned on, on account of the wartime policy of conserving electricity, and the houses behind their discreet arelia hedges were wrapped in an atmosphere of exclusive respectability.

The young woman waiting at the bus stop was not in the least nervous, in spite of the wave of panic that had been sweeping the city about bands of hooligans roaming the streets after dark and assaulting unprotected women. She was a sensible young woman to begin with, who realised that one good scream would be sufficient to bring a score of respectable suburban householders running to her assistance. On the other hand she was an American, and fully conscious of the tradition of American young women that they don't scare easily.

Even that slinking blacker shadow that seemed to be slowly materialising out of the darkness at the other side of the street did not disconcert her. She was only slightly curious now that she observed that the shadow was approaching her.

It was a young man dressed in conventional shirt and pants, with a pair of canvas shoes on his feet. That was what lent the suggestion of slinking to his movements, because he went along noiselessly; that, and the mere suggestion of a stoop. For he was very tall. And there was a curious look as of a great hunger or unrest about the eyes. But the thing that struck her immediately was the fact that he was black; the other particulars scarcely made any impression at all as against that. In her country it is not every night that a white woman would be likely to be thus nonchalantly approached by a black man. There was enough of novelty in all this to intrigue her. She seemed to remember that any sort of adventure could happen to you in one of these tropical islands of the West Indies.

'Could you give me a light, lady?' the man said.

True she was smoking, but she had only just lit this one from the stub of the cigarette she had thrown away. The fact was she had no matches. Would he believe her, she wondered.

'I am sorry, I haven't got a match.'

The young man looked into her face, seemed to hesitate an instant and said, his brow slightly in perplexity: 'But you are smoking.'

There was no argument against that. Still she was not particular about giving him a light from the cigarette she was smoking. It may be stupid, but there was a suggestion of intimacy about such an act, simple as it was, that, call it what you may, she just could not accept offhand.

There was a moment's hesitation on her part now, during which time the man's steady gaze never left her face. There was something of pride and challenge in his look, and curiously mingled with that, something of quiet amusement too.

She held out her cigarette toward him between two fingers.

'Here,' she said, 'you can light from that.'

In the act of bending his head to accept the proffered light, he had perforce to come quite close to her. He did not seem to understand that she meant him to take the lighted cigarette from her hand. He just bent over her hand to light his.

Presently he straightened up, inhaled a deep lungful of soothing smoke and exhaled again with satisfaction. She saw then that he was smoking the half of a cigarette, that had been clinched and saved for future consumption.

'Thank you,' said the man, politely; and was in the act of moving off when he noticed that instead of returning her cigarette to her lips she had casually, unthinkingly flicked it away. He observed all these things in the split part of a second that it took him to say those two words. It was almost a whole cigarette she had thrown away. She had been smoking it with evident enjoyment a moment before.

He stood there looking at her, with a sort of cold speculation.

In a way it unnerved her. Not that she was frightened. He seemed quite decent in his own way, and harmless; but he made her feel uncomfortable. If he had said something rude she would have preferred it. It would have been no more than she would have expected of him. But instead, this quiet contemptuous look. Yes, that was it. The thing began to take on definition in her mind. How dare he; the insolence!

'Well, what are you waiting for?' she said, because she felt she had to break the tension somehow.

'I am sorry I made you waste a whole cigarette,' he said.

She laughed a little nervously. 'It's nothing,' she said, feeling a fool. 'There's plenty more where that came from, eh?'

'I suppose so.'

This would not do. She had no intention of standing at a street corner jawing with – well, with a black man. There was something indecent about it.

Why didn't he move on? As though he had read her thoughts he said. 'This is the street lady. It's public.'

Well, anyway she didn't have to answer him. She could snub him quietly, the way she should have properly done from the start.

'It's a good thing you're a woman,' he said.

'And if I were a man?'

'As man to man maybe I'd give you something to think about,' he said, still in that quiet even voice.

In America they lynched them for less than that, she thought.

'This isn't America,' he said. 'I can see you are an American. In this country there are only men and women. You'll learn about that if you stop here long enough.'

This was too much. But there was nothing she could do about it. But yes there was. She could humour him. Find out what his ideas were about this question, anyway. It would be something to talk about back home. Suddenly she was intrigued.

'So in this country there are only men and women, eh?'

'That's right. So to speak there is only you an' me, only there are hundreds of thousands of us. We seem to get along somehow without lynchings and burnings and all that.'

'Do you really think that all men are created equal?'

'It don't seem to me there is any sense in that. The facts show it ain't so. Look at you an' me, for instance. But that isn't to say you're not a woman the same way as I am a man. You see what I mean?'

'I can't say I do.'

'You will though, if you stop here long enough.'

She threw a quick glance in his direction.

The man laughed.

'I don't mean what you're thinking,' he said. 'You're not my type of woman. You don't have anything to fear under that heading.'

'Oh!'

'You're waiting for the bus, I take it. Well that's it coming now. Thanks for the light.'

'Don't mention it,' she said, with a nervous sort of giggle.

He made no attempt to move along as the bus came up. He stood there quietly aloof, as though in the consciousness of a male strength and pride that was just his. There was something about him that was at once challenging and disturbing. He had shaken her supreme confidence in some important sense.

As the bus moved off she was conscious of his eyes' quiet scrutiny of her, without the interruption of artificial barriers; in the sense of dispassionate appraisement, as between man and woman; any man, any woman.

She fought resolutely against the very natural desire to turn her head and take a last look at him. Perhaps she was thinking about what the people on the bus might think. And perhaps it was just as well that she did not see him bend forward with that swift hungry movement, retrieving from the gutter the half-smoked cigarette she had thrown away.

Shabine

Hazel Simmons-McDonald

p.207

'Look me here, yu see me? Yu stan up over deh watchin me, yuh tink ah don see you? Look me here. I goin stan up under de light for you to see me good, good. Come from de shadow. Yuh wan tuh see me? Well, come see me.' Justine rose slowly from the old soap box on which she sat. Beneath the full, flared skirt of the red dress she wore most nights and which now cascaded from her hips, he could see the outline of firm buttocks, the slender shapeliness of her thighs. His heart beat faster, as much from excitement as from fear as to what she would do now that she had discovered him. They said she had a vicious temper, that her red hair which hung down to her shoulders in a thick woolly tangle was testimony of that and she could do nothing about it even if she tried.

Once, he had seen her burst through her front door, spitting profanities as she threw stones at the boys who had stood facing her house on the other side of the street, taunting her with the chant they had composed about her, singing it first in Kwéyòl, the local lingo, and then in English.

Lò ek danjan tout sa mwen ni	Gold and silver that I have
Tchwi ek diamants sa mwen pa ni	Copper and diamonds I don't have
Ou wè mwen, ou wè mwen	You see me, you see me
Vini bo mwen, vini bo mwen	Come kiss me, come kiss me
Doudou Jamette.	Darling whore.

And they would press their palms to their mouths and make an exaggerated kissing sound.

Justine had two sons whom she called Gold and Silver. Gold had the reddest crop of thick woolly curls and a shock of red bushy eyebrows that inevitably drew one's eyes to his freckled face, to the surprise of grey eyes and a vulnerable mouth that trembled as though he were always on the verge of tears. Silver was blond, sort of. His straight close-cropped, sun-bleached white hair stood out like spines from his head. He was fearless and would stand on his side of the street giving back taunt for taunt, repeating as a litany the only swear words he seemed to know. 'Chou manma'w, yuh muddath athss,' he would lisp through his large front-toothed gap. Gold would be there too, tugging at Silver's sleeve, trying to pull him away before the words erupted in a war of stone-throwing, or before Justine appeared to end it with her own assault of words and stones, the inevitable slap on Silver's rump and the admonition 'How many times I tell you not to interfere wif dese inyowan? How many times? Now you behavin ignorant like dem. Go inside before I get real vex and cut yu tail.'

'Dey trouble me first, an dey call you jamette. I don want dem to call you dat.' And sometimes, Justine would hug Gold and Silver fiercely as if willing her embrace to erase the taunts, the slurs, the hurts that the residents of Riverside Road tossed her way. She had lived in the two rooms that adjoined the large two-storeyed dwelling at No. 30 Riverside Road as long as she could remember. Her mother was Madame Cazaubon's maid and she had let her live in the servants' quarters with her little girl, Justine. Her mother died when she was seventeen, from what everyone said was too much rum and grief because Misié Cazaubon had never kept his promise to her to acknowledge Justine as his daughter and to send her to Convent School. Instead, he allowed Manm Cazaubon to confine them to the two rooms in the yard and to treat Justine as though she were a servant too. That was the thing that seemed to annoy her mother the most and the times she seemed to get angry were when Manm Cazaubon would order Justine to fetch this or that.

'Pa palé ba li kon sa,' her mother would say sharply. 'Don talk to her like dat. She not your maid, yu hear?'

'Well! And who do you think you're talking to? This is my house, don't you forget that. And you'll never replace me here, slut!' And Madame Cazaubon would swish her skirt and stalk off into the drawing room where she would sit in the high chair next to the window muttering under her breath until Mr Cazaubon got home. Then she would let loose a stream of invective in which she accused him of bringing shame, trials and tribulation into their home and making her the subject of gossip and ridicule among the neighbours on Riverside Road. And Mr Cazaubon would gobble his food, go into his room and shut the door against the high-pitched whine of her voice.

Now Justine stood in the circle of light from the street lamp. One hand on her hip, the other twirling the thick woolly curls at the back of her neck. One strap of her dress fell off her shoulders and even in that faint light he could see the spray of chocolate freckles dotting her skin.

When he was much younger his grandmother, who lived in the house next to the Cazaubons on Riverside Road and with whom he spent the long vacations, had warned him not to tease the Shabine, and if she found out that he had, she would make his bottom spit fire. That was a long time ago when he and Justine were both young. She couldn't have been more than two or three years older than he was. She had always fascinated him and, unknown to his grandmother, he would walk along the river wall to the Cazaubon's back yard and leave a paradise plum on the gate post. He would then climb the Julie mango tree in his grandmother's yard and, from the shelter of the thick spray of leaves, peek to see what Justine would do.

Soon enough, she would come to the fence, take the paradise plum, look directly at the mango tree, pretend that she didn't see anyone, seem bewildered, slowly unwrap the paper, place the paradise plum on the tip of her tongue and slowly curl it back into her mouth. And he would sit motionless on his perch, watching this ritual of unwrapping and savouring, and hold his breath until she went into the house.

Then one year he had come and his grandmother told him on the very first day of his visit that even though he was a grown young man of eighteen, he needed to listen to his betters who knew more than he thought they knew. She warned him again about enticing the Shabine. She told him that while he had been away, Justine's mother had come to complain about his giving of paradise plums and putting ideas in Justine's head and upsetting her life. She wanted him to keep his distance.

Yet, one wet afternoon, while he sat reading quietly in the front room, preparing for his examination, he could hear the rush of the river rising, and he smelt the fragrance of paradise plums and he had the strongest urge to taste one. He crept out of the house and looked into her yard from the shelter of the Julie mango tree. He saw her leaning against the post, looking longingly at the river. Her hair seemed more exuberant, the chocolate freckles more stark against her pale skin. She seemed to sense that she was being observed and turned to stare, for what seemed to him to be an eternity, at the Julie mango tree, and he could see that her stomach was swollen and full of Gold.

He had walked with leaden footsteps back to the house and had picked up his book, but the word *Shabine* filtered into every line of the play he was studying '(Shabine) makes hungry where most she satisfies.' He put down the book and sighed. He wondered why some of the people on the street called her 'Shabine' with such contempt. He knew what the word meant literally. It defined her pale, reddish skin colour, the mass of coarsish red hair that resembled the wool of sheep, the grey eyes that looked directly at him only to glance away coyly, the chocolate freckles.

She wasn't like anyone else he knew; not high coloured like Misié Cazaubon, or white like the sailor he saw her mother usher surreptitiously into her house the last time he had visited, and certainly not Negro like her mother. She was a blend, a half-breed and to him more beautiful because of her difference. As the words 'Shabine makes hungry' filtered into his thoughts again, he began to feel angry at the boys who taunted her by tossing the words *Shabine* and *Jamette* at her every time she passed by. He felt angry at the distance between his grandmother's yard and hers, at the fact that no matter how often he traversed the wall space between their yards he would never be able to enter there; angry at the waste of paradise plums he had left for her to pluck off the post in her yard, and angry at the mother for inviting the white stranger in.

As he stood now, watching her beneath the lamp, he wondered whether she too smelt the fragrance of paradise plums. She turned to face him directly where he stood in the shadow.

'Yuh see me?' she asked softly. 'Yuh see me? Maybe yu wan come kiss me too? Maybe?' She stared hard and long at him while his heart raced and the sound thundered so loudly in his ears he thought she must hear it. Then she turned, shoulders drooping, and walked slowly back through the gate into the room in the yard and shut the door.

And he thought that if things had been different, if there wasn't that stretch of wall between his house and hers, that if in those early days they could somehow have claimed the afternoons by the river, savouring the paradise plums together, that perhaps, just perhaps, there might have been plenty of Copper.

Blood Brothers

John Wickham

p.207 The sun was boiling hot and the house was stifling him, so Paul took his pencils and his water colours and went to sit under the casuarina trees. The air was still and it shimmered in the noonday heat and Paul felt sleepy, but he fought against the sleep; and, gripping the pencil in his fingers, set about the sketch he was about to make. The picture he wanted to paint he could see in his mind more clearly than with his eyes. For all of his thirteen years, he had seen the things he was seeing now and they were etched in his memory, an indestructible part of him, indivisible from himself and his own thoughts, a part of him that not even his twin brother Benjy and his insufferable complex of superiority could destroy. The long grass bent in the wind, the hibiscus flowers shone violent red in the sunlight and the casuarinas swayed and spoke in sibilant whispers. It was cool under the casuarinas and Paul stuck the pencil in his mouth and, lying flat on his back, looked up through the gossamer lacework of the trees' foliage to the sky.

Funny, thought Paul, that in the daylight casuarina trees could be so tall and graceful and slender and lovely, swaying in the wind and bending, whispering ever so languidly like lovely ladies in pictures; and yet at night, by starlight and moonlight, they assumed such fantastic, frightening, ghostlike shapes.

Casuarinas at night! Paul shuddered at the memory. He and Benjy had set out for a walk with their father after dinner one night. Paul remembered even now, after six or seven years, that the moon was rising when they left home and Benjy had been in even gayer spirits than usual; he had just discovered that he could whistle. Paul remembered too that Benjy's laugh had mocked him because he had not yet learned to whistle, and he had been silent at this added proof of his brother's superiority. He hated Benjy for this small triumph and for his sneering contemptuous way of being able to do everything better than he; for treating him with his air of studied disdain, as if he were a little girl who had to be helped over fences, who wasn't expected to climb trees and bring down birds with catapults, and who would burst into tears for nothing that he, Benjy, could understand.

Paul remembered that, when they had turned into Garnet Road, the casuarina shadows were lying across the road in fantastic shapes, delicate shadow, diffuse in the soft light, weird and macabre; and the wind was whispering thinly through the trees with the unearthly voice of a ghost. The whole picture was faintly lit by the spectral light of the moon slanting through the trees, and he had been afraid.

He had clutched his father's hand and his father had, it seemed, understood that he was afraid and had squeezed his hand in reassurance. Only Benjy, unaware and unafraid, hopped and danced along the road, exploiting his newly discovered whistle and flaunting his own complete lack of fear, his own blatant intrepidity in the face of the wraithlike shadows and the ghostly voices of the trees. As Paul pieced together the memory of long ago, his heart filled with a full-blooded hate for his blood brother.

Paul looked up through the trees at the sky and knew that in Benjy's eyes he was a coward. It was no solace to his wounded spirit to know that Benjy had never called him coward. His brother's own lack of fear, his recklessness and his arrant devil-may-care swagger was, to him, an unspoken insinuation of his own cowardice, and he felt the stigma of his own timidity each time Benjy and he played together, his self-contempt and distaste for his own chicken-heartedness implicit in his slavish, albeit unwilling, hero worship of his twin brother.

Paul hated Benjy with a bitter passionate venom; and with all his heart's fierceness, he hated and despised himself for hating him. In quiet moments, as now, alone with himself staring up at the blue pool of the sky or sketching on the hill with the wind in his ears, it was easy for him to love his brother as himself. When he rose early in the morning and walked through the dew-wet grass to his spot on the hill, he wished that Benjy could be with him: he would like to talk to him, to tell him that he really wasn't a coward, that there were all sorts of queer little goings on inside him, that he knew the way of the blue mist on the green hills, the way of the white pigeons flying in joyous circles around the house. He yearned with every fibre of him, with a fervour not damped by these many years of vain wishing to share with Benjy the secret ways of his heart. He wanted to link arms with Benjy, to tap from his limitless reservoir of courage some measure of it for himself, so that the two of them could walk together as one. He yearned for this so deeply that he was afraid, afraid that Benjy, 'the little man', so universally applauded for his daring, so consistent in his acts of heroism – climbing to the top of the tamarind tree careless whether he fell, daring to crawl under the house to search for the hens' eggs in the darkness, breaking his arm and betraying not so much as a wince when the doctor at the hospital set it – afraid that Benjy would reject his offer and interpret his overture as another proof of his cowardice. Paul hugged his secrets close and retired into himself, his thought buried so deep inside him that they turned sour and the germ of his potential love turned to bitter hate.

Sometimes, the violence of his hate frightened Paul and he trembled, unable to contain within his frail body the seething tumult of his inner conflict – the love he bore his brother, the admiration he had for his popularity and the twinkling smile in his eye contending in his heart with his own envy, the timid sense of his own timid spirit and his own tongue-tied shyness; and out of the turmoil inside him, there sprouted his own violent hate, deep and morbid because it was rooted and nurtured in the fertile compost heap of his own unavowed love. And always, Paul hated Benjy's presence for reminding him of the night of the ghostly shadows and the thin whisper of the casuarinas.

Benjy sauntered through the back gate, his teeth biting deep into a piece of bread. Paul guessed that he had rifled the larder; for Benjy, it seemed to him, would do that and glory in the doing. Benjy swaggered past Paul, lying on his back under the trees, in an exaggerated goose step of triumph, secure and unassailable in the citadel of his own good humour and blithe spirit, never dreaming that there could be anyone in the whole wide world who did not wish him well, and caring less than a row of pins for anyone who wished him evil. Paul's hate grew big. Look at him, he said to himself, strutting like a cock; he knows I'm watching him, he's only pretending that he doesn't care.

Benjy sat under the tamarind tree and finished his bread. When he had finished, he got up and began throwing stones idly across the pasture. He grew tired of this after a short while and Paul's eyes were on him when he tossed his head in defiance of the boredom that was setting in. He called out to Paul; 'See who can throw farthest!' he shouted.

'No,' Paul answered back. His voice was abrupt and held no hint of the longing in his heart to share games with Benjy. 'And besides,' he went on in an effort to prove himself superior, 'it's farther.'

The hint was, to Benjy, like water off a duck's back. He ignored it and started to climb the tamarind tree.

'Let's play Tarzan,' he invited, letting out the apeman's blood curdling yell.

Paul did not bother to answer. He sat brooding on his brother, and his hate flooded through his body and the blood pounded in his ears.

'Let's go over to Mac,' he suggested, undeterred and with his sunniest smile in spite of Paul's refusals; and Paul, because in the end Benjy always made him do what he wanted, subjected his will and walked along with Benjy.

Mac was the old shoemaker in the village and his shop was the meeting place of the boys during the holidays. Today the shop was empty, except for Mac, who was sitting on his little bench at the door stitching a shoe. The twins strolled into the tumbledown shop.

'Hello, Mac,' said Benjy, and went through the back door to the guava tree in the yard.

'Hello, Mac,' said Paul, and took a seat on the floor behind the shoemaker's back.

'Hello, boys,' said Mac, and went on with his stitching.

Paul picked up one of Mac's awls and began making holes in an old piece of leather he found on the floor. Benjy, out in the yard, was tearing off the bark of the guava tree with his teeth and pretending he was a wild animal.

A few minutes passed. Then Benjy shouted, 'Come and play, Paul.' But Paul did not answer, he only sat idly punching holes in the piece of leather with the sharp awl. Benjy strolled back into the shop. Paul felt him enter but he didn't look up, he just went on pushing the awl through the leather and pulling it out again. Benjy walked across to him and touched him on the shoulder.

'Oh, come and play,' he pleaded.

At the touch of his brother's hand, Paul's blood surged within him and all the pent-up hate and fear and envy, all the accumulated jealousy and worship of the years flooded through him. His blood was hot inside him and he was blind with anger. He dropped the piece of leather from his hand and with one violent push, hurled Benjy into the corner. He ran across the room and stood over him, the awl poised in his right hand for a swift murderous blow.

Then he saw the look of incomprehension on his brother's face, the look of why, what have I done, the look of puzzlement and surprise, and he saw the wide-eyed look of horror and fear in Benjy's eyes.

The awl dropped from Paul's hand and he turned away.

Mac had not even looked up, so sure was he that the boys were playing, so swiftly had the action moved. Paul passed Mac at his little bench and walked silently home, trembling and confused and frightened by the violence of his action; but purged of hate, and happy in the discovery that his brother also knew fear.

Buried with Science

John T. Gilmore

 p.208

Wilbert Gittens could not take any more of the salt-fish and stodgy corn-meal coucou, thick as half-set concrete, but he tried not to show the disgust he felt. Nevertheless, Judith noticed the minute he put down his fork on the plate.

'You ain't like my food? What the hell give yuh de right not to like my food? Yuh don' pay nothing fuh it!'

'You know the boy ain't got no work, so how he is to pay?' his brother Alfred intervened. 'The times hard, Judith.'

'If he did want work, he could get work. He should go out an' look fuh some, 'stead o' stan'ing up in de yard de whole time lif'ing weights …'

At this point Wilbert decided, not for the first time, that attempts at tact were wasted on his sister-in-law, and got up from the table. As he went out the door, Judith's voice went up through being simply raised in anger to a scream: 'You t'ink yuh goin' be some big body-buil'ing champion, or what?'

Walking up the road, Wilbert reflected that it was not his fault that the firm for which he used to work had gone bankrupt, or that he had only had a job for five months in the two years since he had left school. Jobs were not like the recent rains, coming down from the sky bucket a drop. What he would like was a second-hand van, and a lawnmower and a few tools, and he could start up a little landscaping business. There would be plenty of work round all the Parks, and Heights, and Gardens, and Terraces, that were building these days. But right now he didn't even have the money to go into town and see what kind of action was showing at the cinema. Alfred was still paying off the bank for that shiny car he got, and couldn't afford to help him out, even if Judith would let him.

Sammy Pinder and his great-uncle Ernest Cadogan were sitting at the table when Wilbert came into the rum-shop. Ernest had worked on the nearest plantation all his life, and was not what you would call rich, but he had children overseas who would send him a money order from time to time and he was always prepared to buy a drink for the boys. As Wilbert sat down, he pushed an ice-cold bottle of stout over to him. 'Fire one wid muh.'

There was a crowd round the pool table at the other end of the shop, but it was still early and the news was just coming over the TV which was fixed above the bar.

'… and local archaeologists excavating the foundations of a prehistoric house today reported a sensational discovery. They found the skeleton of what is believed to be a young man who died some one thousand years ago. Buried with the skeleton were a number of items, including a small gold plaque bearing what may be the representation of a bat. This is the first piece of Amerindian gold to be discovered in the Eastern Caribbean, though one similar piece is known from Jamaica.'

'Topping our regional stories, Trinidad garment manufacturers today …'

'Dah is a bat?' was Sammy's incredulous comment on the picture which briefly appeared on the screen.

'Dey don' mean a cricket bat, yuh molly-booby,' said Wilbert.

'I ain't such a idiot, Wilbert. I know is suppose to be a leather-bat, but it still don' look like needer one to me.'

'But why dey must go an' dig up a dead just to get a little piece o' gold,' said Ernest, adding some more rum to his rum and coke, 'dah is wha' I don' un'erstand.'

'You mean yuh frighten fuh duppies, Uncle Ernest?' giggled Sammy.

'I ain't frighten fuh nothin' in this world, but I know if yuh don' trouble trouble, trouble don' trouble you, an' I know better dan to laugh at what I don' un'erstand.'

'So Ernest, yuh mean if dere was a whole heap o' gold, or money, or something so in a ol' grave, you would just lef' it there?' asked Wilbert.

'If? If?' The old man sucked his teeth as if it was the stupidest question he had heard in his life. 'Yuh know de wall-in place dey got in a cane-piece 'bout half a mile from here wid de t'ree tombs in it?' Wilbert and Sammy nodded. 'Well, when I did a small boy, my fader help to carry ol' Massa Duke in he lead coffin an' put he in one o' dem. "I am to be gathered unto my people: bury me with my fathers," he said, like Jacob in God's Holy Book. He was de las' o' he fambly tuh own de plantation. Dem tombs full up wid de ol'-time white people an' don' let nuhbody fool you is only ol' nigger believe in obeah, 'cause dey got plenty white people believe in it too, an' all o' dem up dere is buried wid science. De reason de Dukes don' have de plantation nuh more is because ol' Massa Duke granfader fader so blasted greedy he tek most o' de fambly money when he gone. It say plain as anyt'ing, write up 'pon top de tomb, dat he buried wid all his particulars.' Ernest emphasized each syllable of the word, tapping his finger on the table in front of the boys. 'But nuhbody goin' interfere wid it.' He took a large gulp of rum and coke and refilled his glass. 'Solly Brathwaite go looking for it, an' dey have to come an' tek he away an' put he in de Mental. Rawle Skeete go looking for it, an' a Jack o' Lantern come for he, an' carry he all cross de canefields, till he fall down a suck an' brek he blasted neck. You never hear bout Jack o' Lanterns?'

'Of course, man,' said Wilbert, contemptuously. 'Muh mudder nuse to tell we bout dem, tuh mek sure we ain't get too far from de house at night.' He did not feel it necessary to add that he had once believed these tales of mysterious lights which led the unwary to their doom.

'So yuh can see,' Ernest continued, unruffled by Wilbert's tone, 'dat when it got money buried in graves, yuh best lef' it alone, 'cause all o' dem buried wid science. Now,' he stood up, finishing his drink, 'I gwine home.'

The boys watched the old man leave, and then looked at each other in silence for a moment. It was Sammy who spoke first.

'Yuh t'ink it really got money up dere?'

'It ain't gwine do us no harm to check it out.'

'Yuh mean – go inside de tomb?'

'Yuh frighten fuh duppies, Sammy?'

'No man, I ain't believe in none o' dat foolishness.' He paused, and then asked, 'What kind o' particulars it would mean, Wilbert?'

'I ain't know. Could be gold, or di'mon's, or a ches' full o' silver dollars, like in all o' dem pirate stories. Dah is it – a coffin full o' silver dollars. How yuh would like dat? Or of course it could jus' be a big rock. But you listen to me –' He dropped his voice, though what with the television and the noise which they were themselves making, the pool-players would have been hard put to eavesdrop. 'Anyt'ing up dere is fuh we two self, an' nuhbody else is to know wha' plans we mekkin. Yuh hear muh?'

Sammy was a little startled to learn that they were in fact making plans, but he nodded, and Wilbert continued. 'Tonight is Saturday night, an' dere goin' be too much people 'pon de road de whole week-end. Monday night we meet at de place –'

'Wait, Wilbert – you mean we is to go in a tomb 'pon de night-time?'

'Sammy, we ain't want nuhbody to know what we is doing! I thought yuh did tell muh you ain't scared o' duppies?'

'I ain't scared! But why we can' go long dere togeddah?'

Wilbert steupsed in exasperation. 'Yuh want we to lef' de village togeddah? An' walk out to de canefields at night? You does want everybody to t'ink we funny? We goin' meet at de place. Eleven o'clock should be late enough. I can bring a flashlight an' some mason tools I got from when I was working, an' you mus' bring a collins. An' have de sense to wrap it up in a crocus bag, yuh hear?'

By now Sammy was feeling rather the way he had felt when, at the time he was ten and Wilbert was eleven, Wilbert had persuaded him to take part in stealing mangoes off the Rector's tree and they had got caught. But there was nothing to do except nod assent once more.

'Besides,' continued Wilbert cheerfully, 'We might want de crocus bag to carry home what we goin' find.'

******

And so it was that a quarter past eleven on the Monday night found Sammy standing by a wall twenty yards into a field of half-grown canes. He was alone, though he had purposely come late in hope of finding Wilbert already there. A sliver of moon hung in the sky, thin as the handle of a tinnin' cup; it cast bizarre shadows without providing any real illumination. There was a sudden noise: the crack of a broken branch being trodden on.

'Lord, Wilbert! Is you!'

'Yeah man. I had to wait fuh Alfred and dah nasty woman to go to sleep. Come round away from de road-side.'

The wall was barely five feet high, and the top was broken in places, so that it was easily scaled. The enclosure was some thirty feet by thirty, and, unlike the carefully cultivated canefield which surrounded it, was overgrown with long grass and bush. Wilbert demanded the collins from Sammy and switched on the lamp he had brought with him, a large battery-operated affair which boasted two twelve-inch fluorescent tubes. With this in one hand and the collins in the other, he worked his way through the obstruction to where a substantial tree grew out of an altar tomb. The inscription on the top was reasonably intact, though cracked and broken by the tree's roots, but Wilbert did not need to understand the Latin elegiacs which proclaimed the many virtues of a long dead slave-owner to realise

23

that this was not what he was looking for. A large vault nearby bore a small oval of marble with a set of initials and a date: there appeared to be nothing else.

Some distance away, another vault was built into a corner of the enclosure. Wilbert made his way over to it, and climbed on to its roof, which sloped upwards to a large flat surface.

'Sammy! Come here, nuh.'

Although it meant moving from one side of the enclosure right over to the other, Sammy came. At least Wilbert was where the light was.

The top of the vault was a large blue marble slab. With the aid of the lamp the inscription was perfectly legible:

Sacred to the Memory of

the Honble Alured Popple Duke,

for many years a member of

His Majesty's Council

in this Island,

who departed this life 23rd Octr 1795,

in the 72nd Year of his Age.

His remains at his own particular

desire were deposited

in this place.

'You see dat?' said Wilbert. 'I see de word "particular", but I ain't see nothing about no "particulars".'

He climbed down again, Sammy following, and moved round to where a cutting some three feet wide led down to the vault's entrance. It was lined with coral-stone blocks and there was a set of steps of the same material.

'Hand muh de bag o' tools.'

By the time Sammy returned, Wilbert was already at the bottom of the steps, with only his head and shoulders above ground level. The vault was built of irregular pieces of coral stone, cemented over to give a smooth finish. An arch of about a man's height provided the entrance; it was completely filled in, with no gaps visible, although in one or two places the cement had come away to reveal the stone underneath. Weeds had taken root in a number of cracks, and there were about six inches of earth and decaying vegetable matter under Wilbert's feet. He ignored Sammy's suggestion that there might be centipedes, and made him hold the lamp while he himself took a hammer and chisel to the top of the arch. Several pieces of cement came away in large chunks, but it was soon apparent that the masonry behind was solidly constructed and not going to yield easily. After a few minutes Wilbert said, much to Sammy's relief, 'Dis ain't no use. Lewwe go home.'

******

The young men were not disposed to tell anyone else what they had been doing, and that might have been the end of it, had it not been for the fact that, when they met again on the Wednesday evening, Ernest insisted on telling a long and involved story about another victim of Jack o' Lanterns. He wound it up by remarking how strange lights had been seen round the canefield graveyard only the previous night.

Wilbert's interest was immediately aroused. 'Last night yuh mean? Yuh certain it was last night?'

'Last night fuh true! Is Ottokar Boyce tell me so, an' you know as how he is a man that don' drink,' was the reply.

As soon as Ernest had gone home to his usual early bed, Sammy found himself agreeing to another nocturnal expedition. After all, as Wilbert put it, 'If somebody was round dere last night, since we was dere, it must mean dey know somet'ing about what in de tomb, an' I ain't see why dem should have what should belong to we.'

They got there to find that the top half of the entrance to the vault had been neatly covered with fresh cement, in which a large cross had been incised.

'Well, I can tell yuh it ain't no Jack o' Lantern do dat,' was Wilbert's comment. 'Hol' de light fuh muh.'

The new cement was only a thick layer, and the stone blocks filling the arch had been loosened. As Wilbert managed to pull one of them out, Sammy gave a shriek.

Inside the vault, just at eye-level, was a skull. A few wisps of reddish-brown hair still adhered to the temples.

'Don' mek summuch noise,' said Wilbert, taking the lamp from Sammy and peering inside 'He dead. He ain't goin' trouble yuh.'

He returned the lamp, and continued to remove the stone blocks down to the point where the old workmanship proved as solid as ever. Four piles of coffins filled the vault, four or five on top of each other in each pile, most of them lead. The weight of those above had caused several of the lower coffins to collapse, so that the piles were all askew. The skull which had alarmed Sammy was perched on one corner of a coffin which leaned over at a considerable angle.

Making Sammy hold the lamp closer to the entrance, Wilbert climbed into the vault and examined its contents more closely. Where to begin? A child's coffin on top of the right-hand pile seemed to be the obvious answer. It was heavy, but not too hard to shift. He passed it out to Sammy, who took it with reluctance, putting down the lamp in order to do so. They brought it up to the top of the steps and shone the lamp on it.

It was copper, rather than lead, and a name and a date were punched on the top: Abigail Thomasina Duke had died more than a century earlier at the age of fourteen and a half months. Along one of the seams the rivets had come undone, and Wilbert was able to push back the top of the coffin, which turned out to be filled with plastic bags. Unaware that this might be an anachronism, he took one out and opened it, finding several smaller bags. Only when he undid one of these did he let out a startled 'Jeezus! You know wha' dis is?'

'Dat is de particulars?' said a puzzled Sammy, staring at the fine white powder.

'Boy, you really is a idiot. Come, we better run an' call de police.'

They telephoned from Sammy's mother's house. The Station Sergeant was not pleased to be disturbed with such a Nancy story at that time of night, and it was with the greatest difficulty that Wilbert managed to persuade him to send around a car and two constables to investigate. When they saw the contents of the coffin, however, they radioed for Central at once.

The police gave the boys a stern lecture about grave-robbing, but in due course paid out a substantial reward, even though it proved impossible to discover who had hidden what turned out to be the largest cache of illegal drugs ever found in the island. Sammy and Wilbert each bought a brand new bicycle, and a senior police officer got Wilbert a steady job as a gardener. Judith is no longer quite so nasty to him, and he will soon be able to buy that second-hand van.

Emma

Carolyn Cole

p.208

My last fifty cents. She'll never hit me. She wants to tonk out. That's why I'd rather play with Maria. Grown-ups get tired too fast. And when they get tired they can think of zillions of ways to end a good game. Maria would have hit me. And if she'd won my last quarter, she would loan me some more. The game would never end. Never, not until a grown-up would say, 'You've got to go to bed now.' Maria told me that is Emma's favourite.

Maria knows a lot of things, especially about Emma. I do, too. We've decided to be just like Emma when we grow up. We'll play games with the children, read stories to them, take them shopping and to New Orleans. Even when their daddy doesn't want them to go. We'll let them dress up in our pretty red dresses and long white beads. Not the long ones that hang all the way down to your waist. Not those kinds. Not like the lady at the train station.

When we're grown up, we'll go to dinner and to parties. We'll wear long black dresses with real wide skirts. Skirts that spread way out like umbrellas when you spin around. And we'll wear lots of sparkling jewellery. We won't leave home until ten at night. And when we come home, it'll be real late – almost the next day. The house will be quiet and real, real dark. The children will be in bed. But we won't forget about them. We'll tiptoe into their rooms and kiss them on their heads. We'll make sure they're still asleep first. That's the way Emma does.

I like the long black dress. It's shiny and it smells good. When Emma walks, it sounds like paper rattling. That makes me think about presents. She always brings presents back for me and Maria, wrapped in real pretty paper. But not Christmas paper. Maria and I will always remember to bring presents for the children. Maria likes the long black dress, too. She says you should only wear it at night like Emma does. I guess the lady at the train station doesn't know that.

The next morning Maria and I will call each other on the phone and talk for hours about the latest dances and our aching feet. I'll say, 'Such fantastic food and wine.' Maria will say, 'We really should do this more often.' I'll throw my head back and laugh. I'll twist my hair around my fingers, get real serious, and ask Maria, 'Was "she" there?' – like Emma does. I asked Maria if 'she' meant the lady at the train station. Suddenly, for no reason, Maria would get this real mean look on her face. She'd press her lips together real tight. 'You've gotta promise to never tell Emma, Dory, or I'll get in trouble.' I asked her what kind of trouble. When she wouldn't tell me, I told her I'd tell Emma. But she grabbed my arm and twisted it real hard. 'I'll break it!' she yelled.

Sometimes she'd squeeze my arm so tight that I thought she was really going to break it. I'd scream real loud and she'd let go. I knew she wouldn't break it. She's my best friend in the whole world. But sometimes I'd keep right on screaming just to see how loud I could scream.

I heard Emma scream one time. Daddy was fussing at her. She picked up the phone. Then she dropped it and just stood there screaming. Daddy tried to cover her mouth like Maria does me. But she bit him. He snatched his hand back real fast. They stood at the end of the bed, staring at each other. I held my breath 'cause I knew that was going to be it. But they just started laughing real crazylike. Just laughing and rolling all over the bed. One day I'm gonna bite Maria. Maybe she'll think it's funny, too. Yeah, she'll think it's funny. She knows it's just a game. She told me about it.

Maria said grown-ups have a special grown-up game to play. That's the game they play with the lady at the train station. I'm not sure how to play this game. All I know is that I want to play on Emma's side. I don't want her to lose this game. She's my mommy. I think it's fair for me to be on her team. So I asked Maria a lot of questions about it. She said what she always does. 'Dory, you ask too many questions. All you need to do is play fair. Like when we play spades. You wouldn't look in someone else's hand and tell that they have the little joker when the big joker is the card that beats everything. Now would you?' I told her no. But when I know who has the little joker I can play my other cards smarter. I told her that, too. All she said was, 'Fine, Dory, fine. You're gonna do what you want to do anyway. You're a spoiled brat and you just want to have everything your way.' She never sounded like herself when she said stuff like that. She sounded like a grown-up. Emma says Maria is growing up. She's nine years old. She said I'll probably sound just like that next year.

Yesterday Maria was trying to work a puzzle. She hates for people to talk to her when she's trying to work those puzzles. But I kept talking anyway, begging Maria to tell Emma just a little bit about the lady at the train station. She said we could give Emma a hint right after lunch. But when she came back, she didn't want to tell Emma anything. I knew it was because of her mama. But she was mad enough already. I don't like it when she gets too mad at me. She always gets mad at me when she's really mad at somebody else. Mrs Robinson must have done something to her when she went home for lunch. She's always doing something to make Maria mad. On Saturday she fixed Maria's hair in corn rows. Maria hates corn rows. Last time Maria asked for sneakers, her mama bought bobos. Mrs Robinson's kind of weird. One time I heard Emma tell Miss Watson that she has a green-eyed monster. I don't know where she keeps him, but I don't go in that house. I don't think Maria knows about him. I don't think she'd go back home if she did.

I felt Emma kick my leg under the table, but not real hard. 'Are you going to play in this life or the next?' she asked me. 'Huh?' I asked. She held up the cards, almost showing me what she had in her hand. 'Do that one more time,' I said. She made a funny face and pressed the cards to her chest, acting like a little girl. She pushed her hair back and looked up at the clock. I knew what she was going to say next. 'We've been playing for an hour, Dory. It's getting late. I think you're tired. You really should go to bed now.' I begged, 'Please, just a little longer, Emma?' Oops, it slipped. I covered my mouth. 'What did you call me, Dorian?' she asked. I told her that I was sorry. That's what Maria and I call her when we're playing grown-up. She kind of smiled and didn't say anything. So it must have been okay. She looked at the clock again. Then she looked at her watch. I knew she was waiting for him. I wondered if he was still with the lady at the train station. I hate it when he makes us wait like this. 'Do you want to do something else, Mommy?' I asked. Before she answered, I said, 'I know what we can do. We can play hang the man.' She shook her head. 'Monopoly?' She shook her head again. 'I know,' I said, 'let's dance.' I stood on my chair to turn on the radio. I knocked over the sugar can. She caught it as it rolled off the counter. She pulled me back down into my chair. 'No, we will not dance,' she said. 'Well, then, here,' I said, pushing the book across the table. 'Let's finish *Little Women*.' She smiled a little bit. I think she was going to do it, but we heard Daddy's car pull into the garage. Emma threw her cards on the table and ran to the back door. She was so happy to see him. She acted like a puppy licking and kissing his face. He was sort of happy to see her. But not happy like when he sees the lady at the train station.

Every night I would sit at the top of the stairs next to their door. Sometimes I could hear him telling Mommy that he loved her. She would ask, 'Only me?' Daddy said, 'You're the only woman in my life, Emma.' They would talk some more and the bed would squeak a lot. I couldn't hear them talking anymore so I would go to my room. I told Maria about it. She said, 'See, I told you, Dory. It's all just a part of the game.' I told her, 'Humph, it's not much of a game to me. I don't like this game at all.' It just seems to me that Emma should know who has the little joker.

The next morning when I woke up Emma was bouncing up and down on my bed singing, 'Wake up, sleepyhead.' I sat up on my elbows so I could see if the sun was in Mr Teddy's cup. When Grandaddy was here last summer, he teased me a lot about staying in bed too long. He said Emma did the same thing when she was a little girl. Grandaddy has lots of funny ideas. He propped Mr Teddy on the rocker and tied my yellow cup on his arm. 'Now, Dory,' he said, 'when the sun is in this cup, it's twelve noon. All little girls should be up by then.' 'Why?' I asked. 'So you won't miss anything,' he told me. When I asked him how he knew it was noon, he said it was because he lived on a farm and farmers just know about these things. Grandaddy told me a long story about farmers. There was a lot of stuff about chickens and getting up early.

I told Maria. She thought I was real smart. Grandaddy said even Emma could tell time by the sun. Maria liked that part a whole lot. That's why she let me teach her how to tell time in Mr Teddy's cup. Grandaddy said this was our little game. We shook hands and all that stuff. I liked Grandaddy. He always came to my room to talk to me. Daddy never came in my room unless it was to get Mommy. I hugged Grandaddy every day that he stayed with us. His gray whiskers stuck in my face, but I hugged him harder anyway. He'd pick me up so I could almost touch the light. Then he'd bounce me on my bed a while and just stand there staring out the window. Sometimes he took his pipe out of his pocket and beat it in his hand. He told me that holding the cup would keep Mr Teddy busy. 'That's funny,' I said, 'cause Mr Teddy needs something to keep him busy, and Daddy said you need something to keep you busy.' That made him laugh. Then he said the strangest thing. He said Daddy was busy enough for both of them. Then he called me Emma. Grandaddy had a strange look on his face when he said that. 'I'm not Emma,' I told him. 'I'm Dory.' He pulled my braid and said, 'You seem to be one and the same to me, Dory.' I wasn't sure what he meant, but I liked him thinking I was the same as Emma.

We had a real good time that summer. Daddy came home early every night. He even stayed home from work one day. He wore blue overalls like Grandaddy. Emma and I wore some, too. We dug up the backyard and planted a garden. We worked in it all summer, getting dirty and laughing a lot. Maria worked in the garden with us. Mrs Robinson never came over, but Emma sent vegetables to her. Sometimes she sent them back cooked into vegetable pies. I didn't really like them, but Emma and Grandaddy liked them a lot. So I pretended to like them, too. When summer was almost over, Grandaddy went back to his farm. Daddy drove him to the airport early one morning before the sun was in Mr Teddy's cup. Emma sat on the steps with me and Maria and watched them drive away. She started to cry. Maria and I cried, too. I missed him. He made everybody happy at our house. I forgot about the lady at the train station. I think Daddy forgot about her, too.

One day Maria told me that she wanted to live on a farm when she grew up. 'I thought you wanted to be like Emma,' I told her. 'I do,' she said. 'Emma lives here.

You can't live on a farm and be like Emma,' I said. But she told me that she could be Emma when she used to live on a farm. Maria didn't even know Emma then. I asked her how she could do that, but she told me not to worry about it. I didn't have time to worry about it because Emma came to the door talking real fast about new school clothes, a busy day, and hurry.

Mrs Robinson was already in the car when we got to the garage. It didn't take long to get downtown. We went to a lot of shops. Emma had me trying on all kinds of stuff. I lost Maria for a while. I guess Mrs Robinson had her someplace trying on a bunch of stuff, too. We found them and drove to the mall. Maria and I talked about our new clothes. Emma and Mrs Robinson were talking, too. I wanted to listen, but they were so quiet. Besides, Maria kept talking. When we got to the mall, Maria and I went to the arcade. We played Ms Pac Man until we ran out of tokens. 'What do we do now?' I asked Maria. I knew what Maria wanted to do. We said it at the same time. 'Let's go to Gino's and eat with Emma.' I added, 'And your mama, too.'

Emma and Mrs Robinson were sitting out front at Gino's watching the ice skaters. Maria wanted to ice-skate, but I wanted to roller-skate. After she found out that I put her roller skates in the car instead of her ice skates, she was a little bit mad. She kept calling me a brat. It didn't matter as long as I knew she was going to the train station to skate with me. Mrs Robinson and Emma were talking with their heads close together. Emma's black hair and Mrs Robinson's red hair looked pretty. It looked like they had one head with two colors. Like Jabo, the downtown clown.

Then Maria said, 'Let's play Emma and Ruby. You can be Ruby and I'll be Emma,' she told me. I like to play grown-up, but I don't like it when I have to be Maria's mama. Maria and I got into another fight. She wanted me to be her mama 'cause I'm short like her mama. I might be short like her mama, but I dress like my mommy. When I told Maria that, she just said, 'Well, then, your stupid Teddy Bear could be Emma 'cause it dresses just like her, too.' That made me mad because Mr Teddy is a boy. I yelled at Maria. She got angry and grabbed my arm. She squeezed it real tight. I screamed, but she wouldn't let go. I screamed again. She tried to cover my mouth with her hand. I was going to bite it when her mama yanked her away from me. Mrs Robinson pushed Maria into a chair. 'I'm surprised at you two,' she said, 'making all these loud noises in public.' She didn't sound surprised to me – just long and boring. No wonder Maria wants to be Emma, I thought. Mrs Robinson kept talking on and on. I kept waiting for her to stop, but it was taking a long time and Maria was making some awful faces. Mrs Robinson waved to a lady passing by. I whispered to Maria, 'Okay, you can be Emma.' Maria smiled. Emma touched both of us on the hand and said, 'Now, isn't this much better than fighting?' Mrs Robinson said, 'They're both impossible. You should have both of them, Emma.' Emma smiled and winked at us. 'Maria would pack up and leave with you at a moment's notice,' she said. Emma said, 'That would be nice. Dory needs a sister to share her things. It will keep her from being spoiled.' I said, 'I'm not spoiled, Mommy.' She pulled my braid, 'You're not spoiled too bad,' she said. I pushed her away. I always pretended not to like it when she did that. It always made her do it again.

The waitress came over to our table. I was already waving my hand, telling everybody that I knew what I wanted. Maria squeezed my hand under the table. I pulled it away, trying to pretend I didn't know what she wanted. Then she kicked my knee. I knew what she wanted then. I licked my tongue at her. She grinned at Emma. 'You order first. I'm having whatever you have.' So Emma ordered a hot fudge sundae and a glass of water. Mrs Robinson said, 'Does that mean you and I are on a diet, Dory?' I mumbled, 'I guess so.' She ordered frozen strawberry yogurt and coffee. Mrs Robinson went to the bathroom. When Maria wasn't looking, Emma fed me her sundae, drank my coffee, and ate that awful yogurt. When Mrs Robinson sat down again, she smiled at me. 'I see you like yogurt, Dory.' I smiled back and made a face when she wasn't looking. She leaned over and asked Emma, 'Why don't you have another child?' Emma made a face and said, 'Heavens, no! Jack wasn't ready for Dory. We're not going to talk about another baby until he gets the business of Dory straight in his head.' Mrs Robinson said, 'I guess it was a big change for him, from the great player to the great father and husband. That is quite a change.' Emma said, 'I was thinking more of the things that we gave up as a couple.' Mrs Robinson said, 'I can't tell that he's given up anything. It seems to me you've given up everything.' Emma sat back in her chair and looked at Mrs Robinson like she looked at me when she didn't understand something that I had done. I was staring at Mommy. I guess she didn't like that either. She reached into her pocketbook and handed me a deck of cards. 'Play with these and stop listening to my conversation,' she said. I pushed the cards over to Maria. She pulled her face out of her bowl and opened the cards. Mrs Robinson said, 'I could keep Dory for you, sometimes.' Emma said, 'Thank you, but we need to spend time with Dory. Besides, Miss Watson comes whenever I need her.'

Mommy bent down to put her pocketbook on the floor. Mrs Robinson smiled that awful smile. When Mommy sat up she said, 'You know, he's a very handsome man, Emma.' She smiled and drank some coffee. 'He makes good money,' she added. She smiled again and drank some more coffee. Mommy shook her head. 'Yes, he's handsome and he does earn good money.' Mrs Robinson said, 'There's a lot to be said for men and their money.' She smiled a third time and picked up her cup. She touched it to Mommy's glass. 'Here's to a man with money,' she said. 'Wish we all had one.' Mommy snatched her glass back so fast she spilled the water in her lap. Mrs Robinson smiled as Mommy tried to wipe the water off her dress. She kept right on talking like nothing happened. 'And to their ladies of leisure,' she said. Mommy bit down on her lip like Maria does when she's getting ready to twist my arm. She just looked at Mrs Robinson for a long time. Then she said, 'I think we should drink to minority business loans and women who work hard to make men's dreams come true. Or better yet,' she said, 'let's drink to ambitious women who bleed men dry.' She slammed her glass down hard on the table. Mrs Robinson stopped smiling. Mommy looked at me. I was staring at them with my mouth open. I guess she didn't like that either. 'Play with those cards,' she said. She looked up like she was talking to God and said, 'That child will repeat every word of this tomorrow.' I pushed the cards over to Maria. She pulled her face out of her bowl and opened the cards. Mrs Robinson said again, 'I could keep Dory for you sometimes if you'd like to go with your husband more.' Emma said, 'Thank you, but it's like I told you, we need to spend time with Dory.' Maria squeezed my arm. 'Would you please stop staring at them and play cards with me?' I didn't want to play. Something was going on. Emma was getting mad, and Mrs Robinson acted like she wanted her to.

Mrs Robinson said, 'Emma, why don't you put Dory in boarding school or get a live-in housekeeper?' Mommy was looking at the ice skaters. I guess she didn't hear Mrs Robinson. So Mrs Robinson kept on talking. 'I would if it were me,' she said. 'I'd put Maria in a boarding school in a minute.' Maria looked at Mrs Robinson kind of madlike for a long time. You heard that, I thought. Mrs Robinson didn't seem to mind, though. She kept right on talking. 'You better go with him, protect your interest,' she said. 'I'm afraid that's not all there is to it,' Mommy said slowly. 'That's all there was to it when Frank left me,' said Mrs Robinson angrily. 'Jack is a player, just like Frank,' she went on. 'Men like that don't want women and kids. Why don't you admit it? And don't give me that responsibility shit either.' Me and Maria's eyes got real big. We covered our mouths. Ooh! Mrs Robinson said a curse word. Mommy said, 'That's enough, Ruby,' real loud. Mrs Robinson looked real scared then. Maria and I sat real quiet, pretending to put the cards back into the box. Finally Mommy said, 'Come here, Dory.' She held up the prettiest ribbons I had ever seen. They were supposed to be for school, but I talked her into letting me wear mine now. Maria got a present, too. She gave Maria a box of headbands with a lot of different colours, just like my ribbons. It was so funny when Maria told Mommy thank you, 'cause she slipped and called her Emma. I thought it was funny, but Mrs Robinson started fussing at her. She would have fussed a whole lot, but Mommy said, 'Ruby, please, let's not make a big deal of it.' Mommy pushed her chair back and stood up. She had a big wet spot on her pink dress where the water spilled on her. 'I've got a few more things to pick up and I can go home and … and get out of this wet dress.' Me and Maria finished the sentence for her. All of us started laughing, even

Mrs Robinson. I still didn't feel like being around her anymore, so I asked if Maria and I could take the bus to the old train station and skate. Mommy said, 'No,' but Mrs Robinson said she thought it was a good idea. Mommy said, 'Ruby, all kinds of people go there. The worst kinds.' I turned around for her to tie my ribbons. 'Why do you like that place anyway, Dory?' she asked. 'Why don't you let me take you to a nice clean skating rink?' I said, ''Cause I like to skate outdoors.' Maria said, 'Me, too. And I like the smooth pavement. All the kids go there, Mrs York.' Mrs Robinson said, 'See, you have nothing to worry about.' 'Okay, okay,' Mommy said, 'if you like old run-down buildings, rusty pipes, broken windows, and peeling paint, go right ahead.'

Mrs Robinson wanted to come by the train station and pick us up. I told her we could walk home. 'Fine, Dory, just do whatever you want to do.' She sounded just like Maria. After we got our skates from the car they waited with us until the bus came. Me and Maria hugged Emma before we left, but I still didn't feel good about leaving her. I just kept thinking that me and Maria had taken Mrs Robinson's side against her. I would never do that.

I was looking out the window, thinking about my mommy and daddy. I wanted to grow up as quickly as possible, so I could understand things like Maria. I tugged on Maria's arm. She stopped gooing and cooing with the baby across the aisle. 'What's a player, Maria?' I asked. 'Just someone who plays like a card player or a baseball player or a piano player,' she said. I asked, 'Are you sure, Maria?' She just gave me that look. I was just looking to make sure she was telling me right. She'll be a grown-up soon. And I know they don't tell you everything. Anyway, I wanted to know what a boarding school was and all that other stuff I heard Mommy and Mrs Robinson talking about at Gino's. I turned back to the window. Maria went back to her cooing and gooing with the baby across the aisle. I thought about Mrs Robinson trying to get my mommy to have another baby. I almost fell out of my seat trying to see the baby across the aisle. It was wrapped in a yellow blanket with only its head showing. It looked like a turtle. I sat back in my seat. I hate turtles.

When we got to the train station, Maria and I strapped on our skates and moved in with other kids. We skated fast and held hands. We were skating around and around the big poles when we saw the lady sitting on the steps wearing her black dress and long white beads. Maria pulled me over behind an old boxcar. 'It's her, Dory,' she whispered. 'I know,' I whispered. 'But I think this game is over, Maria. Grandaddy told my daddy something when he was here that made him forget all about that lady. Remember how he came home early every night. I told you, Maria, he said Mommy was the only woman in his life.' Maria smiled. 'I don't think he's coming either.' We watched her as she walked up one side and down the other, looking all around. She almost caught us looking at her one time. She sat down on the steps again. We watched her cross her legs and sway back and forth like she was listening to the music. We heard footsteps. She heard them, too. I saw my daddy's shiny black shoes and gray pants. She jumped up and ran toward the old passenger waiting shed. She threw her arms around my daddy's neck. He kissed her just like she was Mommy. He was turning her around and around like he does Mommy. I smelled his perfume all over the train station. The train station was just like Mommy's room when Maria and I sprayed too much perfume. Mommy always said, 'Don't spray too much; it'll make you sick.' It was too much perfume. It was just too much. It made me sick.

I looked at Maria. She stood there with her hand over her mouth. Then she said, 'She's not tall like Emma.' I said, 'She doesn't have pretty black hair like Emma.' Maria said, 'She doesn't have pretty white teeth like Emma. Not even a pretty smile like Emma.' I said, 'To tell the truth, she's kind of fat. She can't even walk pretty like Emma.' A freight train passed by, blowing its horn long and loud. When the last car rolled by, Emma and Mrs Robinson were standing there like they had just gotten off the train. Mommy rushed over to me, brushing my hair and dusting off my dress. 'Look at you, Dory,' she said. 'You're a mess.' Mrs Robinson saw Daddy and the lady on the other side. 'Well, well,' she said with that same smile on her face, the smile she had at Gino's. 'I think you've got a bigger mess than that on your hands.' She pointed right at Daddy and the lady. Mommy looked at them. She walked closer to them, looking like she wasn't sure they were there. I looked at Mrs Robinson. She still had that weird smile on her face.

Mommy screamed real loud and ran away. Daddy called out for her to come back, but she kept walking and running real fast. When she ran past me she almost knocked me down. She was crying, crying real hard. I tried to catch up with her. It was hard to run in skates. But I caught up with Mommy at the bottom of the hill, waiting to cross Georgia Avenue. Daddy ran up behind her and caught her by the arm. She snatched away from him and ran into the street. I don't know exactly what happened. After that, I was lying in the street. People were standing over me talking loud. Red lights were flashing. Some lady was yelling, 'Oh, my God!' and a crazy man was yelling, 'I didn't see them.' I sat up on my knees. My head hurt and blood was dripping from my nose. A man in a white coat said, 'Don't move, little girl. Help is coming for you.' I didn't need help. I just needed my mommy. My arms were bleeding, but they didn't hurt. I stood up, looking around for her. Mommy was there, lying on the ground. Her face was real bloody. It didn't look like Mommy. The men from the hospital were doing something to her. They said they were going to make her all right. But they didn't. Daddy was crying and saying her name over and over. Mrs Robinson had her arms around him, patting his back and saying a bunch of stuff. But where was Maria? I was going to get Maria to help me. That's when the man hit my mommy real hard with his fist. There was a real loud scream. Loud and long like when I heard Mommy scream before. But not just like it. The scream was getting closer and closer, louder and louder. It was Maria. She put her arm around me. She was screaming and saying, 'We've got to do something, Dory!' Me and Maria tried to push the policeman, so we could help Mommy. But the man in the white coat shoved us away, real hard. 'Somebody get these kids!' he yelled. The policeman picked me up. I saw a lot of people looking at me – a lot of people I had never seen before. I saw Mommy's pocketbook open on the ground. Everything was scattered on the street. My cards were everywhere. I started counting, looking for all of them. The last one was lying beside Mommy's hand, the little joker, bloody. She was lying there like a broken doll. I knew we couldn't play with those cards ever again.

Emma never came home after that day. I wish she had. I missed her. Everything was different in our house. No one ever talked to me about anything, except Maria. She did all the things with me that Emma used to do. She even played Monopoly with me. She used to hate Monopoly. Sometimes we would stare at the picture of Emma in the hall for a long time without talking. It was real lonesome for me and Maria, just like when Grandaddy left. We tried to be good. That's the way Miss Watson said Emma would have wanted us to be, real good, not causing any trouble for anybody. We were good, but we could never be good enough for Mrs Robinson. She always fussed at us. Something was always wrong. One day she told me and Maria that she was going to get rid of us soon as she could. She pulled my hair real hard – not the way Emma used to, but real hard. 'The very next thing you do, I'm sending you away from here,' she said over and over again. I wondered how she could send me away. I didn't live at her house, and she wasn't my mommy.

******

She's playing that game that grown-ups play. I told Miss Watson about it. She fussed with Mrs Robinson. But it doesn't matter now 'cause she's sending us all away now, even Miss Watson. Daddy and Mrs Robinson put me and Maria on the train early one morning. Mrs Robinson was smiling that awful smile. Daddy never looked up at me and Maria, not even when he said goodbye. Maria told me that we were going to Saint Agnes House, a boarding school in the country. Maria stopped talking. She was staring out the window. I looked where she was looking. Mrs Robinson and Daddy were kissing. I told Maria about her mama in Emma's bed that night when I heard it squeaking. It's because of me that we had to leave. I told Maria about telling Miss Watson, and how she fussed at her mama. 'I'm sorry Maria,' I told her. 'I wouldn't have gone in the room, but I thought Emma had come home again.' Maria didn't say anything for a long time. She was pointing at trees and houses passing by like she was counting them. I didn't know what to say, so I just didn't say anything. Maria stopped counting or pointing or whatever. 'It's not your fault,' she said. 'It's just grown-ups and all those games.' I don't know if I want to grow up,' I said. Maria was crying. I didn't know what to do, so I held her hand the way Emma used to hold my hand when I cried. Maria told me that she was afraid that we would die just like Emma. But I told Maria that we wouldn't because I learned a lot about this game. When it's our turn to play, we'll play smarter. Maria smiled. It was a nice smile like Emma's smile. It was good to see Maria smile again. She said she was going to take care of me and Mr Teddy, so I told her that when we get to Saint Agnes House she can be Emma when she used to live on a farm.

Two Boys Named Basil

Mark McWatt

p.208
Basil Raatgever and Basil Ross were born three days apart in the month of November, 1939. Basil Ross was the elder and from the beginning their lives seem to have been curiously and profoundly interrelated. They were both born to middle-class Guyanese parents of mixed race and their skins were of almost exactly the same hue of brown. They were not related and although their parents knew of each other – as was inevitable in a small society like Georgetown at the time – there was no opportunity for them to be friendly, because Mr Ross was a Government dispenser who was posted from time to time to various coastal and interior districts, while the Raatgevers lived in Georgetown, where Mr Raatgever was some kind of senior clerical functionary in the Transport and Harbours Department.

The two boys met at the age of ten, when Basil Ross began attending the 'scholarship class' in the same primary school in Georgetown which Basil Raatgever had attended from the age of six. Basil Ross had been sent to the city to live with his maternal grandparents so that he could have two years of special preparation in order to sit the Government scholarship examinations, which were the basis of entry into secondary school. The two Basils found themselves seated next to each other in the classroom and from that moment on their lives and fortunes became inextricably intertwined. Before the scholarship class neither child showed any particular aptitude for scholarly pursuits. They both did well enough to get by, but the fourth standard teacher had already warned Mr Raatgever not to hope for too much of Basil in the scholarship exams; he was restless and easily distracted, though he seemed to have the ability to do fairly well. Basil Ross, on the other hand, possessed great powers of concentration and could occupy himself enthusiastically and obsessively with a number of demanding hobbies, but for him school work was a burdensome chore unworthy of his sustained attention and something to be done with great haste and little care, so that he could return to his more interesting pursuits.

From the time they were placed together in the same class, however, all of this changed entirely. There seemed to occur between the two boys an awakening to the pleasures and possibilities of scholarship – or perhaps it was simply to the instinct to compete, to see which Basil was better; in a strange sort of symbiosis they each seemed to draw energy and inspiration from the other. At the end of the first term in scholarship class Basil Ross was first in class, beating Basil

Raatgever into second by a mere four marks overall. At the end of the second term the positions were the same but the margin was only two marks, and after the third term – at the end of the first year – Basil Raatgever was first in class, beating Basil Ross by a single mark. And so they continued. The change in both boys was great and the marks they achieved were so astonishing that their teacher, Mr Francis Greaves, remarked to the Headmistress that they seemed like two halves of a single personality – feeding off of each other and challenging each other to achieve more and more.

They both easily won Government scholarships to the high school of their parents' choice, and although the ranking was never publicly announced, rumour had it that Basil Raatgever had scored the highest mark ever achieved in the scholarship examinations and this was two marks higher than Basil Ross's mark. The scholarships they won, in fact, nearly put paid to their remarkable joint development and achievement, for Basil Ross was a Roman Catholic and opted to attend St Stanislaus College, whereas Basil Raatgever's family, though nominally Anglican, did not practise any religion, and wanted Basil to attend Queen's College, as his father had done. This proved to be a major crisis for the two boys who, at this time, were the best of friends and were almost literally inseparable. The two families met and discussed the problem with the boys' teacher, Mr Greaves. He reminded everyone that the boys' remarkable development as scholars began only when they were placed together at adjoining desks, and continued as a result of their strong friendship and preoccupation with each other. He offered the opinion that to send them to separate schools might cause them to revert to the same kind of underachievement that had characterised their earlier classroom efforts. In the end it was reasoned that, although Queen's College was considered to have the edge academically, the difference was small and the boys seemed to need each other more than they needed top quality teaching; then, too, since religion was of no consequence to the Raatgevers, but of great importance to the Ross family, the boys would go to St Stanislaus College.

In the first two years at high school, the boys continued as they had done in the scholarship class, taking turns, as it were, at placing first and second in class; but their strange competitiveness and hunger for achievement began to manifest itself in other spheres and activities, notably on the sports field. Despite their inseparability and the similarity of their accomplishments thus far, the boys were not really similar physically. Basil Raatgever was tall for his age and very thin, while Basil Ross had a somewhat shorter, more muscular build. This difference became more evident as the boys grew older, so that when they took to competing in sports they had to settle for achieving equal prowess, but in somewhat different spheres. In cricket, for example, Basil Raatgever was a tall and elegant opening batsman, while Basil Ross used his more muscular, mesomorphic physique to good effect as a fast bowler and a useful slugger and scrambler for runs in the lower order. In athletics there was no one in their age-group who could beat Basil Ross in the sprint events and no one who could jump higher than Basil Raatgever. In this way the boys' symbiotic relationship, their friendship and their remarkable dominance in all the areas in which they chose to compete, continued for the first few years at St Stanislaus College.

Their schoolmates always spoke of them in the same breath – 'Ratty and Ross' – as though they were a single person, and boasted to outsiders about their achievements.

It was in the third form that the trouble between the two Basils began. It started, as always, with little things, such as the fact that Raatgever was the first to manifest the onset of puberty. After a brief period of dramatic squeaks and tonal shifts in his voice, especially when chosen to read in class, Basil Raatgever soon acquired a remarkably deep and rich baritone, which seemed all the more incongruous coming from such a slender body. Basil Ross' voice took longer to change, and in any case did not 'break' dramatically like that of his namesake, but deepened slightly over time, so that by the end of that school year it was different, but still high and somewhat squeaky, compared to Raatgever's. The other boys began to call them 'Ratty and Mouse'.

Then religion played a part in dividing the two Basils. They both did equally well in religious studies, and Raatgever although not a Catholic, attended weekly Benediction and Mass on special occasions with the other boys. But in the third form Basil Ross was trained as an altar-boy and, on one or two mornings a week, according to the roster, he got up early and rode down to the Cathedral to serve at seven o'clock Mass. On those days he went straight on to college afterwards and did not cycle to school with Raatgever as they had done since the first day of first form.

Basil Raatgever pretended to take it in his stride – he knew he was not a Catholic and could not serve Mass, and he discovered that he did not really want to, but at the same time he was resentful that Ross had found a sphere of activity from which he was excluded. Basil Raatgever sulked and in small and subtle ways, he began to be mean to Basil Ross in revenge for being excluded. One day, when he knew that Ross would pass by for him, unfastening the front gate and cycling right under the house while whistling for him, Raatgever 'forgot' to chain the dog early in the morning as he always did. The result was that Skip attacked Basil Ross, forcing him to throw down his bike and school books and clamber in haste onto one of the gate-posts, putting a small tear in his school pants. Raatgever came down and berated the dog and apologised, but Ross had heard, above the noise of the falling bike and barking dog, his muffled laughter coming from the gallery above.

There were other such pranks and, as with everything they did, Basil Ross tried to outdo his friend in this area as well. By the end of that year, when promotion exams were in the offing, each boy ostentatiously cultivated his own circle of friends and the two factions waged a continuous verbal warfare. Then one day Raatgever said:

'Ross, now that we're no longer best friends, I hope I won't find your name under mine when the exam results are put up – try and come fifth and give me a little breathing space.'

Ross had replied: 'Ha, you wish! You know I will be coming first in class and I'm certain you will be swinging on my shirt tails with a close second as usual – but believe me, nothing would please me more than to put a dozen places between us – even if I have to throw away marks to do it.'

Immediately he had said this both boys were struck with its implications, and, unknown to each other, both were determined to show that the friendship and equality with each other were at an end. The profoundly shocking result was that Basil Ross and Basil Raatgever were ranked a joint 10th in class in the promotion examinations! Even when they were determined deliberately to do badly, each did so to exactly the same extent – in fact they got identical overall marks – and of course, none of their teachers were fooled as they had lost marks with silly, obvious 'mistakes'. They were both sent in to see the headmaster on the last day of the term and letters were sent to their parents along with their reports.

This incident had the effect of making both boys more irritated with each other and, at the same time, more certain that there was some uncanny chemistry going on between them that prevented each from breaking free of the other. They felt trapped in an involuntary relationship that began to seem stifling.

Then there was Alison Cossou. Alison Cossou was a bright, vivacious convent girl who boarded with relatives in the house next door to the Raatgevers' because her parents lived in Berbice. Basil Raatgever had known her for years and had found her quite pleasant and easy to talk to, but was never conscious of any amorous feelings towards her. Basil Ross too had known her casually, as his friend's next-door neighbour, but when Alison began attending seven o'clock Mass at the cathedral and Ross, serving Mass, saw her in a different context, he developed a serious crush on her. He would make sure that he touched her chin with the communion plate; this would make her eyelids flicker and she would smile and Basil Ross would thrill to a sudden tightness about his heart. Then they took to chatting on the north stairs after Mass. When he began stopping outside her gate and chatting with her in full view of the other Basil next door, the latter became incensed and felt that he was being out-manoeuvred on his own doorstep, as it were. So Basil Raatgever launched a campaign to woo and win Alison Cossou from Basil Ross and this new rivalry intensified the bitterness between them as well as the hopeless sense that their lives would always be inextricably interrelated.

This situation continued throughout fourth and fifth forms and the boys' mutual hostility and constant sniping at each other began to irk the teachers as well as their classmates. They were still considered inseparable and still spoken of in the same breath, but the unpleasantness surrounding them caused their fellows to adjust significant letters of their joint nickname, so that 'Ratty and Ross' became, derisively, 'Batty and Rass'. All the time they drew energy and competitive zeal from each other so that St Stanislaus won all the interschool sports events in those years as the two friends/enemies swept all before them.

A month before the O-level exams began, one of the Jesuit masters at the college – one whom all the students respected – had several sessions with them of what, at a later period, would be called 'counselling'. He sat them down, spoke to them as adults and reasoned with them. He listened carefully to all the recriminations and made them *see* that the main problem for each was his sense of entrapment – the sense that each was denied the privilege of autonomy, that they did not seem to have the freedom to be separate and authentic persons, but must always in some way, feed on each other in order to survive and to achieve.

When they could see this, the priest told them it was indeed a serious situation and in a sense their bitterness towards each other was a natural reaction as they grew towards the self-assertion of adulthood. He then told them that the problem was that they did not know how to deal with their dilemma and with each other, but if they promised him to try, he would help them devise strategies to either extricate themselves from, or to survive, the suffocating relationship in which they had found themselves for so long.

O-levels were thus written under a truce and in the sixth form, with the help of the Jesuit Father, their relationship steadily improved. Alison Cossou and two other girls from the convent joined them in the sixth form since the subjects that they wanted to do were not available at the convent. The girls had a calming effect on the class and especially on the two Basils who outdid each other in being courteous and pleasant. In the sixth form too, the Basils discovered parties and dancing and it didn't take long for everyone to observe with wonder that there was no equality of achievement between the boys in that sphere. Basil

Raatgever was a natural dancer – he was self-confident and stylish on the floor and could improvise wonderfully in order to flatter the abilities of all the girls. The girls were enchanted by him – especially Alison Cossou who declared one day: 'The man that will marry me must be able to dance up a storm, because I love to dance.'

Basil Ross heard this with dismay but he admitted defeat to himself and considered that Raatgever had won her – for now. It was not that Basil Ross couldn't dance – he made all the correct movements and had a fair sense of rhythm, but he did not attract attention as a dancer the way his friend did and even Ross himself loved to watch the sinuous perfection of his friend Raatgever on the dance floor.

No one will ever know how the relationship might have developed after school, nor where it might have taken the two Basils for, just after writing A-levels, there occurred a shocking and mysterious event which is still unexplained to this day, and which is presumed to have claimed the life of one of the boys and to have altered irreparably that of the other.

The priest who taught Religious Knowledge and Latin to the sixth forms, Father De Montfort – the same priest who had counselled the two Basils earlier – accompanied the entire final-year sixth on a trip to Bartica to unwind after the A-level exams. The year was 1957, the third consecutive year that such a trip was arranged, the previous two having been very successful and much talked about at the college. No one guessed at the time that that year's trip would be the last. There were eight boys, the three convent girls and Father himself, and they stayed in the presbytery next to the little St Anthony parish church in Front Street. The girls shared a room upstairs and the boys slept rough on the floor in the large front room downstairs, stowing away their bedding before Mass each morning so that the place could revert to its regular daytime uses.

On their second night in Bartica it was full moon and the young people from Georgetown went walking along Front Street, past the police station and the stelling, around the curve at the top of the street and ended up at the Bernard's Croft Hotel overlooking the confluence of the rivers. There they ordered soft drinks from the bar and bottles of the still new Banks beer and chatted loudly, imagining that they were behaving like adults. There was a jukebox near the bar and they played music and it wasn't long before some started dancing. Basil Ross, who had enjoyed the trip so far, began to feel uncomfortable; he knew that soon everyone would be admiring and applauding Basil Raatgever as he glided across the floor with one or other of the girls. He told himself it was silly to be jealous, especially now, when he and Raatgever were on very good terms again and everyone was in high spirits on this trip, after the long slog of preparing for A-levels. Ross told the others he was feeling hot and would take a walk along the river wall to get some air: if he didn't see them when he returned, he would make his own way back to the presbytery.

The moonlight was brilliant and quite beautiful on the water. Basil Ross walked quite slowly along the wall, breathing deeply and remembering some of the interior districts where he had lived and gone to school as a child, and where he had later spent his school holidays with his parents. He sat on the wall not far from the little Public Works jetty and looked at the moonlit river and willed himself to be happy. He thought how good it was to have got through the exams feeling confident of good results, and slowly his irritation eased. He was happy to be at that spot, pleased that his troubled friendship with Raatgever was secure forever, and while Ratty might be in love with dancing and the girls, he, Ross, was in love with the whole world, especially the part of it that he could see in front of him, touched magically by the silvery moonlight. He sat on the wall a long time, deciding eventually to say his night prayers and his rosary there. Then he got up and headed back to the hotel. The jukebox still played, at lower volume, and there were a few men at the bar, but no sign of any of his classmates, so he made his way back to the presbytery. There people were unfolding bedding and getting ready to sleep, so he did the same. Then he noticed that Raatgever was not there. 'He and Alison went off walking somewhere with a couple of Bartica fellows we met at the hotel,' someone told him, and he began to feel uneasy again.

After the others had gone to sleep he was still awake, waiting. Some time around two o'clock Basil Raatgever and Alison Cossou came in. They seemed to Basil Ross so mature and self-confident, he felt a pang as they moved carefully about in the almost-dark room. At the foot of the stairs he heard Raatgever whisper: 'See you tomorrow,' and Alison tiptoed upstairs, but not before Ross could notice, despite the dim light, that Raatgever had given her a gentle tap on her bottom as she ascended. Ross felt another pang.

When Raatgever settled into his sleeping bag next to Ross, he pretended to wake up and asked the other where they had been. Raatgever told him that there had been a dance somewhere in Fourth Avenue and they were invited by the two local fellows. He told Basil Ross that the music was good, and Alison wanted to dance so they did, for a while, but that most of the men seemed intent on getting drunk and the women looked fed up and uninteresting. He and Alison had left, walked back to the hotel and sat on the wall and chatted for over an hour in the moonlight and then came home. Raatgever did not ask how he, Ross, had spent the evening.

The next day they left early by boat to visit a small waterfall somewhere in the lower Mazaruni, where they would bathe and picnic for the day. The boat pulled into an uninviting section of riverbank near a small, forested island and the students noticed the beginning of a trail that seemed overgrown. The trail opened out a bit as they got further into it but, although quite distinct, it had not been cleared for some time, indicating that their waterfall was not a much-frequented local attraction. The trail crossed a swift-flowing creek by means of a half-submerged log and they soon began to hear the sound of the waterfall.

In time they emerged into a small clearing and Father De Montfort announced: 'This is it, Baracara Falls.' There in front of them the creek cascaded over a stone ledge about twenty feet above their heads and tumbled, foaming and splashing over a heap of large boulders and into a widened pool, the edges of which were covered in cream-coloured foam. The boys thought the waterfall was small, but quite impressive, and the water looked cool and refreshing. While their classmates put down baskets and haversacks and prepared to strip and stand or sit on the boulders and let the falling water cool them down after their brief hike, the two Basils, already in swim trunks, were climbing the falls, one on either side.

Father De Montfort shook his head and smiled and one of the others remarked: 'Look at Ratty and Ross climbing the fall – trust them to make a contest out of it.' It was not difficult to climb, despite the volume of descending water, as there were many ledges and hand-holds among the boulders. It seemed as though Ross reached the top first, but soon both boys were standing on the ledge looking down on the others, the water curving high about their calves. After a while those below saw them turn and walk along the rocky ledge away from the lip and along the creek-bed, disappearing into the trees and bushes behind the waterfall. Ross was in front and Raatgever behind him. That was the last anyone ever saw of Raatgever – even Ross, if you believe his story.

The rest of the party of students bathed in the cold, falling water or in the little pool at the base of the boulders; a few of the other boys eventually climbed to the ledge as the two Basils had done, but did not venture far along the creek in pursuit of them – all accepted that Ross and Raatgever were quite extraordinary people and at times it was best to leave them to pursue their own joint agenda. The group had arrived at Baracara Falls just after 10 a.m. At 12.30 they had lunch, making sure to leave some for the two Basils who had wandered off. Just before one o'clock Ross appeared on the lip of the waterfall looking troubled.

'Did Ratty come back?' he shouted to the others. When they told him that he had not Ross seemed more agitated.

'We thought he was with you, we saw him follow you into the bush,' Father De Montfort said.

'I thought he was behind me all the time, but when I did turn around he'd disappeared. I'm going back to find him.'

And that, essentially, is the story. Pretty soon everybody was topside the falls looking for Raatgever, except the rather corpulent Tony D'Andrade and two of the girls. Alison Cossou had sprinted up the falls quicker than most of the boys. Ross took them to the spot where he said he had turned around for the first time to say something to Raatgever, only to discover that he had vanished. The others were astounded how far they'd gone along the creek, and it was quite difficult going in places – there were swampy patches and places that were quite deep and other spots that seemed particularly gloomy and sinister; they could not understand why the two Basils would want to trudge through all that – it could hardly be anyone's idea of fun. Ross said that he and Raatgever had spoken to each other from time to time and that he'd heard Ratty's footsteps splashing behind him – although when he did turn around it was partly because he had not heard anything from Raatgever for a while. The whole story sounded improbable and one of the other boys said:

'The two of you concocted this whole thing to play a trick on us – it's just the kind of thing you two would do. I'm sure Ratty's hiding in the bush somewhere, or else he's back at the falls by now, sharing the joke with fat D'Andrade and the girls.'

This immediately seemed plausible to all, including the priest, and they were ready to abandon the search and return to the waterfall, but it was hard not to believe Ross, who was by now visibly disturbed and swore that it was no trick. For more than an hour they shouted Raatgever's name and searched up and down the creek for him, making forays into the bush wherever it seemed that there was an opening in the undergrowth through which the missing boy could have walked off into the surrounding forest. There was no response and no sign of any kind that might have indicated that Raatgever had been there.

The group assembled back at the falls at 4.30 p.m., the three who had remained at the foot of the falls having grown anxious at all the distant shouting and thrashing around they could hear – and at the passage of time. The boatman then came along the path from the river to discover why the group was not waiting on the riverbank at 4.15 as planned, and there was a moment of panic as everyone was speaking and shouting at the same time. All were silenced by a loud and desperate shout of 'Ratt-a-a-a-y!' from Alison Cossou, who then burst into tears. At that point a profound gloom seemed to settle on the group. Led by the

Jesuit Father, they prayed that they would find Raatgever – or that he would find them – and then they prayed for his family and the repose of his soul if anything tragic had happened to him.

When it began to get dark and they prepared to leave, Basil Ross announced that he was not going – he would spend the night there waiting for his friend: 'He would do the same for me,' he said firmly, and could not be persuaded to leave and return in the morning with the search party. In the end Father De Montfort decided to stay with him. Next morning the others, along with a large and curious group from Bartica, arrived at first light to find Ross and the priest wet and hungry and miserable because there was still no sign of the missing boy.

For two days people searched the forest around the creek and far beyond; the next day a party of policemen arrived from town with dogs and they spent two days combing the area, but no one discovered any sign of Raatgever. The speculation was that he had wandered far into the forest, got lost and was eaten by a jaguar or had fallen into a bottomless pit. Some said that if he knew how to survive he could wander around the Mazaruni-Potaro jungle for months – but months, years, decades have since passed, and there has never been a satisfactory explanation of the mystery. There are those who harbour the suspicion that Ross may somehow have done away with Raatgever – those who remembered their intense rivalry of a few years before; but no one could provide a plausible account of how he might have accomplished this without leaving a body, let alone a trace. What cannot be imagined is difficult to believe. What about Ross himself? What does he think? That night that he spent at the foot of Baracara Falls with Father De Montfort was a harrowing time for him. He told the Father that he felt responsible for Raatgever's disappearance. It crossed the priest's mind at the time that Ross may have been about to confess to having done some harm to Raatgever, and he blessed himself quietly and asked the boy if he felt he needed to go to confession. Ross replied that he didn't know; he claimed that he had been quarrelling with Raatgever as they walked single file up the bed of the stream. He'd been jealous and angry that his friend and Alison Cossou seemed to be in love with each other and then he'd been annoyed with himself for having these feelings. At the top of the falls that morning Ross was irritated anew at the fact that he and Raatgever couldn't seem to get away from each other and that it had occurred to Raatgever to climb the waterfall at the same time that he'd begun ascending the rocks. Then Raatgever had followed him up the stream. After they had walked some distance he had told Raatgever that he was fed up with him and he claimed that at first his friend had replied tauntingly, saying: 'You'll never be rid of me, I'm your doppelganger, wherever you go I will follow, like Ruth in the Bible.' Ross claimed that this made him more angry and he refused to look back at Raatgever, although the latter eventually began to plead with him:

'I'm only joking, Ross, look at me, I'm your best friend, I always was and always will be.'

'I wish you'd disappear for good,' Ross had told him.

'You would suffer most if I did,' was the reply that came from behind him. 'Hasn't it occurred to you yet that we are nothing without each other? It's your wonderful Catholic religion, Ross, that makes it impossible for you to accept the truth: we are two halves of a single soul. Please, Ross, forgive me whatever it is that I've done to wrong you: forgive me and accept me – accept yourself.'

'I wish to God you'd disappear, just *disappear*! – vanish!' Ross had heard himself insist in a terrible, hissing voice.

Then, he told Father De Montfort, there was a long silence before he thought he heard Raatgever say, very quietly:

'All right.'

After that he didn't hear any sounds from behind him, and after it seemed to him that they had stood silently in the stream for several minutes, he looked back. There was no sign of the other boy and Ross turned and walked further up the stream, convinced that Raatgever was hiding somewhere to make fun of him. Some time later he had turned back, looking carefully along both banks of the creek, but refusing to call his friend's name, thinking that Raatgever meant to teach him a lesson by remaining hidden. He'd then returned to the top of the falls. He told Father De Montfort that he still expected Ratty to show up triumphantly, perhaps early next morning, and that his friend was doing this to punish him – adding after a pause that he (Ross) deserved to be punished for what he had said.

But hours later that night, after it had rained and they began to hear the noises of bats and animals in the surrounding forest, and Ross began to feel cold and despondent, he said to the priest, as though continuing a current conversation:

'Unless he really disappeared, Father – unless I made him disappear …'

'And how could you have done that, child? How does one make a human being disappear?'

'I don't know, Father.' And Ross began to weep.

Father De Montfort tried to comfort Ross and, at the boy's insistence, gave him absolution for the sin of having become angry with his friend and for having wished for his disappearance. Father De Montfort convinced him that, if he was telling the truth, it was illogical to feel guilty, since it is not possible to make a human being disappear by wishing it. The priest also advised him not to repeat the story he had told him, since it would feed the superstitions of the ungodly and, in any case, was unlikely to lead to the recovery of his friend.

In August that year it was announced that Basil Raatgever was awarded a scholarship to do university studies, based on the results of the A-level examinations. Ross was named proxime, having achieved the second best results in the country. In the absence of Raatgever, Ross accepted the scholarship, reflecting sorrowfully that he and his achievements still seemed to be tied to his vanished friend. Ross studied law in England, returning to Guyana after four years. He worked for a while in the Public Prosecutor's office then, in the mid-1960s, he was appointed a legal officer in the Attorney General's office, and he has remained there to the present.

Basil Ross became a taciturn, solitary individual; he played no games, never competed with anyone in any way and never married nor pursued the opposite sex. He seemed to live for his job and he became an institution at the office, gaining a reputation as an excellent draftsman of complex legislation and legal opinions, though in the nature of his job he did all this anonymously, since his own name was never formally associated with the work he authored. This struck Ross himself as being peculiarly appropriate: Raatgever had disappeared partly because of him, and for years his own existence was partial – he worked each day, but there was no identification of self or personality with the work he did. He was strangely comforted by the thought that Basil Ross had disappeared almost as completely as had Basil Raatgever. He refused to accept appointments to other, more prominent positions in government service. His superiors relied more and more on his knowledge and experience, and many were happy to claim the prominence he eschewed. Ross, in turn, relied on his secretary Miss Morgan – an efficient, old-fashioned civil service spinster – to keep the office running smoothly and to shield him from too much public exposure. The country had long forgotten the mystery of Raatgever's disappearance, although on one or two occasions, not long after his return from England, Ross permitted himself to be interviewed about the incident, more in the hope that the interviewer may have thought of some new angle that had not been explored than out of any conviction that he himself had anything useful to add to all that had been said before. He had been disappointed on each occasion, and decided he would not subject himself to any more such journalistic probing into his painful memories.

People who knew him said that Basil Ross had changed physically after the incident: he had become thin and ascetic-looking and, as the years passed, his physique seemed similar to that of his vanished friend. He lived a life of careful routine – home to office, office to home. He visited his close relatives occasionally, but said very little and seemed to find casual conversation difficult. He remained devout in the practice of his religion and he was careful, in those oppressive times, to keep himself strictly above politics.

Then, in the mid-1990s, Basil Ross had a revelation. A number of ecotourism resorts had opened in the Essequibo-Mazaruni area and one of these, located on a small island in the Mazaruni River, not far from Baracara Falls, had rediscovered the falls, cleared the path and constructed a bridge over the little creek. They took their visitors to see and to bathe in the falls: a bath in the 'therapeutic waters' of Baracara Falls was advertised as one of the attractions of their tour package. It was an advertising brochure for this company that had caught and riveted Basil Ross's attention when he saw it in 1996. On the brochure there was a small picture of Baracara Falls with a few tourists in swim-suits arranged on the top ledge of the falls and on the boulders. Behind a veil of falling water next to the vertical edge of one of these boulders, Basil Ross imagined he saw a face. He knows it is not a real face, but he was struck by the fact that it was the first thing that he noticed when he had looked at the photograph. He visited the office of the tour company, spoke to the proprietor's son and then the proprietor himself, found out who had taken the photograph and, with some difficulty and expense, managed to locate the negative and have a large blow-up made. This confirmed his belief that the face behind the veil of water is that of Basil Raatgever – the face of his sixth-form classmate of 1957: the large forehead, the eyes, the wide mouth, the shadow of a moustache. Raatgever, Ross saw, was smiling.

No one else could see the face, though some agreed that there was a suggestion, in the pattern of water falling over rock, of eyes and a mouth – but only after Ross had pointed these out to them. The fact that no one saw quite what he saw did not surprise nor discourage Basil Ross in the least; he saw the face quite clearly and had no trouble recognising it. He had the enlarged photograph framed and hung on the wall of his bedroom and a smaller version stood on his desk at work. He became convinced that the face of his lost friend was made visible to him in this way in order to free him from his years of guilt and sorrow, and he felt truly liberated. Basil Raatgever was *there* after all – had been *there* all along, there in the falls – he had reappeared in the place where he had made himself disappear in response to his (Ross's) angry wish. At the office they noticed that Mr Ross was more relaxed and approachable. He smiled with uncharacteristic frequency and seemed more inclined to stop and chat with his fellow office-workers. Many surmised that he had mellowed with age and was perhaps looking forward to his retirement in a few years.

One day, shortly after people began to notice these changes, Basil Ross stopped before the desk of his faithful secretary:

'Miss Morgan, I don't quite know how to say this, but … Well … The fact is that I find myself in possession of two tickets for something called an 'Old Time Dance' – I understand that there will be music that was popular in the fifties and sixties and refreshments of some sort. I was wondering if you –'

'Oh, yes, OK, Mr Ross, I'll take them off you – you know I can't pass up a good dance; I'll get one of the friends in my little group to go with me – you're giving me the tickets, or I have to pay?' she asked, looking at him sharply, but with a twinkle in her eye.

'Well … You see, Miss Morgan …'

But Miss Morgan didn't see … She didn't see why Mr Ross was making such a fuss and seemed so awkward this time – he had passed on many such tickets to her over the years … She couldn't help thinking that by now people should have realised that Mr Ross doesn't go to public events of that kind …

'Well, the truth is, Miss Morgan,' Basil Ross continued, 'I thought I would rather like to go myself – for a change, you know … to remind myself of my youth, so to speak … Oh, I don't know, but I was wondering if you would do me the honour of allowing me to escort you …'

Miss Morgan opened her mouth, but no sound issued from it; she was stunned '… the honour of allowing me to escort you …' The words rang in her head for a long time before she could work out that Mr Ross was in fact asking her out to a dance, and it took her still more time to recover the power of speech and to respond.

The evening at the dance was a revelation to Miss Morgan; she had never associated Mr Ross with any social skills or with any activities engaged in simply for pleasure: she had thought that she would have to humour him and be embarrassed on his behalf for his awkwardness – and she told herself that all this she would cheerfully endure while savouring the complete novelty of the situation – she and Mr Ross at a dance … But in fact Mr Ross danced like a man possessed – he was lively and fluent in the quicker numbers: he twirled her around and pulled her towards him with the utmost grace and perfect timing – but it was the slow, soulful hits of the sixties that he seemed to like best. As the music sobbed rhythmically over the large floor, Mr Ross swayed and glided and his hips and shoulders seemed to drift effortlessly with the waves of sound, and his feet seemed hardly in touch with the floor. It took all of Miss Morgan's considerable skills to keep up with him and she noticed, not without genuine pleasure, that they had begun to attract quite a lot of attention: several couples had stopped dancing to watch them. Mr Basil Ross was entirely oblivious – he was floating, he was free. It was as if a long lost dimension of self had reawakened within him and was asserting its presence and its hunger for pleasures long denied it. One or two of the older folk at the dance thought they remembered seeing someone dance like that before – a youngster, long, long ago.

Victory and the Blight

Earl Lovelace

 p.209 Victory didn't even good open his barbershop when Brown reach to play draughts, with him a stringy bushyhead fellar who Victory see once or twice about the town. Right away Victory face changed. To have draughts playing in the barbershop before he began working was sure to blight him for the rest of the day. And to make it worse, the fellar with Brown was a stranger. As he was thinking how to tell this to Brown, Pascal came in and sat down for a trim. Though now, technically, he was about to work, Victory still had this feeling that Brown and his pardner bring with them a blight to his barbershop this Saturday morning.

'The draughts board underneath the bench,' Victory said, with stiff aloofness, not even looking at Brown. 'When you finish with it, put it back where you get it.'

Brown didn't even hear him, he was so busy introducing the pardner who had come in with him. 'This fellar new up here. He working on the farm, with Walker and Carew and them.'

Victory looked at the fellar, not wanting to appear to be interested.

'My name is Ross,' the newcomer said. 'From Arima.'

'And the man you looking at,' said Brown, 'is the great Victory. If you want to get the run of this town, stick close to him. Sports, fete, woman, Victory is the boss.' Pointing to the photographs on the wall, Brown added, 'You see him there on the wall? Tell me which one you think is him?'

The fellar named Ross stood before the photographs, cut out from magazines and framed and his eyes went over Joe Louis and Jack Johnson and Sugar Ray Robinson and Mohammed Ali, and over the West Indies cricket team with Worrell and Weekes and Walcott and Sobers and Hall and they came down to the Wanderers cricket team, the team with Rupert and Manding and Hailings and Slim and Cecil and the Ramcharan brothers and to Penetrators football team with Berris and Mervyn and Campbell and Bass and Jacko and Breeze, and then he pointed to a photograph with Victory in a blazer, standing in the back row of the Wanderers team.

'That is the year they went to Tobago,' Brown said in a kind of glee. 'And that one,' he said pointing to the photograph of a young muscular fellar on a rostrum receiving a trophy from a middle-aged white woman, 'Tell me, who that is?'

'That is you?' the fellar named Ross asked.

'Fifteen years ago,' said Victory. 'Victor ludorum. Hundred, two hundred, long jump, high jump. That is the Warden wife giving me the prize.'

'Didn't know he was an athlete too, eh,' Brown said gleefully. 'I tell you the man is everything.'

Slightly appeased Victory took up the cloth to put around Pascal's neck to keep the hair off his clothes. He shook it out, flop, flop, flop, went around behind Pascal and fit it over him, then he pinned the cloth at Pascal's neck. Brown, in the meantime, had picked up the draughts board and was moving out the bench so he and his pardner could sit astraddle for their game.

'And don't block the door,' Victory said. 'And that bench. One of the legs ready to fall off. People sit down on that bench like they riding a horse.'

Brown and his pardner were setting up the knobs.

'Wait,' Victory said. 'You better wait 'till I start to trim this head before you move a knob. I really don't want a blight to fall on me today.'

'Okay, chief,' the fellar named Ross said.

'Chief?' Victory looked directly at him. 'I thought Brown tell you my name.'

'Okay, Victory,' the fellar named Ross said.

Victory had his scissors at ready; but, now, Pascal was fiddling with the cloth pinned at his neck. 'If it too slack,' Victory cautioned, 'hair will get on your skin.'

'Too tight,' Pascal said.

Without another word Victory unpinned the cloth, slackened it and pinned it again. Somehow he felt today wasn't going to be his day.

'How you want your trim?' he asked, clicking his scissors over Pascal's ear.

'Clean it,' Pascal said.

Victory paused, 'Think a clean head will suit you?' Then, he chuckled, 'Look at the nice head this man have to take a good trim and he telling me clean it.' He chuckled again, the chuckle turning to a smile, the smile widening his lips, swelling his face, 'Like you want to put me out of business. Like you want me to leave this trade and go and drive taxi or something.' He clicked his scissors again, faster this time, 'Clean it, you say?'

'Okay. Trim me how you want,' Pascal said. 'My head is in your hands.' He was laughing too.

'Trim you how I want?' Victory stopped his scissors. 'I can't do that. Your head is not my head. I here to do as the customers say. If you say clean, is clean. I would clean it.' A seriousness was creeping into his voice, 'Look, I have one of those machines here that you could just plug in … they call it a clipper. I could just plug in the clipper and put it on your head and bzzz! Just like that, and all your hair gone. But, I don't call that barbering. Barbering is playing music. Everything have to flow. Things have to fit.'

'Victory, just give me a good trim, not too low,' Pascal said, trying with a light tone to ease the heaviness of the mood he felt descending.

Victory started his scissors clicking again, but did not touch it to Pascal's head, 'No. Serious. I mean it. I could just plug in that machine, that clipper and put it on your head, and you will give me the same three dollars and bzzzz! Your head will be clean.' He touched the scissors to Pascal's hair, 'Everything in the world losing taste, everything quick, quick quick … And you know how I get this clipper? A pardner send it from the States for me. The latest. You know who send it? Rupert, the fast bowler from Wanderers. He gone up there in the States and see this clipper and he say, "Victory will like this" and he send it for me.'

'How long he away now?' Pascal asked.

'Four, five years. Last time I hear about him he was living in New Jersey. I always wonder why he send me the clipper.'

'Maybe he didn't like how you used to trim him,' Brown said.

After the laughter, the barbershop was filled with the sound of the clicking scissors, with Brown and the fellar named Ross intent on their game.

'Those was the days when Wanderers was Wanderers,' Brown said. 'This barbershop was the centre. On a Saturday morning you couldn't get in. All the young teachers and civil servants lined up to talk cricket and boxing and waiting to trim. Those days real draughts used to play, with Castillo and Cecil and Mr Arthur leaving Libertville to clash with Paul. Now Paul, too, gone away.'

'The worst thing this government do is to allow people to go away,' Victory said. And he swung the barbering chair around to get to tackle the other side of Pascal's head.

Tugging at the cloth pinned loosely at his neck, Pascal held up a hand to stop Victory, 'You know this thing kinda slack.'

'Hair scratching your skin,' Victory said with undisguised triumph, and began to unpin the cloth once more. 'Pascal, you know what wrong with you. You always feel it have an easy way in everything. Some things aint have no short cut. You just have to do them. No short cut,' he said, tightening the cloth at Pascal's neck, and pinning it.

Suddenly there was an uproar from the draughts game. 'Come and see how this man dead and he don't know! Come and see play!' Victory couldn't believe it. It was the fellar named Ross making this big uproar. The first time this man step into my barbershop, and not even for a hair cut and hear the noise he making, Victory thought, stopping his barbering to allow Pascal to see the position of the game.

Brown countered well, they swapped a few knobs and the tension eased. Victory clicked his scissors and Pascal settled back in the chair.

'So, Victory, what is going to happen to your side now?' Pascal asked, idly. With Victory working on the front of his head, he was looking at the photographs on the wall.

'Which side?' Victory answered.

'You know who I mean, Wanderers. Your side.'

'Wanderers is not a side. Wanderers is a club. A club is not a side. A side is when you pick up eleven fellars to play a match and next week you have to look to pick up eleven fellars again. A club is solid. It is something to belong to.'

'What going to happen to your club when all your players gone away?'

'All? All the players?'

'Well, the stars. Prince, your fast bowler going to Canada. Murray going. Ali gone to the States.'

'Who else going?' Victory asked. He didn't like this talk.

'Is your club. You should know.'

'What you want us to do? They going to study. They have to think about their future. They have to get their education. Just now, just from the fellars who leave and go away from Cunaripo and they come back with their BAs and MAs and Ph dees they could run the government.'

'I wish I was one of them going,' Brown said. He was relaxed now. Ross has miscalculated.

Victory was ready now to clean the edges of Pascal's head with the razor. Quickly, he lathered the shaving brush and brushed it across the edge of hair he was going to remove, then, tilting the chair, bending at the knees, he swept the razor in brisk, deft strokes at the base of Pascal's head and behind his ears, nobody saying anything, Pascal sitting very still. Then Victory attacked the head once more with the scissors; then, with a powder puff, he puffed some white powder over the places where he had wielded the razor. He took up a comb and handed it to Pascal. He was going to do the final shaping of the hair now.

'Comb out your hair,' he said to Pascal. 'Wait. Is so you does comb your hair?' he asked, seeing Pascal combing from back to front.

'I combing it *out*. I usually comb it backwards.'

'Well, comb it backwards, just as you does comb it when you dollsing up.' Watching Pascal comb his hair, Victory continued talking. 'You build a club to last, to stand up. They say nothing can't last in Cunaripo. They say we can't build nothing. And you build a club and next thing you know, bam! fellars you building it with gone away.'

'What you want them to do?' Pascal asked.

'You think I going to stay here just to play cricket?' Brown said.

'*Just*?' Victory asked. '*Just* to play cricket? How you mean *just* to play cricket? What you think put us on the map, make us known in Pakistan, England, Australia? You all don't know what to care about?'

'You have to be able to afford to care,' Brown said. 'How you expect a fellar like me scrambling for a living, to care about cricket?'

'And how you will care about anything? Somebody will pay you to care? They will give you money and then you will care, eh, Brown? Money will make you care?' Victory had stopped work on Pascal's head.

'I would go away to better my position,' Brown said. 'Not because I don't care.'

'Betterment? By the time you come back you stop playing cricket, you seeing 'bout wife and children, you get fat. It was like if you was never here. Sometimes I look through the scorebook and see the names of players who used to play: Bridges, Kedar, Housen, Francis, Lee, Bisson, Griffith. Was like they was never here. Maybe the government should give a subsidy to care, eh, Brown, eh?'

'Is not the going away,' the fellar named Ross said.

Victory turned upon him, 'Is not the going away? Wait! You come in this barbershop a stranger and making more noise than anybody and now you telling me "is not the going away"?'

'Is not the going away,' Ross said, holding his ground in the now silent barbershop, 'What it is? Is what they do while they here … I see Housen. I see him play in Arima and I see him play in 'Grande. I remember him like today, and is how long ago I see him play? He bring an excitement, a magic, a life. You see him on the field and you see life. You see yourself. Is like that, I miss a man like Housen. I glad he was here.'

The silence deepened in the barbershop.

'Is true, Victory,' Pascal said. 'I play against him once. He playing for Dades Trace, I playing for Colts, and when he finish bat … I mean, when we at last get him out, the whole field was clapping, not because we out him, because of the innings he play. Is true. The man coulda bat.'

Victory spun the chair around and crouched and looked at Pascal's head, then he spun the chair again and looked at the head as a surveyor looking for an angle. Then he rose up.

'So you does play cricket?' Victory asked, turning now to the fellar named Ross, his scissors clicking once again. 'What you do? Bat? Bowl?'

'Open bat and bowl medium pace. Inswing mostly, but now and again I does get one to move away.'

'Ross, you say your name is? From Arima. It had a fellar used to work with the electricity company. Gerome Ross. Tall, kinda good looking, always with his hair cut neat and his moustache trimmed?'

'Gerome? That is my first cousin.'

'When he was up here, he was my good pardner. Neat, clothes always sharp, dressed to kill when he playing cricket, but he couldn't play fast bowling. Bounce one at him and he start to dodge away. Rupert used to have him hopping. What about him?'

'He get kinda fat,' Ross said.

Victory looked down at his own middle, 'Just now I have to start some jogging. Or maybe start to referee some football. Pascal, you don't remember Gerome? Coulda kick a football *hard*. Goalies used to cry when they see him coming.'

Brown had been studying the draughts board and now, as if he had the whole game worked out, he pushed a knob and said to Ross, 'Your play.'

Victory finished touching up Pascal's head, went around behind him and unpinned the cloth, taking if off carefully so that the hair wouldn't fall on Pascal's clothes. He brushed the tufts of cut hair off the cloth into a heap on the floor, then went to the door and holding the cloth with two hands dusted it out, flap, flap, flap, then he began to fold it. When he turned it was to see Pascal standing in front of the mirror looking at his head admiringly.

'You still think I shoulda clean it?' Victory asked, still folding the cloth.

Pascal turned his head this way and that. Then a smile broke onto his face, 'How much I have for you?'

'The price aint gone up,' Victory said.

As Pascal put his hand in his pocket, Brown let out a big exclamation and slapped a knob down on the draughts board, same time springing to his feet just as the legs of the bench gave away, upsetting the whole game, but not before Ross, with a quickness that amazed Victory, had leapt from the falling bench. Victory thinking, yes, he's an opening bat in truth.

'I tell you,' Victory said sternly. 'I tell you the legs of that bench not good. I don't have money to pay compensation when somebody break they back. People sit down on that bench like they riding a horse. Brown,' he said, his tone changing,

'You better come tomorrow with your hammer and fix that bench before somebody get kill.'

Ross had moved to the mirror and was looking at his head. Then he lowered himself into the barbering chair, 'You think you could give me a trim, Victory? I does really trim in Arima, but I going to be up here now.'

'How you want it?' Victory asked, picking up the cloth once again.

'Now,' said Ross. 'It mustn't be too low. Cut down the sides, level off the back, and leave my muff.'

Victory unfolded the cloth, went to the doorway and dusted it out, flop, flop, flop, then he came around behind Ross to pin the cloth around his neck, 'And, you know,' Victory said as he drew the ends of the cloth securely around Ross' neck, 'When you step through that door this morning, I sure you was a blight.'

Child of Darkening Humour

Noel D. Williams

p.209

Gold, 1973

Mrs Beverly Segree (her husband had died in a spectacular crash, she had informed a vacationing American at the beauty parlour a few hours ago, and her little boy was approaching fourteen and quite a prodigy) almost collapsed from laughter one evening, minutes before Mrs Hart and her husband finally left. She had been preparing to go out (it was her birthday) to dinner with the Doctor, and then the playhouse, and had welcomed the Harts graciously, hoping to suggest (as she had learnt to with difficult people and complainants at the Tourist Office) that the timing of their visit was distressingly wrong. While Mr Hart was parked placidly before the television, a picture of the courtroom composure he had worked hard to master (the pipe-smoking lawyer, ingeniously detecting false evidence), Mrs Hart had slipped off and was perched on the pink spread of the large bed, talking vociferously. She was relating at that very moment, while Mrs Segree skipped from bathroom to dressing mirror pausing only at the hushed point before the climax of a scandalous disclosure, an incident circulating in talk relay among the men and women of the university community. About a foreign lecturer in physics and a city prostitute. 'My dear, it is quite frightening sometimes, the things that go on up there. You'd never believe it. The man was led to believe she was a medical student …' Mrs Segree had interrupted, suddenly serious-faced, and shouted to Gran in the living room to listen for the Doctor's car. He was not a very patient man. He announced his arrival by giving three short blasts on the horn, and waited, the motor still running, for her to join him outside. Once in an inexplicable rage he drove off and left her standing, well-dressed and fumbling with the latch of the gate. She had stayed in Montego Bay (where her office was located) for over a month and a half before coming home to Gran and her boy and the neighbours who must have forgotten the whole thing.

Gran was sitting in an easy chair pretending to be engrossed in the newspaper. She made little attempt to converse with Mr Hart except to ask him, as a polite matter of course, whether he wanted anything to drink. He had refused, tucked a pipe at the side of his mouth and was preparing to light up the tobacco. She did not like him at all, and had turned on the television minutes before he had entered trailing after his wife's breathless chatter and handbag smile (he had delayed to lock up the car and to inspect it again, as if inviting the secret approval of the world whose satisfaction he acknowledged with a practised, stiff gait and pencil moustache and the studied inattention of a half-successful, brooding man). She had hoped he would be tempted to watch, and he had indeed nestled (it was close to a programme of world news) into that thought-tidy, scrupulous sobermanliness with which he approached the tumult of every ungodly event, encapsulated and reported now in the satisfyingly grave tones of the local newscaster.

She thought he was quite unlike her son and glanced at him, photographed and framed on the piano. She had heard, however, that he was an impressive lawyer, given to colourful speeches on behalf of destitute clients. His English wife was much more the talker during social visits. She chirped solicitously, asked serious questions about quaint local customs and told hilarious anecdotes about other people which only foreigners to the island could relate with such peculiar zest, such human world-weariness. She had attended the courts once and had said after, about Mr Hart, that he displayed (Gran remembered her exact words) 'a poet's remarkable sensitivity to their unlettered terror of farcical procedure and legal rigmarole'. She was a lecturer at the university. Their marriage was the trump-charged hand of bridge players in the field, a contract of concealment, without child.

But he sat before the television and sorted out from all the screen intensity information about seemingly unstoppable upheavals in far-flung parts of the globe. He had grown familiar with the 'trouble spots', the 'psychopaths' to the left and right, and at weekends (often after strenuous afternoons of lawn tennis and over frothy beer at the club's bar) he turned his thoughts incisively on the 'painful absurdities' here at home.

Gran turned to the centre pages and looked through the windows half-expectantly. She wondered about Morgan, her grandson, who had retired to his room earlier that evening, and she feared an interruption, another display of bad manners which his mother had, after one unforgettable evening, spoken to the Doctor about, believing that his accident when still a baby had caused serious damage to his brain as well. Recently he had been given a chemistry set (his mother always returned home with an expensive gift; she felt it made up for her long absence and would help to *motivate* the boy).

It was when she caught the first vagrant whiff of an offensive smell that Gran knew the little demon was concocting gases or something. She rose to speak to him but heard at the same moment the sound of a car approaching the house which meant (she tensed in every patient muscle) the Doctor. The door of the bedroom had opened and Mrs Hart came out still running her tale but preparing to leave. Mrs Segree looked slightly agitated and glanced towards the door. But the car had stopped, the motor had gone silent, and shortly after (Mr Hart was also slowly, and with visible regret and annoyance, detaching himself from the news) the Doctor came through the door. He was a smooth-shaven man of middle height, wearing an informal jacket, a neckerchief and flashing white shoes. His gruffness of greeting softened into tasteful silence as he found himself being quickly introduced, nodding politely at the English woman and shaking Mr Hart's hand (the name, the name didn't register).

They seized a few moments of chatter, in a small impromptu circle in the living room. It was their rubber dinghy of sharing a rare warmth amidst the dark choppy waters of the island's disorder. And Gran hoped they would not notice the smell which had intruded and was becoming stronger. But Mrs Hart, warming instinctively to a new island acquaintance, unwrapped a story about the day she arrived on the island.

'We had just left the airport,' she was saying in confidential tones that promised intrigue, 'and we had reached that stretch of road, you know, where you get your first marvellous view of the sea and the mountains. Well, all of a sudden, there, right in front of us, was this positively revolting figure of … a black man. Absolutely stark naked!' The group perked up and shuffled. The Doctor folded his arms and waited. And Mrs Hart, now feverish and inspired, rushed on up to the intimacy she had flagged down. 'He just stood there, trying to stop our car. He was almost in the middle of the road and we were, oh, about fifty yards or so away, when suddenly he threw up his hands as if he were about to die or fling a curse at us or something. We had to swerve to avoid hitting the man. We might have run right over him.'

(Mr Hart had hissed, 'My God! The mentality of these people …' as if passing a traveller's cheque of self-advertisement, or a scribbled note of apology to the flabbergasted witness of the world.)

'I turned to my husband and I said, "Darling, are we really home?" I asked. Of course we all laughed and he said that for a moment he was not quite sure, that, maybe, we *were* home, back on the mainland somewhere. It really was the most incredible sight. I haven't met him since, the man I mean, though you never can tell where next he'll turn up.'

Gran had slipped away while the introductions were being made. By the time she returned to the living room having spoken sharply to Morgan about his inconsiderate conduct (he had not even looked up at her), the Harts, to her great relief, were getting into their car. She seemed to recall a voice shouting farewell, hoping perhaps the sound would locate her wherever she was in the house and deliver its ringing good cheer. The Doctor was standing before the television, impatience beginning to swell in his neatly dressed figure; for Mrs Segree was back in her bedroom attending to finishing details, but appearing to delay longer than was necessary. Gran was on the point of taking up the newspaper again (there was little she could say to the Doctor in that mood) when he swore and exploded with trembling anger.

The newscaster was reporting on army and police operations in the hills. Gran had noticed a similar report in the newspapers outlining new plans to combat disorder and crime. The operation was designed to smoke out criminals believed to be holding out in the hills. There had been rumours of secret training camps and an unearthed cache of weapons, and it seemed a big swoop and gunbattle had taken place in which three men had been fatally shot.

The face on the screen affected deep concern but there was just a hint of compensating triumph in the announcement which did succeed, however, in comforting the Doctor. He swore loudly again (Mrs Segree was running to the bathroom, shouting an excuse and promising to be right out) and broke out in a tense perspiration. He fumbled for a handkerchief.

'Hooligans … morbid anatomy and laziness, that's what it is. And all these strikes, killings, all this *indecency*. Nothing but morbid anatomy. Damn lazy, hooligans, predatory on the hard-working. A heap of unhygienic rabble, look at them!' The screen was showing a small group of captured men being handcuffed and pushed into waiting jeeps by cinematically-clad troops, bristling automatic weapons. 'And those other dreamers blaspheming our sight with their self-righteousness, polluting our ears with foolish lamentation and drums! I'd castrate the whole pack of them. Make all that innocence and holy rage into the impotence they conceal and robe in seediness and ignorant prophecy. It is the morbid anatomy of the victim, badly wanting insult and courting our complicity and reluctant hand in rituals of defilement.'

He was wiping his face, fresh and wet and slapped from some coiled serpent sleep, and he was apologising to Gran as if she were a patient on a crowded hospital bed, staring at him through a film of bewildering pain; as if he had committed an irrevocable error, with his blunt authority of scalpel and stainless white jacket and hypocritical wedge of an oath he could not now renounce, like a cancerous disposition. He was sorry, he said.

Gran wished them a good night and waited until the car had taken off before rising to peer through the window. The darkness outside prowled away and assumed the stillness of a drowsy, half-attentive jury. She felt strangely soothed by its absence of stress, its accommodating ocean depth (there were lights up in the distance, of dwellings she could see clearly during the day). She turned off the television, lights in empty rooms, and decided she would speak again to Morgan before she retired.

He had never known his father, Gran's only son and bridgehead of an unexamined privilege of birth and the stolen right to make a name for himself. That was a self-made man, she always said. He had not gone abroad to pursue and fulfil an impossible island yearning, and to return shot down by treacherous, doubtful homesickness. And ingeniously clever, he had shown an early interest in building model planes. On Sunday afternoon he went to a playing field nearby where scruffy, slum youth, fighting over football, stopped, squatted on haunches and watched as the model plane circled and dipped through space. And later in his life when his position in the insurance company allowed it, he had paid down for a private plane, the airship (it was his charming way of describing the Cessna), and flew around the island. On the day he died (Morgan was one year old then) she felt as if the light of day over the island had dimmed to an almost permanent state of mourning for the loss of his kind of daring inventiveness.

She had not attended the funeral (she was too weak, and the light seemed to hail her with a coded message she struggled, through deeply private sadness, to decipher). She had read a report in the newspapers (a vulgar piece, she thought, by some exuberant trainee) which reported a man from a distant village as saying that the airship had shot out, 'had come tumbling out' of the sky. There had been a photograph on the front page. The nose of the airship had lodged in the ground, one wing had tilted at a ludicrous angle. It seemed so utterly beyond repair. They had spared her details of the tragedy and had made arrangements for a quick burial (the doctor had been extremely helpful in making all preparations). Within one week he was buried and when Mrs Segree returned that afternoon from the funeral, her eyes reddened with weeping, she found Gran studying a framed photograph of her son, handsome and in full vigour, almost indestructibly modest.

But calamity had struck again soon after. Mrs Segree was giving Morgan a morning bath when the child slipped from her fingers and fell to the cold tiles. She had screamed, and was hysterical for several weeks. The doctor had been summoned and Morgan was taken to hospital. After months of what Gran imagined, with a sigh, to be the best in local consultative care, he was brought back home but it was feared he would grow up unable to walk. It was a year of unbelievable tragedy for the family but they survived the worst months quite well. Mrs Segree had taken this job with the Tourist Board, and Gran had assumed the responsibility of bringing up Morgan.

Above all, she was careful to educate him. She sat with him and watched television programmes which brought the troubled world into their living room; she read him children's classics, fairy tales (he was fascinated with stories of forests and monsters, and old men with white hair), and before he was ten he was coping with Dickens and even Shakespeare. She was honestly amazed at his quicksilver mind and imagination, and when one day (it was two days after his twelfth birthday) he appeared suddenly in the dining room, attempting bravely to walk, she stared at him and felt an oncoming dizziness. When she could see properly again and had focused on Morgan, he was telling her about the first science-fiction book he had just read but she was only half-listening. It seemed that the light had assumed a sharper edge, almost too strong for her ageing eyes. It was as if some trapped animal, after years of despairing waiting, had released itself; as if some shrunken leg and spirit had found its way back to a half-remembered lair. It was a miracle of forgiveness for which, it seemed, there was no one to thank amidst the vulgar confusion and foolish, struggling human war with the tight-lipped patient of life.

When Morgan was moving around the house (not too steadily; he walked with a stick, an absurd prop to his natural brilliance, Gran felt) she watched him with even greater anxiety. She would wait for him to approach with some marvellous question about the island or the world (he was given, however, to uttering elliptical statements of late, and often stood gazing blankly into space as if hoping to catch a chance communication, or scribbled note dropped from the beak of some winged intimation).

Her life was the routine and blessed compensation of the ageing. She went through the regular motions of, first, unlatching the kitchen door for the maid to get in at five-thirty; of answering the phone and informing callers (frequently male voices that sounded alarmingly familiar) that Mrs Segree was not in the city; and assimilating the sounds of domesticity in their quiet neighbourhood.

She did not have much to say to the neighbours, hardly finding the occasion to meet them. Across the road and beyond their high hedge lived, she knew, a French engineer, his daughter and a rather fierce dog. She had glimpsed him several times, washing his car or reading on the patio, and could hardly avoid raising a hand in respectful greeting. She was more intrigued with the little girl with short blonde curls, who romped on the lawns with the fierce dog. She felt Morgan would find her interesting to talk with. She seemed incredibly happy. And charmingly wicked, for they waited (dog and solitary girl) many afternoons until a noisy dishevelled group of children from a public school in the area passed by on their way home, then the dog would be set to give chase, scattering the children screaming in all directions. At precisely three every day the girl practised on the piano, first rapid up and down scales, then simple melodies of left and right hand delicacy. And Gran, listening from across the street, forgot the dryness and heat, the dust and hill fires, the mad hammerstroke of the sun. She slipped gently into the reflective pool of the melodies. It was the soothing hand of eternity upon the withered brow of her years.

But on Sundays, each week and every month, there was a visitor at the gate. A woman who travelled from a village in the hills all the way down to the city to sell her vegetables, oranges, breadfruit and cane. Gran had stopped her once, had found her land produce cheap and her peasant manners quite pleasing. She had told the woman to reappear at six in the morning, not before and not much after, but as early as five-thirty the woman and her boy (she had taken to bringing him along to introduce him to the mistress, and to allow him a taste of the city) and a mule bearing two heavy baskets were waiting at the gate. The woman knew perhaps she had arrived too soon. Gran was careful to go out shortly after six, her greeting tones suggesting that the woman seemed to have no understanding of what time meant.

On this Sunday (two days after Mrs Segree's birthday; she had flown off from the city), Gran went to the gate holding the collar of her dressing gown tightly against the morning chilliness. She enquired about the boy's health and inspected the baskets, all the while complaining to the world about the rising prices, the city problems of water and electricity, and her good fortune in conducting gentle transactions with the woman. When she was ready to withdraw (she never purchased very much but received, always as a generous offer from the heart, more vegetables and fruit than she could use) she listened as the woman spoke of her recurring illness. Recently she had received an injury which now compelled her to limp (she pulled up the hem of her long, plaid dress to display a stained bandage strapped around her left calf). Gran commiserated as best she could, exalting the woman's private distress to the battered, suffering status of the world. It was the poignant melody and game of lament played by the untidy island in the open, dark field of the world.

'Wha's happening to us, ma'am?' the woman pleaded suddenly, as if seeking a golden nugget of unearthed feeling, truth to take back from the city to her tiny village in the hills.

Gran felt a strange shudder in the morning light and looked up, as if a huge wing-tip had brushed by her heart, flying dangerously low and radioing its message and rhetorical plea for incredible salvation. The large markings of the woman's obvious disquiet lay folded and wet, jettisoned in haste upon the chilly dawn by some callous deliverer, or anguished victim of miscarriage.

'Our suffering is …' she was wrestling with a swelling irritation and sadness but she seemed to detect, in an infinite flash of sympathy, the ancient sigh nestling in the impulse of the woman's question.

'Our suffering,' she tried again, 'is like the rude loss of a treasured son, an emptiness …' (It was coming through, rushing up, plummeting down to an unmistakable clarity of disclosure.) 'I mean, the illegitimacy of such dank unfairness … it will be … unclaimed or reclaimed … Christ or Christophe … It will be, you'll see …'

But the woman and her son and the mule had reached a bend of the road where the curving hedge took them gently out of sight. Gran looked around her, thinking she had addressed some stray dog or an upstart wind panting at the back door of her heart for all that she had sown and gathered and stored away from all the hideous contemporary seriousness and frantic grope. It was (she hastened now to the house) the awesome, quivering bloodstain and issue of a dark wrong and amputation which no physician or magic healer from the sky could join, with all the skill aboard this grounded ship of an island, together again.

When she came into the living room she sat down in an easy chair to catch her breath. Her ageing heart was heaving with the thought of facing anew the intrusion of the world's curse and ugliness, its shoddy vagrancy and dropped anchor of innocence. And now, more menacingly than ever, this new insolence with which its wandering beggars, cast ashore and freed, dared to march into her island and boldly set up their shacks of human refusal to accept the logic and sentence passed over and upon them.

It was too much for her frayed soul (she wished her son were alive, he would know how to deal with this) and she lapsed into a troubled sleep.

It was the sound of someone hailing the Godharboured day of rest which brought her to her feet (each hovering sound was now a startling signal). What she saw when she looked outside almost felled her with its seeming lack of reason. Morgan was (What was he doing out there? And what time of day was it?) conversing with a strange man who seemed to be selling yard brooms. She recognised the man and shivered anxiously. He was one of the mad cultists. He wore a pouch of a hat, a thick, black beard, and a towel or rag was draped across his left shoulder.

'Morgan,' she shouted from the door, 'come inside at once. Get away from that man. You, sir, what do you want?'

The man had seen her peering the first time through the window. He smiled and replied, 'Selling brooms, ma'am, yard brooms.' He broke off knowing he could sell nothing here and, leaving a whispered prayer or password or sealed pact with the boy, he stalked off, tossing in the air the weirdest song and laughing lyric, or knife of a trick artist:

God is Dog/In-land is I-land

In and I and Out

I-land is I-world

God is Dog

in the spell of the Master

I-mind

Morgan was flabbergasted and stared after the man, his nose tracking the strangest aroma, receding breath of illumination, forbidden and outlawed from his steep diving hands until that moment, until the man selling yard brooms had approached the gate.

'Come in here at once,' Gran called, 'come away from the gate. That man is dreadful. They're dangerous. They kill.'

Morgan turned slowly, paused and started forward uncertainly. (He seemed so brave and frail out there, Gran thought, confronting the unpredictable, the shocking indecency out there.) He started up the path to the house, prowling lion of a child, in a webbed lair of self-possession from which, on occasion, he pulled out or snapped the unfairest of sleeping questions. He was muttering to himself.

'No wonder,' (she could hardly catch his words), 'no wonder we take off in quest of new orders to sell, new orders to celebrate, or cerebrate. It is this obsessional hunting of a destitute prey. Foolish compensating raids on a praying community by legions of the saved, privileged to disdain or patronise as the dripping fat of profits or scandal decrees.'

'An incensed, islanded love,' (was he trying, the foolish boy, to balance the whole earth on his left foot? He almost fell), 'and the suffocating incense of the dead dog in humanity.'

'Gran, what have your eyes seen?' (He was looking, through uncountable trees of bewilderment, at her.) 'Who piloting this damn airship? Chinese racehorse owner? Coat-and-tied Black? Syrian money eater? White grab 'n flee? God is Dog, see him there …?'

He pointed and knew, where the man selling yard brooms hailed songs to the heavens, his laugh and lyric looping back through the air like raw meat tossed from the butcher shop of his heart, whetting its patient knife for a humble sale.

Morgan looked at the gazing hills, then took the deepest breath to exhale its burning tremor of the future. Its hewn face of secrets, he knew, was the runaway spirit that once sought its green slopes for a refuge and forge of its angry breathing. Its smoke, curling in ascent, was the signal to a gloomy patient (refusing to grieve, planting new seed) finally free from the groping fingers counting the fee for a fumbled job or flight of mercy (commission of the sensitised doctor, rummaging an island wound for the beloved hem that dragged an unswept ocean floor; commission of the brooding lawyer, exhibiting the dried blood on a curious murder weapon to a jury convinced of the savage and unsalvageable in humanity).

It was growing dark, alarmingly dark upon the island, above the dog/shot kennel of the world.

Gran shuddered, turned, stumped a pealing toe, entered the house, shut and bolted the door.

The Man of the House

Frank O'Connor

p.210

When I woke, I heard my mother coughing, below in the kitchen. She had been coughing for days, but I had paid no attention. We were living on the Old Youghal Road at the time, the old hilly coaching road into East Cork. The coughing sounded terrible. I dressed and went downstairs in my stockinged feet, and in the clear morning light I saw her, unaware that she was being watched, collapsed into a little wickerwork armchair, holding her side. She had made an attempt to light the fire, but it had gone against her. She looked so tired and helpless that my heart turned over with compassion. I ran to her.

'Are you all right, Mum?' I asked.

'I'll be all right in a second,' she replied, trying to smile. 'The old sticks were wet, and the smoke started me coughing.'

'Go back to bed and I'll light the fire,' I said.

'Ah, how can I, child?' she said anxiously. 'Sure, I have to go to work.'

'You couldn't work like that,' I said. 'I'll stop at home from school and look after you.'

It's a funny thing about women, the way they'll take orders from anything in trousers, even if it's only ten.

'If you could make yourself a cup of tea, I might be all right later on,' she said guiltily, and she rose, very shakily, and climbed back up the stairs. I knew then she must be feeling really bad.

I got more sticks out of the coalhole, under the stairs. My mother was so economical that she never used enough, and that was why the fire sometimes went against her. I used a whole bundle, and I soon had the fire roaring and the kettle on. I made her toast while I was about it. I was a great believer of hot buttered toast at all hours of the day. Then I made the tea and brought her up a cup on the tray. 'Is that all right?' I asked.

'Would you have a sup of boiling water left?' she asked doubtfully.

''Tis too strong,' I agreed cheerfully, remembering the patience of the saints in their many afflictions. 'I'll pour half of it out.'

'I'm an old nuisance,' she sighed.

''Tis my fault,' I said, taking the cup. 'I can never remember about tea. Put the shawl round you while you're sitting up. Will I shut the skylight?'

'Would you be able?' she asked doubtfully.

''Tis no trouble,' I said, getting the chair to it. 'I'll do the messages after.'

I had my own breakfast alone by the window, and then I went out and stood by the front door to watch the kids from the road on their way to school.

'You'd better hurry or you'll be killed, Sullivan,' they shouted.

'I'm not going,' I said. 'My mother is sick, and I have to mind the house.'

I wasn't a malicious child, by any means, but I liked to be able to take out my comforts and study them by the light of others' misfortunes. Then I heated another kettle of water and cleared up the breakfast things before I washed my face and came up to the attic with my shopping basket, a piece of paper, and a lead pencil.

'I'll do the messages now if you'll write them down,' I said. 'Would you like me to get the doctor?'

'Ah,' said my mother impatiently, 'he'd only want to send me to hospital, and how would I go to hospital? You could call in at the chemist's and ask him to give you a good, strong cough bottle.'

'Write it down,' I said. 'If I haven't it written down, I might forget it. And put "strong" in big letters. What will I get for the dinner? Eggs?'

As boiled eggs were the only dish I could manage, I more or less knew it would be eggs, but she told me to get sausages as well, in case she could get up.

I passed the school on my way. Opposite it was a hill, and I went up a short distance and stood there for ten minutes in quiet contemplation. The schoolhouse and yard and gate were revealed as in a painted picture, detached and peaceful except for the chorus of voices through the opened windows and the glimpse of Danny Delaney, the teacher, passing the front door with his cane behind his back, stealing a glance at the world outside. I could have stood there all day. Of all the profound and simple pleasures of those days, that was the richest.

When I got home, I rushed and found Minnie Ryan sitting with my mother. She was a middle-aged woman, very knowledgeable, gossipy, and pious.

'How are you, Mum?' I asked.

'Grand,' said my mother, with a smile.

'You can't get up today, though,' said Minnie Ryan.

'I'll put the kettle on and make a cup of tea for you,' I said.

'Sure I'll do that,' said Minnie.

'Ah, don't worry, Miss Ryan,' I said lightly. 'I can manage it all right.'

'Wisha, isn't he very good?' I heard her say in a low voice to my mother.

'As good as gold,' said my mother.

'There's not many like that, then,' said Minnie. 'The most of them that's going now are more like savages than Christians.'

In the afternoon, my mother wanted me to run out and play, but I didn't go far. I knew if once I went a certain distance from the house, I was liable to stray into temptation. Below our house, there was a glen, the drill field of the barracks perched high above it on a chalky cliff, and below, in a deep hollow, the millpond and millstream running between wooded hills – the Rockies, the Himalayas, or the Highlands, according to your mood. Once down there, I tended to forget the real world, so I sat on a wall outside the house, running in every half hour to see how the mother was and if there was anything she wanted.

Evening fell; the street lamps were lit, and the paper boy went crying up the road. I bought a paper, lit the lamp in the kitchen and the candle in my mother's attic, and tried to read to her, not very successfully, because I was only at words of one syllable, but I have a great wish to please, and she to be pleased, so we got on quite well, considering.

Later, Minnie Ryan came again, and as she was going, I saw her to the door.

'If she's not better in the morning, I think I'd get the doctor, Flurry,' she said, over her shoulder.

'Why?' I asked, in alarm. 'Do you think she is worse, Miss Ryan?'

'Ah, I wouldn't say so,' she replied with affected nonchalance, 'but I'd be frightened she might get pneumonia.'

'But wouldn't he send her to hospital, Miss Ryan?'

'Wisha, he mightn't,' she said with a shrug, pulling her old shawl about her. 'But even if he did, wouldn't it be better than neglecting it? Ye wouldn't have a drop of whiskey in the house?'

'I'll get it,' I said at once. I knew what might happen to people who got pneumonia, and what was bound to happen afterward to their children.

'If you could give it to her hot, with a squeeze of lemon in it, it might help her to shake it off,' said Minnie.

My mother said she didn't want the whiskey, dreading the expense, but I had got such a fright that I wouldn't be put off. When I went to the public house, it was full of men, who drew aside to let me reach the bar. I had never been in a public house before, and I was frightened.

'Hullo, my old flower,' said one man, grinning diabolically at me. 'It must be ten years since I seen you last. What are you having?'

My pal, Bob Connell, had told me how he once asked a drunk man for a half crown and the man gave it to him. I always wished I could bring myself to do the same, but I didn't feel like it just then.

'I want a half-glass of whiskey for my mother,' I said.

'Oh, the thundering ruffian!' said the man. 'Pretending 'tis for his mother, and the last time I seen him he had to be carried home.'

'I had not,' I shouted indignantly. 'And *'tis* for my mother. She's sick.'

'Ah, let the child alone, Johnnie,' said the barmaid. She gave me the whiskey, and then, still frightened of the men in the public house, I went off to a shop for a lemon.

When my mother had drunk the hot whiskey, she fell asleep, and I quenched the lights and went to bed, but I couldn't sleep very well. I was regretting I hadn't asked the man in the pub for a half crown. I was wakened several times by the coughing, and when I went into my mother's room her head felt very hot, and she was rambling in her talk. It frightened me more than anything else when she didn't know me, and I lay awake, thinking of what would happen to me if it were really pneumonia.

The depression was terrible when, next morning, my mother seemed not to be any better. I had done all I could do, and I felt helpless. I lit the fire and got her breakfast, but this time I didn't stand at the front door to see the other fellows on their way to school. I should have been too inclined to envy them. Instead, I went over to Minnie Ryan and reported.

'I'd go for the doctor,' she said firmly. 'Better be sure than sorry.'

I had first to go to the house of a Poor Law Guardian, for a ticket to show we couldn't pay. Then I went down to the dispensary, which was in a deep hollow beyond the school. After that I had to go back to ready the house for the doctor. I had to have a basin of water and soap and a clean towel laid out for him, and I had to get the dinner, too.

It was after dinner when he called. He was a fat, loud-voiced man and, like all the drunks of the medical profession, supposed to be 'the cleverest doctor in Cork, if only he'd mind himself'. He hadn't been minding himself much that morning, it seemed.

'How are you going to get this now?' he grumbled, sitting on the bed with the prescription pad on his knee. 'The only place open is the North Dispensary.'

'I'll go, Doctor,' I said at once, relieved that he had said nothing about hospital.

''Tis a long way,' he said, doubtfully. 'Do you know where it is?'

'I'll find it,' I said.

'Isn't he a great little fellow?' he said to my mother.

'Oh, the best in the world, Doctor!' she said. 'A daughter couldn't be better to me.'

'That's right,' said the doctor. 'Look after your mother; she'll be the best for you in the long run. We don't mind them when we have them,' he added, to my mother, 'and then we spend the rest of our lives regretting it.'

I wished he hadn't said that; it tuned in altogether too well with my mood. To make it worse, he didn't even use the soap and water I had laid ready for him.

My mother gave me directions how to reach the dispensary and I set off with a bottle wrapped in brown paper under my arm. The road led uphill, through a thickly populated poor locality, as far as the barracks, which was perched on the very top of the hill, over the city, and then descended, between high walls, till it suddenly almost disappeared in a stony path, with red brick corporation houses to one side of it, that dropped steeply, steeply, to the valley of the little river, where a brewery stood, and the opposite hillside, a murmuring honeycomb of houses, rose to the gently rounded top, on which stood the purple sandstone tower of the cathedral and the limestone spire of Shandon church, on a level with your eye.

It was so wide a view that it was never all lit up together, and the sunlight wandered across it as across a prairie, picking out first a line of roofs with a brightness like snow, and then delving into the depth of some dark street and outlining in shadow figures of climbing carts and straining horses. I leaned on the low wall and thought how happy a fellow could be, looking at that, if he had nothing to trouble him. I tore myself from it with a sigh, slithered without stopping to the bottom of the hill, and climbed up a series of shadowy and stepped lanes around the back of the cathedral, which now seemed enormous. I had a penny, which my mother had given me by way of encouragement, and I made up my mind that when I had done my business, I should go into the cathedral and spend it on a candle to the Blessed Virgin, to make my mother better quick. I felt sure it would be more effective in a really big church like that, so very close to Heaven.

The dispensary was a sordid little hallway with a bench to one side and a window like the one in a railway ticket office at the far end. There was a little girl with a green plaid shawl about her shoulders sitting on the bench. I knocked at the window, and a seedy, angry-looking man opened it. Without waiting for me to finish what I was saying, he grabbed bottle and prescription from me and banged the shutter down again without a word. I waited for a moment and then lifted my hand to knock again.

'You'll have to wait, little boy,' said the girl quickly.

'What will I have to wait for?' I asked.

'He have to make it up,' she explained. 'You might as well sit down.'

I did, glad of anyone to keep me company.

'Where are you from?' she asked. 'I live in Blarney Lane,' she added when I had told her. 'Who's the bottle for?'

'My mother,' I said.

'What's wrong with her?'

'She have a bad cough.'

'She might have consumption,' she said thoughtfully. 'That's what my sister that died last year had. This is a tonic for my other sister. She have to have tonics all the time. Is it nice where you live?'

I told her about the glen, and then she told me about the river near their place. It seemed to be a nicer place than ours, as she described it. She was a pleasant, talkative little girl, and I didn't notice the time until the window opened again and a red bottle was thrust out.

'Dooley!' shouted the seedy man, and closed the window again.

'That's me,' said the little girl. 'Yours won't be ready for a good while yet. I'll wait for you.'

'I have a penny,' I said boastfully.

She waited until my bottle was thrust out, and then she accompanied me as far as the steps leading down to the brewery. On the way, I bought a pennyworth of sweets, and we sat on the other steps, beside the infirmary to eat them. It was nice there, with the spire of Shandon in shadow behind us, the young trees overhanging the high walls, and the sun, when it came out in great golden blasts, throwing our linked shadows onto the road.

'Give us a taste of your bottle, little boy,' she said.

'Why?' I asked. 'Can't you taste your own?'

'Mine is awful,' she said. 'Tonics is awful to taste. You can try it if you like.'

I took a taste of it and hastily spat out. She was right; it was awful. After that, I couldn't do less than let her taste mine.

'That's grand,' she said enthusiastically, after taking a swig from it. 'Cough bottles are nearly always grand. Try it, can't you?'

I did, and saw she was right about that, too. It was very sweet and sticky.

'Give us another,' she said excitedly, grabbing at it.

''Twill be all gone,' I said.

'Erra, 'twon't,' she replied with a laugh. 'You have gallons of it.'

Somehow, I couldn't refuse her. I was swept from my anchorage into an unfamiliar world of spires and towers, trees, steps, shadowy laneways, and little girls with red hair and green eyes. I took a drink myself and gave her another. Then I began to panic. ''Tis nearly gone,' I said. 'What am I going to do now?'

'Finish it and say the cork fell out,' she replied, and again, as she said it, it sounded plausible enough. We finished the bottle between us, and then, slowly, as I looked at it in my hand, empty as I had brought it, and remembered that I had not kept my word to the Blessed Virgin and had spent her penny on sweets, a terrible despondency swept over me, I had sacrificed everything for the little girl and she didn't even care for me. It was my cough bottle she had coveted all the time. I saw her guile too late. I put my head in my hands and began to cry.

'What are you crying for?' the little girl asked in astonishment.

'My mother is sick, and we're after drinking her medicine,' I said.

'Ah, don't be an old crybaby!' she said contemptuously. 'You have only to say the cork fell out. Sure, that's a thing could happen to anybody.'

'And I promised the Blessed Virgin a candle, and I spent the money on you!' I screamed, and, suddenly grabbing the empty bottle, I ran up the road from her, wailing. Now I had only one refuge and one hope – a miracle. I went back to the cathedral, and, kneeling before the shrine of the Blessed Virgin, I begged her pardon for having spent her penny, and promised her a candle from the next penny I got, if only she would work a miracle and make my mother better before I got back. After that, I crawled miserably homeward, back up the great hill, but now all the light had gone out of the day, and the murmuring hillside had become a vast, alien, cruel world. Besides, I felt very sick. I thought I might be going to die. In one way it would be better.

When I got back into the house, the silence of the kitchen and then the sight of the fire gone out in the grate smote me with the cruel realisation that the Blessed Virgin had let me down. There was no miracle, and my mother was still in bed. At once, I began to howl.

'What is it at all, child?' she called in alarm from upstairs.

'I lost the medicine,' I bellowed, and rushed up the stairs to throw myself on the bed and bury my face in the clothes.

'Oh, wisha, if that's all that's a trouble to you!' she exclaimed with relief, running her hand through my hair. 'Is anything the matter?' she added, after a moment. 'You're very hot.'

'I drank the medicine,' I bawled.

'Ah, what harm?' she murmured soothingly. 'You poor, unfortunate child! 'Twas my own fault for letting you go all that way by yourself. And then to have your journey for nothing. Undress yourself now, and you can lie down here.'

She got up, put on her slippers and coat, and unlaced my boots while I sat on the bed. But even before she had finished I was fast asleep. I didn't see her dress herself or hear her go out, but some time later I felt a hand on my forehead and saw Minnie Ryan peering down at me, laughing.

'Ah, 'twill be nothing,' she said, giving her shawl a pull about her. 'He'll sleep it off by morning. The dear knows, Mrs Sullivan, 'tis you should be in bed.'

I knew that was a judgement on me, but I could do nothing about it. Later I saw my mother come in with the candle and her paper, and I smiled up at her. She smiled back. Minnie Ryan might despise me as much as she liked, but there were others who didn't. The miracle had happened, after all.

The Day the World Almost Came to an End

Pearl Crayton

If you haven't had the world coming to an end on you when you're twelve years old and a sinner, you don't know how lucky you are! When it happened to me it scared the living daylights and some of the joy of sinning out of me and, in a lot of other ways, messed up my life altogether. But if I am to believe Ralph Waldo Emerson's 'Compensation', I guess I got some good out of it too.

The calamity befell me back in 1936. We were living on a plantation in Louisiana at the time, close to the earth and God, and all wrapped up in religion. The church was the axis around which plantation life revolved, the Mother to whom the folks took their problems, the Teacher who taught them how the Lord wanted them to live, the Chastiser who threatened the sinful with Hell.

In spite of the fact that my parents were churchgoing Christians, I was still holding on to being a sinner. Not that I had anything against religion, it was just a matter of integrity. There was an old plantation custom that in order to be baptised into the church a sinner had to 'get religion', a mystical experience in which the soul of the sinner was converted into Christian. A Christian had to live upright, and I knew I just couldn't come up to that on account of there were too many delicious sins around to get into. But a world coming to an end can be pretty hard on a sinner.

The trouble began when my cousin Rena came upon me playing in the watermelon patch, running like the devil was behind her. I was making a whole quarter of mud cabins by packing dirt over my foot in the shape of a cabin, putting a chimney on top, then pulling my foot out. The space left by my foot formed the room of the cabin. I'd broken some twigs off chinaberry and sycamore trees which I planted in the ground around the cabins to make 'trees'. Some blooming wild flowers that I had picked made up a flower yard in front of each cabin. It was as pretty a sight as you ever want to see before she came stepping all over everything. I let her know I didn't like it real loud, but she didn't pay what I said any attention, she just blurted out, 'The end of the world is coming Saturday; you'd better go get you some religion in a hurry!'

That was on a Friday afternoon, getting late.

A picture of Hell flashed across my mind but I pushed it back into the subconscious. 'The world's NOT coming to an end!' The confidence I tried to put in my voice failed; it quaked a little. 'Who told you the world is coming to an end?'

'I heard Mama and Miss Daya talking about it just now. There's going to be an eclipse Sunday. You know what an eclipse is, don't you?'

I didn't know but I nodded anyhow.

'That's when the sun has a fight with the moon. If the sun whips, the world goes on; if the moon whips, then the world comes to an end. Well, they say that Sunday the moon is going to whip the sun!'

I wasn't going to be scared into giving up my sinning that easily. 'How do they know the moon is going to whip?' I asked.

'They read it in the almanac. And it's in the Bible too, in Revelation. It says in Revelation that the world is supposed to end this year. Miss Daya is a missionary sister and she knows all about things like that.'

'Nobody knows anything about Revelation, my daddy says so,' I rebutted. 'Ain't never been nobody born smart enough to figure out Revelation since that Mister John wrote it. He's just going to have to come back and explain it himself.'

She acted like she didn't hear that. 'And Reverend Davis said in church last Sunday that time is winding up,' she said.

'He's been saying that for years now, and time hasn't wound up yet.'

'That's what I know, he's been saying it for years, and all the while he's been saying it time's been winding right along, and now it's just about all wound up!'

That made sense to me and I began to consider that maybe she could be right. Then that Miss Daya happened by.

'Lord bless you down there on your knees, baby! Pray to the Lord 'cause it's praying time!'

I hadn't gotten up from where I'd been making mud cabins, but I jumped up quick to let her know I wasn't praying.

'Both of you girls got religion?' she asked, and without waiting for an answer, 'That's good. You're both big girls, big enough to go to Hell. You all be glad you all got religion 'cause the Lord is coming soon! He said he was coming and he's coming SOON!' And she went on towards our cabin before I could ask her about the world ending Sunday.

Rena just stood there and looked at me awhile, shaking her head in an 'I told you so,' and advised me again to get some religion in a hurry. Then she ran off to warn someone else.

Although I was a sinner, I was a regular churchgoing sinner and at our church we had a hellfire-preaching pastor. He could paint a picture of Hell and the Devil in his sermons horrible enough to give a sinner a whole week of nightmares. Nobody with a dime's worth of sense wanted to go to a hot, burning Hell where a red, horned Devil tormented folks with a pitchfork, but I'd been taking a chance on enjoying life another thirty years or so before getting some religion – getting just enough to keep me out of Hell. I hadn't figured on time running out on me so soon, and I still wasn't taking anybody's word before asking my daddy about it first. But it was ploughing time and Daddy was way back in the cornfield where I'd already run across a rattlesnake, so I figured even the world coming to an end could wait until suppertime.

I went around the rest of that day with my mind loaded down. Now I didn't exactly believe that the world was coming to an end, but I didn't exactly believe it wasn't either. About two years before, I'd went and read the worst part of Revelation and it had taken my daddy two weeks to convince me that I didn't understand what I had read, which still didn't keep me from having bad dreams about the moon dripping away in blood and a lot of other distressing visions aroused from misunderstood words.

Those dreams were only a vague and frightening memory the Friday I'm talking about, and Revelation an accepted mystery. Yet things like that have a way of sneaking back on you when you need it the least. I got to 'supposing' the world did come to an end with earthquakes and hail and fire raining down from the sky and stars falling, exactly like it read in Revelation, and 'supposing' the Devil got after me and took me to Hell like folks on the plantation said he would, and 'supposing' Hell really and truly was as horrible as the preacher said it was. The way the preacher told it, in Hell a person got burned and burned up and never died, he just kept on burning, burning, burning. With 'supposing' like that going through it, my mind was really loaded down! I figured there was no use talking to Mama about what was bothering me because that Miss Daya had stayed at our cabin for over an hour, and I was sure she had convinced Mama that the moon was going to whip the sun.

It seemed to me like it took Daddy longer than ever to come home. It was the Friday of Council Meeting at the church, and Daddy, a deacon, had to be there. I knew he wouldn't have much time to talk to me before he'd have to leave out for the church, so I started walking up the turnrow through the fields to meet him. When I finally saw him riding towards home on his slide I ran to meet him.

Daddy always hitched a plank under his plough to keep the plough blades from cutting up the turnrow when he came home from ploughing the fields. The plank, which we called a slide, was long enough behind the plough for him to stand on and ride home, pulled by his plough horse. Whenever I ran to meet him he'd let me ride home with him on the slide.

'Daddy,' I said as soon as he'd put me on the slide in front of him and 'gee'd' the horse to go on, 'is the world going to come to an end Sunday?'

'I don't know, honey,' he replied. 'Why do you want to know?'

I told him about Rena's prophecy. That really tickled him! He laughed and laughed like that was the funniest thing he'd ever heard! I laughed a little too, though I didn't get the joke in it.

'There's always somebody coming around prophesying that the world's coming to an end,' he said after he'd laughed himself out. 'Folks been doing that ever since I was a boy, they were doing it when my daddy was a boy, aw, they've been doing that for hundreds of years and the world is still here. Don't you ever pay any attention to anybody that comes around telling you the world is going to end, baby.'

'But ain't the world *ever* going to end?' I wanted to know.

'Yeah, but don't anybody know when. Only the Lord knows that. Why, the world might not end for another thousand years, then again it might end tonight, we just don't know …'

'TONIGHT! You mean the world might end TONIGHT!'

'Sure. I'm not saying it will but it could. A person never can tell about a thing like that. But if you let that bother you, why you'll be scared to death every day of your life looking for the world to end. You're not going to be that silly, are you?'

'Aw, shucks, no,' I lied. I was that silly. Right then and there I got to looking for the world to end, right there on the *spot*!

Like anybody expecting a calamity, I decided to sit up all night that night but Mama made me go to bed. My room was full of the plantation, the darkest of darkness. Before Daddy returned from church Mama put out the coal oil lamp and went to bed.

The lazy old moon was on its vacation again; there was no light anywhere, not a speck. Although my eyes couldn't see anything in that awful dark, my mind had always been very good at seeing things in the dark that weren't there. I got to 'seeing' how it was going to be when the world ended, the whole drama of it paraded right before my mind. Then my imagination marched me up before the judgment seat to give account for my past sins and I tried to figure out how much burning I'd get for each offence. Counting up all the ripe plums and peaches I'd saved from going to waste on the neighbours' trees, neglecting to get the owners' permission, the fights I'd had with that sassy little Catherine who lived across the river, the domino games I'd played for penny stakes with my sinner-cousin, Sam, the times I'd handled the truth careless enough to save myself from a whipping, and other not so holy acts, I figured I'd be in for some real hot burning.

While I lay there in that pitch-black darkness worrying myself sick about burning in Hell, a distant rumbling disturbed the stillness of the night, so faint that at first I wasn't sure I'd heard it. I sat up in the bed, straining my ears listening. Sure enough there was a rumbling, far away. The rumbling wasn't thunder, I was sure of that because thunder rumbled, then died away, but this rumbling grew louder and louder and LOUDER. A slow-moving, terrible, loud rumbling that was to my scared mind the earth quaking, the sky caving in, the world ending!

I got out of there, I got out of there *fast*! I didn't even think about being dressed only in my nightgown or the awful dark outside being full of ghosts and bogeymen and other horrors, I just ran!

'The world is ending! The world is ending! Run! Run for your life!' I shouted a warning to Mama, and I just kept on hollering as I ran down the road past the other plantation cabins. 'The world is ending! The world is ending! Run! Run for your life!'

Doors opened and folks came out on the cabin porches, some holding coal oil lamps in their hands. They'd look at me in my white nightgown running down the road as fast as a scared rabbit, then look up at the sky rumbling like it was caving in, and a few of them hollered something at me as I passed by, but I couldn't make out what any of them said.

I might have run myself plumb to the ocean or death if Daddy and some other deacons hadn't been coming up the road on their way from church. Daddy caught me. He had a hard time holding me though. The fear of the Devil and Hell was stronger in me than reason. I was dead set on escaping them.

Daddy had heard my hollering about the world ending as I ran down the road towards them, so he kept telling me, 'That's just an old airplane, honey, the world's not ending. That's just an old airplane making all that racket!'

When his words got through the fear that fogged my mind I calmed down a bit. 'Airplane?' I'd only heard about airplanes, never had I seen one or heard one passing by.

Daddy laughed. 'You were just about outrunning that old airplane and keeping up almost as much racket!' He pointed toward the sky. 'Look up there, you see, it's gone now. See that light moving towards town? That's it. Those old airplanes sure have scared a lot of folks with all that racket they make.'

I looked up. Sure enough there was a light that looked like a star moving across the sky. The rumbling was way off in the distance, going away slowly like it had come. And the sky was whole, not a piece of it had caved in! I broke down and cried because I was so relieved that the world wasn't coming to an end, because I'd been so scared for so long, because I'd made such a fool of myself, and just because.

Daddy pulled off his suit coat and wrapped it around me to hide the shame of my nightgown from the deacons. After I'd had a real good cry we walked home.

As we walked up the ribbon of road bordering the plantation on our way home I felt a new kind of happiness inside of me. The yellow squares of light shining from the black shapes of the plantation cabins outlined against the night made a picture that looked beautiful to me for the first time. Even the chirping of the crickets sounded beautiful, like a new song I'd never heard before. Even the darkness was beautiful, everything was beautiful. And I was alive, I felt the life within me warming me from the inside, a happy feeling I'd never had before. And the world was there all around me, I was aware of it, aware of all of it, full of beauty, full of happy things to do. Right then and there I was overwhelmed with a desire to *live*, really *live* in the world and enjoy as much of it as I could before it came to an end. And I've been doing so ever since.

It's Cherry Pink and Apple Blossom White

Barbara Jenkins

p.211 When I was eleven, my family split up. I didn't know then and I don't know now what caused this to happen. All I know is that one day my mother said that we were going to stay with some other people. It was right after I had taken the Exhibition exam for a high school place; the school holiday was about to begin and I remember my confusion as we children always spent the six weeks of holidays with our grandmother, at my mother's childhood home in Belmont Valley.

Maybe our father had decided he wouldn't continue to pay rent for our three rooms in the house in Boissiere Village. He didn't live with us, he visited in erratic pouncings. When his car slid silently to a halt at the house, the message, *Yuh fadda reach*, ran through the neighbourhood and, wherever we were, we scampered home. He sat on the bed, pointing to his left cheek for us to kiss and I wished for sudden death rather than enter his aura of smoke, staleness and rum. My mother made him coffee. One of us carried it to him. He drank it and left. Without his support, perhaps my mother saw the scattering of her brood as her only option when she no longer had a home in which we could all live together.

When she told me we would be going somewhere else, I got a cold, hard clenching feeling in my belly, but I didn't have the words to tell her that. As she was leaving, she stood facing me, held my shoulders and said, 'Be a good girl,' as she did whenever she left me anywhere, but that time my mother didn't look into my eyes; she looked down at the floor. I saw her cheeks were smeared and wet; I was puzzled. I touched her face; the powder she rarely wore came off on my palm. She was dressed as if for a special occasion, a christening or a funeral, and, as she turned away, I caught hold of the skirt of her smoke-grey shantung dress with the tiny pearl buttons like a row of boiled fishes' eyes. My hand left a dull orange smear of Max Factor Suntan. I saw the stain I had made and I felt glad.

None of us was left with family. I was to go to a neighbour; one sister was sent to San Fernando to stay with friends of my mother's – people we children didn't know; where the other went I don't remember, but I do know that our mother took only my one-year-old brother with her, and we didn't know where. I think that she must have been planning this for a while; the far-flung arrangements would have been difficult to negotiate quickly without telephone, and the timing was too convenient to be coincidence.

My new home was a shop. Over the street door was a sign, white lettering on black, 'Marie Tai Shue, licensed to sell spirituous liquors'. I knew the shop well, since, as the eldest, I was the one sent to make message. We children on the making message mission scrambled up with dusty bare feet to sit on the huge hundredweight crocus bags of dry goods stacked against the interior walls of the shop until Auntie Marie called out, 'What you come for?' Nobody but the bees cared that we were sitting on foodstuffs – rice, sugar, dried beans, and the bees only bothered if you sat on a sugar bag without noticing their plump golden-brown stripes camouflaged against the brown string of the sacks, heads burrowed into the tight weave.

Early morning, my mother sent me for four hops bread and two ounces of cheese or salami; mid-morning, half-pound rice, quarter-pound dried beans, quarter-pound pig tail, salt beef or salt fish; more hops bread and two ounces of fresh butter mid-afternoon. I had no money for my shopping; we took goods 'on trust' all week. The items were handed over, the amount owed was noted in Chinese script on a small square of brown paper selected from a creased and curling pack threaded through a long hooked wire suspended from a nail driven into the back wall. I would peer over the counter to watch Auntie go to the dark recesses of the shop, hear the thunk of the chopper as it cleaved through the salted meat into the chopping block, then remember to call, 'Mammie say cut from the middle,' or 'Mammie say not too much bone.' On Saturdays, my mother went herself for the week's supplies: Nestlé's condensed milk, Fry's cocoa powder, bars of yellow Sunlight soap for washing clothes and a single-cup sachet of Nestlé instant coffee, just in case. She'd bring a rum bottle for cooking oil and a can for pitch-oil for the stove. What she was able to take away depended on Auntie's goodwill and on how much of that week's accumulated 'on trust' total she could wipe off.

In my new life I was on the other side of the shop counter with a new family. The six children ranged in age from fifteen to nine. I moved in with a cardboard box and a folding canvas camp-bed which the boys set up in the girls' room, between Suelin's bed and Meilin's and Kanlin's double-decker. One of the boys hammered two new nails behind the bedroom door where my clothes would hang alongside the girls': a Sunday dress, two outgrown school overalls as day clothes and another for the night. That first night, I closed my eyes and saw pictures running behind my eyelids. I saw my cousins at my grandmother's climbing trees, picking and eating chenette, mango, pommerac, playing in the rain and the river. Without me. I saw Miriam, chief rival as my grandmother's favourite, brushing Granny's long silver hair until she fell asleep at siesta-time. Perhaps, with me not there, Uncle Francois was choosing Jeannie to help him pack the panniers of gladioli and dahlias to take to the flower shop. I felt red heat rise and fill my head at my mother for cheating me of what was mine by right. Then I remembered her face when she was leaving me. I wondered why she wouldn't look at me. Did she feel bad about leaving me where I didn't want to be? I felt a tugging tightness in my throat about being glad for spoiling her best dress. I had looked at her downcast face and promised I would be a good girl and not give Auntie Marie any trouble.

Life in my new home seemed one of plenty – the whole grocery to choose from, a shower with a door and latch, toothpaste not salt, their own latrine. I felt lucky. All these luxuries were mine too. On dry days, Meilin and I scrubbed clothes in a tub and spread soapy garments on a bed of rocks in the backyard to bleach in the sunshine. Next day, two of the boys rinsed and wrung out the clothes, draping them over hibiscus and sweet lime bushes to dry. Between us we swept and mopped the floors of the two bedrooms and the common living and dining space at the back of the shop where Auntie slept at night in a hammock of bleached flourbags. After closing the shop at night, Auntie cooked dinner, my first experience of strange food: grainy rice or noodles infused with the salt and fat of chunks of Chinese sausage, patchoi, cabbage, carrots fragrant with thin slices of ginger steamed in a bamboo basket above the simmering pot, meat slivers flashed in a wok. Auntie spoke Cantonese to her children; they answered in English. I listened to tone, looked from face to face, followed the thread and joined in.

The bigger children helped in the shop; I wasn't expected to, but I often sat on a bench, watching and listening and learning. I could fold brown paper so that the edges were straight and, inserting a long, sharp knife, cut to size for half-pound, quarter-pound, two-ounce dry goods and farthing salt, but two tricks of the trade defeated me. The first was twisting a sheet of paper up at two sides around dry goods to make a firm, leak-proof package and flipping the whole over to close the top in a fold. The second was unpicking the ends of the stitching across the top of a crocus bag so that, when you held the two loose ends of string and pulled, the top of the bag fell open to expose sugar or rice, like Moses unzipping the Red Sea to reveal the dry land below, leaving you with a long zigzag piece of twine, perfect for flying kites.

I had long idle spells when I would read – anything, everything. On the narrow shelves along the shop's back wall were goods we seldom had at home. I would pick up these luxuries, hold them, read the labels: Carnation evaporated milk, Libby's corned beef, blue and gold tins of fresh butter, Andrex toilet paper, Moddess sanitary napkins. My hands caressed things from England, Australia, New Zealand, USA and I felt a current connecting me with those places. The boys had comic books that they hid under their beds. I would borrow a comic and steal away to read it quickly and borrow another. Comics pulled me immediately into their unambiguous graphic world where I had the power to do anything. I could save the world from alien invasion, rescue beleaguered innocents from danger, fight forces bent on destroying civilisation. With just Kryptonite, a Batmobile, a two-way wrist radio, Hi-Ho Silver, I leapt over skyscrapers with a single bound, stopped speeding trains with bare hands, deflected bullets to ricochet onto the bad guys, big things, real things. When I stopped reading, I looked at my world, hoping to find some disaster I could avert, but I saw no Martians, missiles or maverick trains, so I opened another comic, and another. I lived in so many other worlds that, for much of the time, I moved through my real world as if it was just something else I was reading and had got lost in. Each new thing I read added to my world, making my own life something I had to let happen, like a story whose pages I was turning, not something I could shape myself.

For the people I lived with, reading brought them the world they had physically left but had carried with them in everything they thought and did. The Chinese community had an informal circulating library of magazine-type papers from China, 'Free' China. Auntie and Suelin would read the Chinese script from the back page bottom right corner and work their way up the columns to the front page. From the synopsis in English, I learnt about Sun-Yat-Sen, saw pictures of Chiang-Kai-Shek with the glamorous cheongsam-clad Madam Chiang-Kai-Shek, and read about Mao-Tse-Tung. The first two were revered, the last hated – he and the Communists had driven them out of China, stealing all they had and then seizing their family. I wondered whether the Communists had captured my mother, forcing her to give us away and if this was so, how did she know that the people she left me with could be trusted not to give me to the Communists in exchange for their own captured family? I didn't think they would do this because they were taking care of me, just as if I was one of the children of their family. But then, maybe they were fattening me up like the witch in Hansel and Gretel, because sometimes they had big gatherings and feasts.

When fellow shopkeepers, laundry owners and restaurant proprietors came to visit on Sunday, the white-shirted men and their jade-bedecked wives would sit round a table quickly assembled from an old door and packing cases, covered with a white sheet. Competing chatter in passionate, high pitched Cantonese – sounds like frantic trapped birds crashing into glass panes – would rise to a clamour, and just when I thought a fight would start, there would be explosions of laughter, the brandishing of magazines, and the pointing at one another with raised chopsticks, still pinching slick black mushrooms and floppy white wantons. There was a constant flow of china bowls and platters bearing translucent rice noodles and bright green chopped chives floating in clear broth, shrimp and pork fried rice, meat, soybean curd, bamboo shoots, water chestnuts, glistening roasted duck, rice wine poured from a ceramic bottle into matching thimble cups, sweet and sour prunes hidden in layers of paper, preserved ginger.

I had never been to a restaurant, had never imagined such plenty of food and noise. I had never before seen this close-knittedness, this exclusiveness of clan bonding. I stayed on the edge, watching. I felt I was both in and at a movie.

On a normal weekday I found other entertainment, watching bar customers. Men came in from mid-morning, ordered shots of rum and single cigarettes, sat on long benches at the wooden table to drink, smoke, play cards for small stakes, talk, argue. On payday they would buy nips and flasks, pour on the dusty concrete floor an offering to those gone before, and lime as long as they could until their women sent children to rescue the residue of the family funds before it was all smoked, drunk and gambled away. We in-house children served the orders, cleared up glasses and ran our own riotous card games in a corner with burnt matches as our stakes.

But best of all was the radio in the bar, a novelty for me. It was kept permanently turned to WVDI, beamed from the American base at Chaguaramas. The call signal, "This is station WVDI, the armed forces radio station in Trinidad," was said in that cool, confident, leisurely, Yankee drawl that conjured up other lives entitled to Wrigley's Spearmint chewing gum, soda fountains, high school sweaters emblazoned with huge single letters, driving on the right side of the road in a convertible, hair blowing in the wind. That year, Perez Prado and his Cuban Orchestra dominated the airwaves with his number one hit, "It's Cherry Pink and Apple Blossom White". Twenty times a day or more, a trumpet wailed the opening bars, that long sustained waaaaaaah, a puppet string of sound, pulling me to my feet, making me forget who, what, where, lifting me into that upswelling blare. I was Scarlett O'Hara, smooth thick black hair curling round shoulders, long slender fingers curved into back of the neck of someone like Rhett Butler, his smouldering eyes scorching mine; my True Romance magazine figure was draped in a V-necked cowl with a flared skirt which swirled and lifted as we two, entranced, mamboed across the dance floor lost to the admiration and applause of all.

When the song was over, Meilin and I, panting with exertion, would collapse on a bench and she would tell me about her school. She had been in high school since last year, when a neighbour brought the newspaper to Auntie Marie to show her that Meilin's name was there, that she had passed the Exhibition exam. Auntie Marie couldn't read English, and she called Meilin to read her own name, to make sure. I wondered if my name would be on the list when the results came out. I wondered how I would know, how my mother would know, as we didn't buy papers. As we talked about Meilin's school, I wasn't sure I liked the sound of it – Bishop's. Their uniform had a funny hat with pointy corners that made them look like the soldiers in history books about Napoleon. St Joseph's Convent girls wore floating white veils and looked like they were little nuns already on their way to heaven. Also, Bishop's girls had gym twice a week and afterwards showered together. This bothered me.

'Does that mean people could see your punky and totots?'

'After a while, people don't bother to look. You get accustomed.'

I'd have to do very well in the exam to win a free place at either school – if I only passed, my mother couldn't pay fees like Meilin's. We made a pact. If I won first place, I told her, I would choose her school. We hooked the little fingers of our right hands to seal this pledge. At times like those, Meilin shared with me her burgeoning knowledge of life. She told me about her monthly bleeding and I said it wouldn't happen to me. She told me what men and women did in secret and I didn't believe her. She told me that babies came out through their mothers' punkies and I knew then that she was just making it all up. We danced through that long holiday, we and Perez Prado singing, 'It's cherry pink and apple blossom white, when your true lover comes your way.' It was about flowers we had never seen, emotions we were too young to understand.

I had seen or heard nothing about my family for a long time, when, one day at the end of August, my Uncle Francois raced up on his bicycle with a bunch of purple and white dahlias in the basket. He gave the flowers to Auntie Marie and the two of them whispered together, glancing towards me while they shush-shushed. I wondered what I had done wrong. He called out, 'Get ready. Your mother coming for you.' Auntie gave me one of her precious brown paper carrier bags. I put my clothes in it and waited. When I first saw my mother, I thought it was my aunt, her twin sister. Her long hair was gone; she looked older, more nervous than I remembered. She looked at me, said, 'You got bigger,' squeezed me tight, patted my head, sat me in the back seat of the waiting car. We were taken to La Seiva, where my grandmother had moved without my knowing. Two men were waiting there for me: a photographer and a reporter. The results of the Exhibition exam were released to the newspaper and my mother had been tracked down through my Uncle Francois, whose flower-growing business everybody knew. I was to be photographed and interviewed for the next day's *Guardian* because I had come first in the College Exhibition exam. Afterwards, Uncle Francois bought a jug of coconut ice cream from a passing vendor's bike-cart, a special treat for me.

The news must have reached our father somehow, because that night he arrived in La Seiva. He and my mother spoke in the gallery for a long time. I don't know for sure why they decided to get back together. Maybe the people to whom we children had been sent had agreed to keep us only for the school holidays. I also think that when the news of my success became public, our father would have felt ashamed among his friends and co-workers, shown up as a man who didn't take care of his children. Our father said he had found somewhere for us to live. He took my mother and me to see the place.

It was in Belmont, two bare rooms at the back of a house. The partition walls of wood with open slats at the top allowed air, sound and smell to circulate freely between the rooms, already home to two other watching, listening families. Standing in the backyard, I took in the dank open-air shower, its door hanging on a single hinge. In the kitchen-shed, coal-pot charcoal sparked red eyes through black smoke; from the sink, grey water splashed into a mossy open drain where, in a crack, a cluster of ambitious tomato seedlings had rooted. My nose trailed the pit latrine to its location, under the silhouetted tracery of branches and leaves of a guava tree at the back of the house. I could touch the neighbour's crumbling house over the sagging galvanised fence; I could hear the wail of a child, a hot, heavy slap – 'Here is something to cry for!' – the heightened wailing. My mother looked straight ahead, silent, hewn. I do not think she saw, heard or smelled anything. I saw her shoulders straighten; I felt mine straighten too.

Next day, we separated children were re-gathered. As silent as strangers, we moved into our new life in the open tray of a Ford truck alongside my mother's other possessions; a two-burner pitch-oil stove, an iron cooking pot, two cardboard boxes of clothes, one of crockery, and her girlhood treasures – a foot-pedal Singer sewing machine and a grand matching bedroom set of solid mahogany: bed, dressing table, stool and wardrobe. All, like us, had been looked after somewhere. My picture was in the papers. I was soon to go to big school. I was a big girl now.

The Boy Who Loved Ice Cream

Olive Senior

p.211

They walked down the path in single file, first the father carrying the baby Beatrice on his shoulder, then the mother, then Elsa. He brought up the rear. Wearing unaccustomed sandals, Benjy found it hard to keep his footing on the slippery path. Once or twice he almost fell and throwing out his hands to break his fall, had touched the ground. Unconsciously he wiped his hands on his seat, so that his new Sunday-go-to-church pants that his mother had made from cutting down one of his father's old jackets was already dirty with bits of mud and green bush clinging to him. But there was nobody behind him to see.

They were already late for the Harvest Festival Sale, or so his father claimed. Papa also said that it was his fault. But then his father blamed him for a lot of things, even when he was not to be blamed. The boy wasn't sure why his father was sometimes so irritable towards him, and lived in a constant state of suspense over what his father's response to him was likely to be. Now, he had been the first ready. First his sister had taken him around to the side of the house for his bath. She held him and firmly scrubbed him down with a 'strainer' covered in soap. Then she had stuck the long-handled dipper into the drum of rain water and poured it over him from head to foot. He made noises as the cold water hit him and would have run, but Elsa always had a firm grip on one of his limbs.

'Stan still yu jumbo-head bwoy or a konk yu till yu fenny,' she hissed at him. Although he knew that her threats were infrequently accompanied by action beyond a slap or two, still he tried to get away from her grip for he hated this weekly ritual of bathing. But Elsa by now had learned to control him and she carried the bath through without mishap for she had whispered, 'Awright. Doan have yu bath and see what happen. See if yu get no ice cream.'

Ice Cream! The very words conveyed to him the sound of everything in his life that he had always wanted, always longed for, but could not give a name to. He had never tasted ice cream.

It was Elsa who had told him about it. Two years ago at the Harvest Festival Sale, Mr Doran had brought an ice cream bucket and had spent the evening the most popular man at the sale, his very customers fighting to get an opportunity to turn the bucket. According to Elsa's description, this marvellous bucket somehow produced something that, she said, was not a drink and was not food. It was hot and it was cold. Both at the same time. You didn't chew it, but if you held it on your tongue long enough it vanished, leaving an after-trace that lingered and lingered like a beautiful dream. Elsa the excitable, the imaginative, the self-assured, told him, think of your best dream, when he didn't understand. Think of it in colours, she said, pink and mauve and green. And imagine it with edges. Then imagine licking it slowly round and round the edges. That's how ice cream was.

But this description only bewildered him more. He sighed, and tried hard to imagine it. But he couldn't because he didn't have a best dream or even a good dream, only nightmares, and his mother would hold him and his father would say, 'what is wrong with this pickney eh? a mampala man yu a raise.' Then the baby had come and he didn't have his mother's lap any more. Now imagining ice cream, he thought of sitting cuddled in his mother's arms again and saw this mysterious new creation as something as warm and beautiful. From Elsa's description, ice cream was the most marvellous thing he had ever heard of. And the strangest. For apart from anything else, he didn't know what ice was. His thoughts kept returning to the notion of ice cream throughout the year, and soon it became the one bright constant in a world full of changeable adults.

Then last year when he would have discovered for himself exactly what this ice cream was like, he had come down with measles. Elsa of course went to the sale for she had already had it, but he had to stay feverish and miserable with only toothless old Tata Maud to keep him company. And Elsa had come back and given him a description of ice cream that was even more marvellous than the first. This time Mr Doran had brought two buckets, and she alone had had two cones. Not even the drops, the wangla, and the slice of light cake they brought him could compensate for missing the ice cream.

This year he was well and nothing would keep him away.

Now with the thought of ice cream the cold water his sister kept splashing on him felt refreshing and he and she turned the bath into a game, both shrieking so loudly that their mother had to put her head out the window and promise to switch them both if they didn't stop.

His mother rubbed him down with an old cloth and put on his new clothes of which he was extremely proud, not noticing that the black serge was stitched very badly with white thread which was all his mother had, and the three buttons she sewed down the front were all of different sizes and colours. His shirt too, with the body of one colour, the sleeves of a print which was once part of Mama's dress and the collar of yet another print, was just, Mama said, like Joseph's coat of many colours.

Then Mama had dressed the baby and she herself had got ready. By this time Papa had come up from the spring where he had had his bath and put on his Sunday suit and hat. Benjy, dressed and bored, had wandered off down to the cotton tree root to have another look at the marvellous colours and shapes of the junjo which had sprung up after the rains just a few days ago. He was so busy that it took him a long time to hear them calling. They were standing all ready to go to the Harvest Festival Sale and Papa was cross for he said that Benjy was making them late.

Papa dressed in his Sunday suit and hat was a sight to see, for he only dressed up for special occasions – funerals, weddings and the Harvest Festival Sale. Papa never went to church though Mama did every Sunday. Papa complained every Sunday that there was no hot food and dinner was always late for Mama never got back from church till late afternoon. Plus Papa never liked Mama to be away from him for any length of time.

Foolishness, foolishness, Papa said of the church going.

Mama didn't say anything but she prayed for Papa every Sunday. She wasn't that religious, but she loved every opportunity to go out. She loved to dress up and she loved to talk to people and hear all the news that was happening out there in the wide world, though she didn't believe half of it. Although Mama hadn't even been to Kingston in her life, if someone came along and said, 'Let us go to the moon,' quick as anything Mama would pick herself up and go. Or if Papa said to her, 'Let us give up all this hard life and move to town where we will have electric light and water out of a pipe and food out of a tin,' Mama would not hesitate. Papa of course would never dream of saying anything of the sort. He was firmly wedded to the soil. She was always for Progress, though, as she sadly complained to the children, none of that ever came their way.

Now the Harvest Festival Sale was virtually the only time that Papa went into Springville these days. He hated to go into Springville even though it was where he was born for increasingly over the last four or five years, he had developed the feeling that Springville people knew something he didn't know but should, and they were laughing at him behind his back. It was something to do with his woman. It was one of those entirely intuitive feelings that suddenly occurred full-blown, then immediately took firm root in the mind. Even before the child was born he had had the instinctive feeling that it was not his. Then as the boy had grown, he had searched his face, his features, to discern himself there, and had failed utterly to find anything conclusive. He could never be sure. The old women used to say you could tell paternity sure thing by comparing the child's foot with that of the supposed father: 'if the foot not the spitting image of the man then is jacket'. He had spent countless surreptitious hours studying the turn of his son's foot but had come away with nothing. For one thing, the child was so thin and rickety that his limbs bore no resemblance to the man's heavily muscled body.

Now he had never known of the woman being unfaithful to him. But the minute she had come back from spending three weeks in Springville that time her mother was dying, from then on he had had the feeling that something had happened. Maybe it was only because she seemed to him so beautiful, so womanly that he had the first twinges of jealousy. Now every Sunday as she dressed in her neat white dress and shoes and the chaste hat which to him sat so provocatively on her head, his heart quickened as he saw her anew, not as the young girl he had taken from her mother's house so many years before, not as the gentle and good-natured mother of his children, but as a woman whom he suddenly perceived as a being attractive to other men.

But now everyone was in a good mood again as they set off down the road to the Harvest Festival Sale. First they walked a mile and a half down their mountain path where they saw no one, until they met up with the main path to the village. Always in the distance ahead of them now they could see people similarly dressed going to the sale. Others would call out to them from their houses as they passed by:

'Howdy Mis Dinah,' said Papa.

'Mis Dinah,' Mama said.

'Mis Dinah,' the children murmured.

'Howdy Mister Seeter. Miss Mae. Children. Yu gone on early.'

'Ai. Yu coming?'

'No mus'. Jus a wait for Icy finish iron mi frock Miss Mae. A ketch yu up soon.'

'Awright Mis D.'

Then they would walk another quarter mile or so till they got to another house perched on the hillside.

'Owdy Mister Seeter. Miss Mae. Little ones. A coming right behin'.'

And another family group would come out of the house and join them. Soon, a long line of people was walking in single file down the path. The family groups got mixed. The adults would walk behind other adults so that they could talk. The children bringing up the rear instinctively ranked themselves, putting the smallest ones in front. Occasionally one of the adults would look back and frown because the tail of the line had fallen too far behind.

'Stop! Jacky! Ceddie! Mavis! Merteen! What yu all doing back there a lagga lagga so? Jus' hurry up ya pickney.'

Then, all the offspring chastised, the adults would soon become lost in a discussion of the tough-headedness of children.

The children paid hardly any attention and even forgot to fight or get into any mischief, for they were far too excited about the coming afternoon.

Soon, the path broadened out and joined the lane which led to the Commons where the sale was being held. Benjy loved to come out from the cool and shadows of the path, through an archway of wild brazilwood with branches that drooped so much the adults had to lift them up in order to get through. From the semi-darkness they came suddenly into the broad lane covered in marl and dazzling white which to him was the broadest street in the whole world. Today the lane was full of people as far as the eye could see, all the men in their dark suits and hats and the women, abandoning their chaste Sunday white, wearing their brightest dresses. Now a new set of greetings had to take place between the mountain people who came from a place called One Eye and were regarded as 'dark' and mysterious by the people who lived in the one-time prosperous market town of Springville. Springville itself wasn't much – a crossroads with a few wooden 'upstairs' houses with fretwork balconies, built at the turn of the century with quick money made in Panama or Cuba. Now even though these houses were so old they leaned in the wind together, and had never seen a coat of paint, to the mountain people they looked as huge and magical as anything they hoped to see. Two of these upstairs houses had shops and bars beneath, with their proud owners residing above, and on one corner there was a large one-storey concrete building with huge wooden shutters which housed the Chinese grocery and the Chinese. A tiny painted house served as the post office and the equally tiny house beside it housed Brother Brammie the tailor. The most imposing buildings in the village were the school and the Anglican Church which were both on the main lane. The Baptists and the Seventh Day Adventists had their churches on the side road.

At Harvest Festival time, all the people in the village forgot their differences and came together to support each other's Harvest Festival Sales. But none could compare in magnificence to the Anglicans'. The sale took place on the Monday after the Harvest Service in the church. On Monday morning at dawn, the church members travelled from far with the bamboo poles and coconut boughs to erect on the Commons the booths for the sale. Because the sale was a secular event and liable to attract all kinds of sinners, it was not held in the church yard but on the Commons which belonged to the church but was separated by a barbed wire fence. Since the most prosperous people in the area were Anglicans, this was the largest and most popular of the sales. After a while it became less of a traditional Harvest Festival Sale and more of a regular fair, for people began to come from the city with goods to sell, and took over a little corner of the Commons for themselves. The church people frowned on this at first, then gave up on keeping these people out even when they began to bring games such as 'Crown and Anchor', for they helped to attract larger and larger crowds which also spent money in the church members' booths. The church members also enjoyed themselves buying the wares of the town vendors, parson drawing the line only at the sale and consumption of liquor on the premises. A few zealots of the village strongly objected to this sale, forbidding their daughters to go to this den of wickedness and vice, but nobody paid these people the slightest attention. The Mothers' Union ladies who had decorated the church for the Harvest Service the day before now tied up sprays of bougainvillea and asparagus fern over the entrance into each booth and radiated good cheer to everyone in their self-appointed role as hostesses.

The sale actually started at noon, but the only people who got there early were those who were involved in the arrangements. Most people turned up only after the men had put in at least a half-day in the fields and then gone home to bathe and dress and eat. They would stay at the sale until night had fallen, using bottle torches to light their way home.

When they got to the Commons, Benjy was the only person who was worried, for he wasn't sure that they wouldn't get there too late for the ice cream. Maybe Mr Doran would make the ice cream as soon as the sale started and then it would all be finished by the time they got there. Then another thought came: suppose this year Mr Doran was sick, or simply couldn't be bothered with ice cream any more. He would have to wait a whole year again to taste it. Perhaps never.

'Suppose, jus' suppose,' he had said to his sister many times during the past week, 'suppose him doan mek enough.'

'Cho! As soon as him finish wan bucket him mek anadda. Ice cream nevva done,' Elsa told him impatiently, wishing that she had never brought up the subject.

But this did not console him. Suppose his father refused to buy him ice cream? It was unthinkable! And yet his father's behaviour towards him was irrational: Benjy never knew just what to expect.

As soon as they turned into the Commons they could hear the sound of Mass Vass' accordion rising shrilly above the noise of the crowd, as much a part of the Harvest Festival Sale as was Brother Shearer's fife and drum band that played at all fairs, weddings and other notable events for miles around.

There were so many people already in the Commons that Benjy was afraid to enter: the crowd was a living, moving thing that would swallow him up as soon as he crossed through the gate. And yet he was excited too, and his excitement won out over his fear so that he boldly stepped up to the gate where the ticket taker waited and Papa paid the entrance fee for them all.

'Now you children don't bother get lost,' Mama warned them but not too sternly, knowing that sooner or later they would all become separated in this joyous crowd.

Benjy was in an agony just to see the ice cream. But Elsa would have none of it.

'Wait nuh,' she said, grabbing his hand and steering him firmly in the direction of the fancy goods stall where Mama had headed. There were cake stalls and pickles and preserves stalls, fancy goods stalls, glass cases full of baked goods and all the finest in fruits, vegetables, yams and all the other products of the soil that the people had brought to the church as their offerings to the Harvest Service. Off to one side was a small wooden merry-go-round and all over the field were children playing and shrieking.

'Elsa, ice cream,' Benjy kept saying, and finally to reduce this annoyance Elsa took him over to a corner of the field where a crowd had gathered. There, she said. But the crowd was so thick that he could see nothing, and he felt a pain in his heart that so many other, bigger people also wanted ice cream. How ever would he get any?

'Nuh mine, Benjy,' Elsa consoled him. 'Papa wi gi wi ice cream. When de time come.'

'Suppose him forget, Elsa.'

'Not gwine forget.'

'Yu remin' him.'

'Yes.'

'Promise?'

'But wa do yu ee bwoy,' Elsa cried. She angrily flung his hand away and took off into the crowd.

He did not mind being alone, for this rich crowd so flowed that sooner or later the same people passed each other.

Benjy wished he had some money. Then he would go and wiggle his way into the very centre of the crowd that surrounded the ice-cream bucket. And he would be standing there just as Mr Doran took out the ice cream. But he didn't know anything about money and had no idea what something as wonderful as ice cream would cost.

So he flowed with the crowd, stopping here and there but not really looking at anything and soon he came across his mother with Beatrice. Mama firmly took hold of his hand.

'Come. Sister Nelson bring a piece of pone fe yu.'

She took him to Sister Nelson who gave him the pone which he stuffed into his mouth.

'Say tank yu chile. Yu doan have manners?' his mother asked.

He murmured thank you through the pone. Sister Nelson smiled at him. 'Growing a good boy,' she said and patted his head.

'But baad!' Mama said, laughing.

Mama was always saying that and it frightened him a little, for he never knew for sure just how he was 'baad'.

'Mama,' he said, 'ice cream'.

'Chile! Yu mout full an yu talking bout ice cream aready!'

Tears started to trickle down his cheeks.

'Now see here. A bawl yu wan' bawl? Doan mek a give yu something fe bawl bout, yu hear bwoy. Hm. Anyway a doan know if there is money for foolishness like cream. Have to see yu father about dat.'

His heart sank, for the day before he had heard his father complain that there was not enough money to buy all the things they needed at the Harvest Festival Sale and did she think money grew on trees. But everyone knew that Papa saved all year for that day, for the town vendors came and spread out their wares under the big cotton tree – cloth, pots and pans, fancy lamps, wicks and shades, readymade clothes, shoes, shoelaces, matches, knives, cheap perfume, plastic oilcloths for the table, glasses with birds and flowers, water jugs, needles, enamelware, and plaster wall hangings with robins and favourite Bible texts. Even Miss Sybil who had the dry goods store would turn up and buy from them, and months later the goods would turn up in her dark and dusty shop at twice the price as the vendors'.

Mama had announced months in advance that she wanted an oilskin cloth, a new lampshade and shoes for the children. She hadn't mentioned anything for herself, but on these occasions Mama usually came home with a pair of new shoes, or a scarf, or a hat – anything that would put her in touch with what seemed another, glamorous life.

Papa, like his son, was distracted, torn between two desires. One was to enjoy the sale and to see if he could pick up anything for the farm or just talk to the farmers whom nowadays he never saw at any other time. Then the Extension Officer was there and he wanted to catch him to ask about some new thing he had heard that the government was lending money to plant crops though he didn't believe a word of it. Then he wanted to go and buy a good white shirt from the town vendors. Mama had insisted that he should. And he wanted to see the new games they had brought. In many ways one part of his mind was like a child's, for he wanted to see and do everything. But another part of his mind was spoiling the day for him: he didn't want to let Mama out of his sight. More and more the conviction had been growing on him that if there had been another man in her life, it wasn't anyone from around here. So it had to be a townman. And where else did one get the opportunity to meet strangers but at the sale. Walking down the mountain path he had started out enjoying the feeling of going on an outing, the only one he permitted himself for the year. But as they got nearer and nearer to Springville and were joined by other people, he became more and more uneasy. The way his woman easily greeted and chatted with people at first used to fill him with pride and admiration that she could so naturally be at ease where he was dull and awkward and clumsy. But by the time they entered the lane this pride had turned to irritation, for now he had begun to exaggerate in his mind precisely those qualities for which he had previously praised her: now she laughed too loudly, chattered too much, she was not modest enough, she attracted attention to herself – and to him, for having a woman so common and so visible. By the time they got to the Commons it was clear to her that he was in one of his 'moods' though she did not know why and she hoped that the crowd would bring back his good humour again, for she was accustomed to his ups and downs. But she didn't dwell on the man's moods, for nothing would make her not enjoy herself at the sale.

Now the man surreptitiously tried to keep her under his eye but it was virtually impossible because of the crowd. He saw her sometimes only as a flash in the distance and he strained to see what she was up to, but he caught her only in the most innocent of poses – with church sisters and married couples and little children. She eagerly tried on hats and shoes. She looked at pictures. She examined tablecloths. She ate grater cake and snowballs. Looking at her from afar, her gestures seemed to him so pure, so innocent that he told himself that he was surely mad to think badly of her. Then he looked at the town folk gathered around the games, hawking yards of cloth, and stockings and ties and cheap jewellery. He looked at them and their slim hard bodies and their stylish clothes and their arrogant manners and their tough faces which hid a knowledge of the world he could never have. And he felt anxious and angry again. Now he turned all his attention to these townmen to see if he could single out one of them: the one. So engaged did he become on this lonely and futile pursuit that he hardly heard at all what anybody said to him. Even the children begging for ice cream he roughly brushed aside. He was immediately full of remorse, for he had planned to treat them to ice cream, but by the time he came to his senses and called after them, they had disappeared into the crowd. He vowed that once he met up with them again he would make up for his gruffness. He would treat them not only to ice cream but to sliced cake, to soft drinks, to paradise plums and jujubs. But the moment of softness, of sentiment, quickly passed for his attention became focused on one man in black pants and a purple shirt and wearing a grey felt hat. The man was tall, brown-skinned and good looking with dark, curly hair. He couldn't tell why this man caught his attention except that he was by far the best looking of the townmen, seemed in fact a cut above them, even though like some of the others his arms were covered from wrist to elbow in lengths of cheap chains, and his fingers in the tacky rings that he was selling. He watched the man steadily while he flirted and chatted with the girls and finally faded out of sight – but not in the direction his woman was last seen.

Now Benjy was crying and even Elsa felt let down. Papa had refused to buy them ice cream! Although she cajoled and threatened, she couldn't get Benjy to stop crying. He was crying as much for the ice cream as for being lost from even his mother so happy and animated among all the people she knew, amid crowds and noise and confusion. Now she had little time for them and impatiently waved them on to 'enjoy themselves'. Elsa did just that for she found everything entertaining and school friends to chatter with. But not Benjy. She could not understand how a little boy could be so lacking in joy for such long periods of time, and how his mind could become focused on just one thing. If Benjy could not have ice cream, he wanted nothing.

Night was coming on and they were lighting the lamps. They hung up the storm lantern at the gate but all the coconut booths were lit with kitchen bitches. Only the cake stall run by Parson's wife and the most prosperous ladies of the church had a tilly lamp, though there wasn't much cake left to sell.

Benjy still stumbled along blindly, dragged by Elsa who was determined to get a last fill of everything. Benjy was no longer crying but his eyes were swollen and he was tired and his feet were dragging. He knew that soon they would have to go home. The lighting of the lamps was the signal for gathering up families together, and though they might linger for a while after that talking, making last minute purchases and plans, children were at this point not allowed to wander or stray from the group for the word of adults had once again become law, and when all the adults decided to move, woe onto the child who could not be found.

So everyone was rounding up everyone else, and in this confusion, Benjy started to howl again for he and Elsa were passing by Mr Doran and his bucket, only the crowd was so thick around it you couldn't see anything.

But just then they ran into Papa again and, miraculously, he was the one that suggested ice cream. Although Benjy's spirits immediately lifted, he still felt anxious that Papa would never be able to get through that crowd in time. Papa left him and Elsa on the fringes, and he impatiently watched as Papa, a big man, bore his way through. What is taking Papa so long? I bet Mr Doran has come to the end of the bucket. There is no more ice cream. Here comes Mr Manuel and Mars Edgy asking if they aren't ready. And indeed, everyone from the mountain was more or less assembled and they and Papa now seemed the only people missing from the group. They told Mars Edgy that Papa had gone to get them ice cream, and Mars Edgy was vexed because, he said, Papa should have done that long before. Now Mars Edgy made his way through the crowd around the ice-cream vendor and Benjy's hopes fell again. He felt sure that Mars Edgy would pull Papa away before he got the ice cream. Torn between hope and despair, Benjy looked up at the sky which was pink and mauve from the setting sun. Just like ice cream! But here comes Papa and Mars Edgy now and Papa is carrying in his hands three cones and Papa is coming and Benjy is so excited that he starts to run towards him and he stumbles and falls and Elsa is laughing as she picks him up and he is laughing and Mars Edgy is moving off quickly to where the mountain people are standing and Papa bends down and hands him a cone and Papa has a cone and Elsa has a cone and Benjy has a cone and the three of them stand there as if frozen in time and he is totally joyous for he is about to have his first taste of ice cream but even though this is so long-awaited so precious he first has to hold the cone at arm's length to examine it and witness the ice cream perched just so on top and he is afraid to put it into his mouth for Elsa said it was colder than spring water early in the morning and suppose just suppose it burns his tongue suppose he doesn't like it and Elsa who is well into eating hers and Papa who is eating his are laughing at him … then he doesn't know what is happening for suddenly Papa sees something his face quickly changes and he flings away his cone and makes a grab for Benjy and starts walking almost running in the direction where Mama is standing she is apart from all the people talking to a strange man in a purple shirt and Papa is moving so fast Benjy's feet are almost off the ground and Benjy is crying Papa Papa and everything is happening so quickly he doesn't know the point at which he loses the ice cream and half the cone and all that is left in his hand is the little tip of the cone which he clutches tightly and he cannot understand why Papa has let go of his hand and is shouting and why Mama isn't laughing with the man anymore and why everyone is rushing about and why he has only this little tip of cone in his hand and there is no ice cream and he cannot understand why the sky which a minute ago was pink and mauve just like the ice cream is now swimming in his vision like one swollen blanket of rain.

Uncle Umberto's Slippers

Mark McWatt

p.212 Uncle Umberto was my father's eldest brother and he was well known for two things: the stories he told about ghosts and strange things that happen to him, and his slippers, which were remarkable because of their size. Uncle Umberto had the most enormous feet and could never get them into any shoe that a store would sell. When I was a small boy I remember him trying to wear the ubiquitous rubber flip-flops that we all wore. Uncle Umberto would wear the largest size he could find, but when he stood in them nothing could be seen of the soles, for his large feet completely covered them – only the two tight and straining coloured straps could be seen, emerging from beneath the calloused edges of his flat feet and disappearing between his toes. They never lasted very long and the story goes that Aunt Teresa, his wife, used to buy six pairs at a time, trying to get them all of the same colour so people would not realize how quickly Uncle Umberto's feet could destroy a pair.

But all that was before Uncle Umberto got his famous slippers. It is said that, on a rare trip to the city, Uncle Umberto stood a whole day by a leather craft stall in the big market and watched a Rasta man make slippers out of bits of car tire and lengths of rawhide strap. When he came home from this trip, Uncle set about making his own unique pair of slippers. It seems that no car tire was wide enough for the sole, so Uncle went foraging in the yard of the Public Works Depot in the town and came up with a Firestone truck tire that seemed in fairly good shape, with lots of deeply grooved treads on it – he claimed he 'signalled' to the watchman that he was taking it and the watchman waved him through the gate. This he cut up for the soles of his slippers. Because they had to be so long they did not sit flat on the floor, but curled up somewhat at heel and toe, keeping the curved shape of the tire – this was of course when they did not contain Uncle's vast feet. Each of these soles had three thick, parallel strips of rawhide curving across the front and these kept Uncle Umberto's feet in the slippers. There were no straps around the heel. Uncle made these slippers to last the rest of his life: they were twenty-two inches long, eight inches wide and nearly two inches thick. The grooves in the treads on the sole were one and a quarter inches deep when I measured them about four years before he died – when I was twelve, and beginning to get interested in my family and its wonderful characters and oddities.

The other detail to be mentioned about the slippers is that Uncle Umberto took the trouble to cut or drill his initials into the thick soles, carving H.I.C., Humberto

Ignatius Calistro – the central 'I' being about twice the height of the other two letters (he always wrote his name with the 'H', but was unreasonably upset if anyone dared to pronounce it. To be on the safe side, we children decided to abandon the H even in the written form of his name, and he seemed quite happy with this). These incised initials always struck me as being completely unnecessary, if their purpose was to indicate ownership, for there could never be another such pair of quarry barges masquerading as footwear anywhere else in the world.

These then became Uncle's famous badge of recognition – one tended to see the slippers first, and *then* become aware of his presence. Quite often one didn't actually have to see them: a muddy tire print on the bridge into Arjune's rumshop told us that Uncle was in there 'relaxing with the boys'. At home (we all live together in the huge house my grandmother built over the last thirty years of her life) my father would suddenly say, 'Umberto coming, you all start dishing up the food.' When we looked enquiringly at him he would shrug and say, 'I can hear the Firestones coming up the hill,' and soon after we would all hear the wooden stairs protesting unmistakably under the weight of Uncle Umberto's footfalls.

******

My grandfather, whom I never knew, was a seaman; as a youngster he had worked on the government river ferries and coastal steamers, but then, after he'd had two children, and had started quarrelling with my grandmother, he took to going further away on larger ships. Often he would not return for a year or more, but whenever he did he would get my grandmother pregnant and they would start quarrelling and he would be off again, until, in his memory, their painful discord had mellowed into a romantic lovers' tiff – at which point he would return to start all over again. When he returned after the fourth child, it was supposed to be for good, and he actually married my grandmother as a statement of this intention, but when the fifth child was visible in my grandmother's stomach, he became so miserable (she said) and looked so trapped and forlorn, that for his own good she threw him out and told him not to come back until he remembered how to be a real man again. In this way their relationship ebbed and flowed like the great rivers that had ruled their lives and fortunes. They had nine children, although it pleased God, as Grandmother said, to reclaim two of them within their first few years of life.

The cycle of Grandfather's going and coming (and of my grandmother's pregnancies) was broken when he got into a quarrel in some foreign port and some bad men robbed him of his money, beat him up and left him to die on one of those dark and desperate docklands streets that I was readily able to picture, thanks to my mild addiction to American gangster movies. At least this is the version of the story of his death that they told me when I was a boy. As I grew into a teenager and my ears became more attuned to adult conversations – especially those that are whispered – I began to overhear other versions: that yes, the men had killed him, but it was because he had cheated in a card game and won all their money; that he had really died in a brothel in New Orleans, in bed with a woman of stunning beauty called Lucinda – shot by a jealous rival; even that he had been caught on a ship that was smuggling narcotics into the United States, and was thrown to the sharks by federal agents who boarded the vessel at sea … At any rate he was still quite a young man when he died.

My grandmother mourned her husband for thirty years by embarking on a building project of huge proportions – the house we now lived in. She decided she would move her family out of the unhealthy capital city on the coast and build them a home on a hill overlooking the wide river and the small riverside mining town in which she herself was born. The first section of the house ('the first Bata shoe box', as my father puts it) was built by a carpenter friend of my grandmother's who had hopes of replacing my grandfather in her affections, and ultimately in the home he was building for her. My grandmother allegedly teased and strung him along, like Penelope, until the new house was habitable; then, becoming her own Ulysses, she quarrelled with him in public and sent him packing. The next section of the house was built when Uncle Umberto, the eldest boy, was old enough to build it for her, and for the next twenty years he periodically added on another 'shoe box', until the house became as I now know it – a huge two-story structure with labyrinthine corridors and innumerable bedrooms and bathrooms (none of which has ever been completely finished) and the four 'tower' rooms, one at each corner, projecting above the other roofs and affording wonderful views of the town, river and surrounding forest. It is to one of these towers – the one we call 'the bookroom' – that I have retreated to write this story.

When Uncle Umberto began to clear the land to lay the foundation for the third 'shoe box' (in the year of the great drought), he said one night he saw a light, like someone waving a flashlight, coming from one of the sandbanks that had appeared out of the much diminished river. Next morning he saw a small boy apparently stranded on the bank and he went down to the river, got into the corrial and paddled across. When he got close to the bank he realized that it was not a boy, but a naked old man, scarcely four feet tall, with a wispy beard and an enormous, crooked penis. This man gesticulated furiously to Uncle, indicating first that he should paddle closer to the sandbank and then, when the bow of the corrial had grated on the sand, that he should come no further. Uncle swears that the little man held him paralysed in the stern of the boat and spoke to him at length in a language he did not understand, although somehow he knew that the man was telling him not to build the extension to the house, because an Indian chief had been buried in that spot long ago.

My grandmother, who had lived the first fifteen years of her life aboard her father's sloop and had seen everything there is to be seen along these coasts and rivers, did not believe in ghosts and walking spirits and she would have none of it when Uncle Umberto suggested they abandon the second extension to the house. To satisfy Uncle she allowed him to dig up the entire rectangle of land and when no bones were found, she said: 'O.K. Umberto, you've had your fun, now get serious and build on the few rooms we need so your brother Leonard could marry the woman he living in sin with and move her in with the rest of the family. It's more important to avoid giving offence to God than to worry about some old-time Indian chief who probably wasn't even a Christian anyway.'

So Uncle built the shoe box despite his misgivings, but the day before his brother Leonard was to be married, there was an accident at the sawmill where he worked and a tumbling greenheart log jammed him onto the spinning blade and his body was cut in two just below the breastbone. Everyone agreed it was an accident, but Uncle Umberto knew why it had happened. Aunt Irene, Uncle Leonard's bride, who was visibly pregnant at the time, moved into the new extension nevertheless and she and my big cousin Lennie have been part of the household ever since. Uncle Umberto, who never had children of his own, became like a father to Lennie and took special care of him, claiming that, from infancy, the boy had the identical crooked, oversized penis that the old man on the sandbank had flaunted. Uncle Umberto also saw from time to time in that part of the house apparitions of both his brother Leonard and the Indian chief, the latter arrayed in plumed headdress and beaded loincloth and sitting awkwardly on the bed or on the edge of Aunt Irene's mahogany bureau.

The others now living in the big house were my own family – Papi, Mami, my sister Mac, my two brothers and I – my Uncle John, the lawyer, and his wife Aunt Monica, my Uncle 'Phonso and the four children that my aunt Carmen had for four different men before she decided to get serious about life and move to the States, where she now works in a factory that builds aeroplanes and lives with an ex-monk who can't stand children. My father's other sister has also lived in the States from as far back as I can remember.

Actually, my Uncle 'Phonso doesn't really live with us either – he is the youngest and, it is said, the most like his father, both in terms of his skill as a seaman and his restlessness and rebellious spirit. He took over the running of my grandmother's sloop (which plies up and down the rivers, coasts and nearby islands, as it always has, engaged equally in a little trading and a little harmless smuggling), and always claimed he could never live under the same roof with 'the old witch' (his mother). So he spends most of his life on the sloop. On every long trip he takes a different female companion ('… just to grieve me and to force me to spend all my time praying and burning candles for his wicked soul,' my grandmother said). Once a year the sloop would be hauled up onto the river bank below our house for four or five weeks, so that Uncle Umberto could replace rotten planks and timbers and caulk and paint it. During this time Uncle 'Phonso would have his annual holiday in his section of the family home.

Uncle John, the lawyer, was the most serious of my father's brothers – though he was not really a lawyer. From as long as I can remember he has worked in the district administrator's office and has been 'preparing' to be a lawyer by wearing pin-striped shirts and conservative ties and dark suits and highly polished black shoes. His apprenticeship to the profession became an eternal dress rehearsal. Packages of books and papers would arrive for him from overseas (though less frequently in recent years) and we would all be impressed at this evidence of his scholarly intent, but as far as I know he has never sat an exam. He and Aunt Monica live very comfortably off his salary as a clerk in the district office, but they have agreed not to have any children until he is qualified. In the early years of marriage the couple was cruelly teased about not having children. Papi would say, 'Hey, Johnno, you sure is Monica Suarez you married, and not Rima Valenzuela?' Rima Valenzuela was a beautiful and warm-hearted woman in town notorious for her childlessness. Since she was a teenager she has longed for children and tried to conceive with the aid of an ever-lengthening list of men (including, it was rumoured, one or two of my uncles). She was said to be close to forty now, and was beginning despairingly to accept what people had been telling her for years – that she was barren.

Every new-year's day after mass people would say to Uncle John, 'Well, Johnno, this is the year; don't forget to invite me to the celebrations when they call you to the bar.' But no one really believes anymore that he will actually become a lawyer. One year Uncle 'Phonso patted him on the back and said consolingly, 'Never mind, brother John, there's a big sand bar two-three miles down river; I can take you there in the sloop anytime you want, and you can tell all these idiots that you've been called to the bar, you didn't like the look of it and you changed your mind.'

In a way, Aunt Monica was as strangely obsessive as Uncle John. Papi said it was because she has no children to occupy her and bring her to her senses. She seemed to dedicate her life to neatness and cleanliness, not only making sure that Uncle John's lawyerly apparel was always impeccable, but every piece of cloth in their section of the house, from handkerchief to bed-sheet to window-blind, was more than regularly washed and – above all – ironed. Aunt Monica spent at least three or four hours every day making sure that every item of cloth she possessed was clean and smooth and shiny. She had ironing boards that folded out from the wall in each of the three rooms she and Uncle John occupied and kept urging the other branches of the family to install similar contraptions in their rooms. Once when my grandmother remarked: 'All these children! The house beginning to feel crowded again. Umberto, we best think about adding on a few more rooms,' Papi quipped: 'Why? Just so that Monica could put in more fold-out ironing boards?' – and everyone laughed.

******

One morning as we were all at the kitchen table, dressed for work and school and finishing breakfast, Uncle Umberto came into the room in his sleeping attire (short pants and an old singlet) looking restless and confused. We all looked at him, but before anyone could ask, he said: 'You all, I didn't sleep at all last night, because I was studying something funny that happened to me last evening.' Everyone sensed one of his ghost stories coming and we waited expectantly. I had got up from the table to go and do some quick revision before leaving for school, but I stood my ground to listen.

'Just as the sun was going down yesterday I went for my usual walk along the path overlooking the river – you know I does like to watch the sunset on the river and the small boats with people going home up-river from work in town. Suddenly, just as I reach that big rock overhanging the river at Mora Point, this white woman appear from nowhere on top the rock. Is like if she float up or fly up from the river and light on the rock. She was wearing a bright blue dress, shiny like one of them big blue butterflies …'

'Morpho,' interrupted my brother Patrick, the know-it-all. And Papi also had to put in his little bit.

'Shiny blue dress, eh? Take care is not Monica starch and press it for her.' But they were both told to be quiet and let Uncle Umberto get on with his story.

'She beckon me to come up on the rock, so I climb up and stand up there next to her and she start to ask me a whole set of questions – all kind of thing about age and occupation and how long I live in these parts and if I ever travel overseas – and she got a funny squarish black box or bag in her hand. Well, first of all, because she was white I expect her to talk foreign, like somebody from England or America, but she sound just like one of we.' He paused and looked around. 'Then after she had me talking for about ten or fifteen minutes, I venture to ask her about where *she* come from, but she laugh and say: "Oh, that's not important, *you're* the interesting subject under discussion here" – meaning me –' and Uncle Umberto tapped his breastbone twice. 'Then like she sensed that I start to feel a little uneasy, and she say: "Sorry, there's no need to keep you any longer, you can continue your walk." By then like she had me hypnotized, and I climb down from the rock onto the path and start walking away.'

'Eh-eh, when I catch myself, two, three seconds later and look back, the woman done disappear! I hurry back up the rock and I can't see her anywhere. I look up and down the path, I look down at the river, but no sign of her – just a big blue butterfly fluttering about the bushes on the cliff-side …'

It was vintage Umberto. Uncle John said: 'Boy, you still got the gift – you does tell some real good ones.'

'I swear to God,' Umberto said, 'I telling you *exactly* what happen. This isn't no make-up story.'

Still musing about Uncle Umberto's experience, we were all beginning to move off to resume our preparations for school and work, when Aunt Teresa began to speak in an uncharacteristically troubled voice.

'Umberto, I don't know who it is you see, or you think you see, but you got to be careful how you deal with strange women who want to ask a lot of questions – you say she had you hypnotized, well many a man end up losing his mind – not to mention his soul – over women like that. The day you decide to have anything personal to do with this woman, you better forget about me, because I ent having no dealings with devil women …'

This was certainly strange for Aunt Teresa, who usually shrugged off her husband's idiosyncrasies and strange 'experiences' with a knowing smile and a wink at the rest of us. Aunt Teresa's agitation seemed to be contagious among the women of the household. I noticed that Mami seemed suddenly very serious and, as Aunt Teresa continued to speak, Aunt Monica, preoccupied and fidgety, came and stood by the fridge next to me and began to unbutton my school shirt. As she reached the last button and began to pull the shirt-tails out of my pants, the talking stopped and everyone was looking at us.

Too shocked or uncertain to react to this divestiture before, I now smiled nervously and said: 'Hey, Aunty, I'm not too sure what we're supposed to be doing here, but should we be doing it in front of all these others?'

There was a general uproar of laughter and Aunt Monica removed her hands from my shirt as if stung; but she quickly recovered, gave me a swift slap on the cheek, and said, 'Don't fool around with me, boy, I could be your mother. Besides, everybody knows that I'm just taking off this crushed-up excuse for a school shirt to give it a quick press with the steam iron and see if I can't get you to look at little more decent. If your mother can't make sure you all children go to school looking presentable (and you, Mr Nickie, are the worst of the lot), then somebody else will have to do it, for the sake of the good name of the family you represent …' By the time she'd finished saying this, she was traipsing out of the kitchen waving my shirt behind her like a flag.

We did not realize it at the time, but Uncle Umberto's story was the beginning of a strange sequence of events that was to befall him and to haunt the rest of us for a very long time.

No one was surprised when he revealed, a few days later, that he had met the woman again, and that she had walked up and down the riverside path with him, but the mystery of the woman was solved for me when she came into my classroom at school one day, along with our teacher, Mr Fitzpatrick, who introduced her as Miss Pauline Vyfhuis, a graduate student who was doing fieldwork for her thesis in Applied Linguistics. She carried a tape-recorder in a black leather case and told us that Professor Rickford at the university had sent her up here to record the people's speech for her research. When I went home and announced this to the family, they all accepted that Miss Vyfhuis must be Uncle Umberto's blue butterfly lady – all except Uncle Umberto himself; he claimed to have spoken at length to his lady and she'd confirmed that she could appear and disappear at will; that she could fly or float in the air and that one day he (Uncle Umberto) would be able to accompany her – floating off the cliff to places unimagined by the rest of us.

'Umberto, before you go floating off over the river,' Papi interjected, 'just make sure you take off them two four-wheel drives 'pon your feet, in case they weight you down and cause you to crash into the river and drown.'

Ignoring Papi, Uncle Umberto went on to tell us that, besides all he'd just said, he had *also* met Miss Vyfhuis, outside Arjune's rumshop, and had even condescended to say a few words into her microphone. She was nothing like his butterfly lady; she was small and mousey-looking, and anyone could see that she could never fly. Also, her tape-recorder was twice the size of the magic black box carried by *his* lady … We shrugged – no one could take away one of Uncle's prized fantasies.

A few months after this my grandmother died one night in her sleep. The family was not overwhelmed with grief; the old lady was eighty-nine years old, and although her death was unexpected, everyone said that it was a good thing that it was not preceded by a long or painful illness. 'She herself would have chosen to go in that way,' Mami said. Uncle Umberto seemed the one most deeply affected by the old lady's passing; he seemed not so much grief-stricken as bewildered. It was as though the event had caught him at a particularly inconvenient time and for days he walked about the house and the streets mumbling and distracted. Uncle Umberto should have become the head of our household, and I suppose he was, in a way, but he seemed to abdicate all responsibility in favour of Aunt Teresa, his wife, who took on the role of making the big decisions and giving orders. Umberto's slippers took their increasingly distracted occupant more and more frequently to the path above the river and he could be seen there not only in the evenings, but now also first thing in the morning and sometimes again in the heat of the day. None of us who saw him ever saw the butterfly woman – nor anyone else, for that matter – walking with him, although there were times when he seemed to be gesticulating to an invisible companion. Mostly he just walked. He haunted the riverside path like a Dutchman's ghost and we all began to worry about him.

One evening not long after this, Uncle Umberto came home dishevelled and distraught, a wild look in his eyes.

'She going,' he said. 'She say is time to go and she want me go with her.'

'Go where?' Aunt Teresa snapped. 'Just look at yourself, Umberto, look at the state you have yourself in over this imaginary creature.'

'I keep telling you,' Umberto pleaded, 'she's not imaginary – I see her for true, swear-to-god, although it seem nobody else can see her. Now she say she going away, and I must go with her – or else follow her later.'

'Tell her you will follow her, man Umberto,' Papi said. 'You know like how a husband or a wife does go off to America and then send later for the other partner and the children. Tell her to go and send for you when she ready. No need to throw yourself off the cliff behind her.'

I was sure Papi was joking, and there was a little nervous laughter in the room, but surprisingly, Umberto thought it was a great idea. His face cleared of its deep frown and he said simply: 'Thank you, Ernesto, I will tell her that and see what she say,' and he went off to his room, followed by his visibly uncomfortable wife.

Two days later Umberto reported that the lady had agreed to the plan; they had said their goodbyes early that morning and she floated off the rock where she had first appeared, and was enveloped in the mist above the river. Umberto seemed in very good spirits and the family breathed a collective sigh of relief. In the weeks immediately following he appeared to be his old self again – having a drink or two with the boys in Arjune's rumshop, joking with the rest of us and talking of replacing the north roof of the house, which had begun to leak again. He never spoke of the butterfly lady.

In just over six weeks, however, Uncle Umberto was dead. He announced one morning that he was taking a walk into town to order galvanize, stepped into his famous slippers and disappeared down the road. It seemed like only minutes later (we hadn't left for school yet) that we heard shouting outside and looked down the road to see Imtiaz, Mr Wardle from the drug store and even old Lall at the forefront of a crowd of people running up the hill, waving and shouting. The only thing that we could make out in the hubbub was the word 'Umberto'.

It seems Umberto had stopped at the edge of town to chat with a small group of friends when he suddenly looked up, shouted 'Oh God! Child, look, out!' and leapt right in front of one of the big quarry trucks that was speeding down the hill. He died where he had landed after the impact, his rib-cage and one arm badly smashed and his face cut above the left eye. The slippers were still on his feet. There was no child – nor anyone else – near to the truck.

Well, you can guess what everyone said: the butterfly woman appeared to him and led him to his death – just when we all thought he was rid of her. The family was devastated. Unlike my grandmother's, Uncle Umberto's funeral was an extremely sad and painful occasion – not least because we saw Umberto's feet, for the first time ever, in a pair of highly polished black shoes. The shoes were large, but not as large as we thought they needed to be to contain Uncle's feet. The thought that the people at the funeral parlour had mutilated his feet and crammed them into those shoes was too much to bear. We all wept, and scarcely anyone looked at Umberto's face as he lay in the coffin – all eyes were on the extraordinary and deeply disturbing sight at its other end. At home, after the burial, we all turned on poor Aunt Teresa – how could she permit the undertakers to mutilate Uncle's feet? My cousin Lennie, his favourite, said tearfully that not even God would recognize Uncle Umberto in those shoes.

'You should have buried him in his slippers; those were his trademark.'

'Trademark, yes,' Aunt Teresa spat, her eyes bright with tears, 'and they made him a laughing-stock – everybody always laughing and making fun of him and his big feet. I wanted that he could have in death the dignity he was never allowed in life, what with Ernesto and John and you and Nickie and the children always making cruel jokes about the feet and the slippers. God knows he used to encourage you all with his antics, it's true, but it always hurt me to hear him ridiculed …'

At that point my brother Patti appeared in the room with the slippers in his hands, saying 'These are fantastic, just amazing – nobody else in the world – just look at them!' And he held them up, tears streaming down his face.

'Give me those!' Aunt Teresa shouted, flying into a rage, 'He only been buried two hours and already you parading these ridiculous things and making fun of the dead. At least you could have a little respect for *my* feelings.'

As she snatched the slippers from Patti I couldn't help noticing with awe that they still had the deep grooves of the tire tread and seemed to be hardly worn. At another time I might have remarked: 'They look as though they have less than a hundred miles on them' (that is, if Papi didn't beat me to it), but now, with Aunty raging, we all kept silent and watched her disappear into her room, clutching the offending footwear.

*****

You might think that the story is now ended, but in fact there is a little more to tell. You must remember that this is not the story of Uncle Umberto, but of his slippers. Several months later, when Aunt Teresa returned from a visit to her sister in Trinidad and seemed to be in a good mood, someone – Lennie, perhaps – casually asked her what had become of Uncle Umberto's slippers. Her face clouded over, but only for an instant. She smiled and said: 'Oh, those things – don't worry, I didn't burn them, only buried them away in the bottom of my trunk. I don't think I'm ready to see them again yet,' and the conversation moved on to other topics.

About a year later, when the house was in general upheaval – because Mr Moses was replacing the rotten north roof at last; because Aunt Lina (one of my father's sisters) was visiting from New Jersey and because my cousin Lennie had just disgraced us all by getting Rima Valenzuela pregnant (and him barely nineteen!) – Aunt Teresa came into the kitchen one night and announced that Uncle Umberto's slippers had disappeared. 'What you mean "disappeared", Aunty?' Lennie said. 'Remember you told us that you had put them in the bottom of your trunk?'

'Yes,' Aunt Teresa said, 'in this big blue plastic bag; but when I was looking for them just now to show Lina, I find the bag empty. Look, you can still see the print of the truck tire where it press against the plastic for so long under the weight of the things in the trunk.' And she held up the bag for us to see.

'But it's impossible for them to just disappear,' Lennie insisted.

Aunt Teresa gave him a look: 'Just like how it's impossible for Rima Valenzuela to make baby, eh? You proud to admit that you responsible for that miracle; for all I know you may be to blame for this one as well.'

'Ow, Aunty,' I pleaded, 'don't start picking on him again.' I was feeling for Lennie, who had taken a lot of flack from the women in the family (and had become something of an underground hero to the men and boys!).

'OK. Look,' Teresa said, 'I don't know who removed the slippers. I would have said it has to be one of you, but I always lock the trunk, as you know, and walk everywhere with the key – in this menagerie of a house that is the only way I can have a little privacy and be able to call my few possessions my own. The disappearance of the slippers is a real mystery to me, but you could go and search for yourself if you want.' And she flung the bunch of keys at us, shaking her head. We did search – the trunk, the wardrobe, the chest of drawers, under the bed, everywhere, but there was no sign of the slippers. It was a mystery in truth.

Eventually the slippers became a dim memory for most of us. Life moved on; we children continued 'to grow like weeds', as my Aunt Monica would say. I went to board with cousins in the city during term-time, so that I could attend sixth form at college, and I found that my life changed, to the point where all that remained of Uncle Umberto and his slippers were memories, dim and fading memories. But.

After I wrote my last A-level exam – just days ago – I returned home at once to spend some time with my family and to prepare to leave them again in a few months, for I had already received provisional acceptance from the University of Toronto. The day after I returned home, about mid-morning, Aunt Teresa ran into the house in a state of shock; in her hands were Uncle Umberto's slippers. She had taken to walking along the path above the river, almost as regularly as Uncle Umberto had in the years before his death – perhaps she did it in memory of Uncle – but that morning, as she passed the large rock on the cliff at Mora point, she saw on the path, just at the base of the rock, Uncle Umberto's slippers. They were placed neatly, one beside the other, as though someone had just stepped out of them to climb the rock. There was no one in sight. Aunt Teresa had almost fainted. The rest of us were in shock as well, at seeing the slippers again, and you can well imagine the wild surmises about how they got to be on the path that day.

But the strangest thing was that the slippers, while undoubtedly Uncle Umberto's (portions of the incised initials were still discernible), had soles that were worn until the thickest parts were less than half as thick as they were when Uncle died; on the sections between instep and the tip of the toe the tire tread was worn away entirely and the rubber was smooth and black. In two and a half years someone – or something – had put ten thousand miles on Uncle Umberto's old Firestones!

The next day I came up here, to the bookroom tower, and began writing this story.

The Creek

Subraj Singh

p.212 Grandfather rowed the canoe, ruffling the still edges of the water as he confidently dipped the paddle and pushed backwards, against the liquid blackness, so that the boat glided gently forwards.

Boy thought it was a peculiar thing. Going backwards in order to go forwards. He felt that it was most unusual and he wondered if the old man was aware of the strangeness involved in his powerful strokes against the current. *Left-side – backwards, forwards. Right-side – backwards, forwards.*

Boy closed his eyes and listened to the slapping of the paddle on the water and the soft sucking of water on the paddle. He liked these days, when it was just him and Grandfather and creek and paddle. It was as if they were discoverers, voyaging on a black river bordered by never-ending expanses of greenery. It was as if they were lords of a new, beautiful, secret world. Journeying through waterways that were as old as mankind. Boy was delighted to be part of the continuum of history that was knotted up in rivers and creeks.

He was impressed with the way the wooden paddle, thin as a spear, sliced through the back of the strong, slithering creek. He was intrigued at how the creek, like some placid black beast, merely murmured at the repeated attacks of the paddle. It just lay there, flat, unmoving, as if sedated, and ignored the sharp thrusts of the paddle.

The creek was a dark mirror, reflecting the sky, turning the blue into an ugly darkness. It was this that showed Boy that despite its mild nature, the creek was still a dangerous force, guarding its treasures in its black belly, protecting the secrets that swam in it from coming to harm.

Boy liked the tussle, the fight, the connection – almost intimate – between paddle and creek. He and Grandfather were watcher and rower, respectively. They relied on both river and paddle to take them where they wanted go and so, did not choose sides. There were times when Boy watched keenly, the way Grandfather taught him to – like a hawk, and he saw that the battle between the paddle and creek may not have been a fight at all. It was almost playful, as if paddle and rivulet were ancient, long-lost friends.

'Boy, wake up! Watch here, watch here!'

Boy sprang up at the sound of his Grandfather's hushed summons, adjusted his cap and quickly looked around to where the old man was pointing. Grandfather was hunched at the side of the canoe, paddle tucked safely between his legs, and pointed, as if he were a compass, at a spot directly across from them, on the right bank of the creek. Boy peered along the line of his grandfather's crooked aim and he was able to make out a shadowy outline moving behind the trees. He grinned eagerly at Grandfather and leaned so far out to see that the old man grabbed the back of his shirt to keep him from slipping over. The silhouette moved closer to the water's edge and it became clearer. Short legs, short snout, sturdy body, dappled grey colour.

'It's a tapir!' Boy shouted excitedly, too loudly.

The small tapir raised its head, took one glance at them and then quickly bolted away, turning into a shadow amid the trees again before completely disappearing. Boy's face crumpled and as his grandfather took up the paddle once more, he averted his eyes from the old man, so Grandfather would not notice the embarrassment in them.

'We will see other things,' Grandfather said, the lines around his eyes crinkling. But Boy knew that it was very unlikely that they would see anything as interesting as a tapir for the rest of the day. He didn't even budge when Grandfather pointed out an hourglass butterfly, golden-brown and glittering in the sunlight, dancing from bank to bank and stopping to circle and hover around them.

When the canoe had gotten further inland, Grandfather stopped once to observe a waterweed that grew in the center of the creek. He marveled at the vibrant violet, mossy leaves and the way they stood out against the black water. To him they were amethysts sunk in molten opals. Boy, on the other hand, was not interested; he still had not gotten over the loss of the tapir. He spent most of his time trailing his fingers in the river, sending drizzles rainbowing in the air.

When they came to a bend in the creek, a low hum drifted towards them and when the canoe rounded the turn, they saw two boats, one operating with a small engine that emitted the hum, the other a canoe much like theirs.

There were two men in one of the boats. They had red faces, with coppery hair. They were dressed in colours that imitated the earth – greens and browns. One of them clutched a sleek rifle in his hands. Their canoe overflowed with cages stuffed with an assortment of animals that screeched and snarled and howled and shrieked and hissed woefully. Snakes – labarias and yellow anacondas –

reared their heads and coiled themselves tightly in glass cases. Tiny green parrots and giant blue macaws flapped in iron-barred cells that rocked in the little canoe. A lone Canje pheasant sat noiseless and spectacular in another cage, its crest poking through the bars. There were even armadillos and labba, but most astounding was a jaguar, so young that its spots had not even developed on its body. Grandfather had told Boy that there were no more jaguars to be found in these parts. It snarled at them as they came closer. A green dragonfly zipped between the boats as everyone surveyed each other.

'Who are you?' Grandfather asked, keeping his eyes on the men, who were heatedly whispering to each other in a language that Boy could not understand. Grandfather clutched his paddle tightly in his arms, his veins plump beneath his dark skin.

'Boy, get to the back now,' Grandfather muttered, pointing at the further end of their canoe. The men stopped speaking and looked defiantly at Grandfather.

'This is my land. Those are my animals. Who are you? Boy, get to the back NOW!'

Boy stumbled as he moved – cowering behind his grandfather's bowed back. The man with the gun smirked at him.

'*Boy*?' he questioned, his strange accent twisting the name and sharpening its edges. '*Boy*,' he sneered. 'Your name is *Boy*?'

Grandfather pushed out his chest to divert the men's attention from his grandson. 'Listen, take the animals and go. I will turn my canoe and go back the way we came, okay? Take the animals and leave.'

The man with the gun raised the weapon and pointed it straight at Grandfather's limp chest. 'Take us to the arapaima, old man. The big fish bring in more money than gold.'

Grandfather hardened his eyes and gripped his paddle tighter. It gleamed wetly in the sunlight, shining like a steel javelin. The creek watched the scene unfolding on its back in silence, refusing to intrude.

'You heard me, old man?'

Boy was starting to get scared. Grandfather knew where the arapaima swam. It was mating season; they would all gather, hundreds of them, in one part of the creek. Grandfather could just take the men there and this would be over. Instead, he said nothing.

'Old man, are you deaf? Do you want me to shoot you? You want me to tie you up and put you in one of these cages like an animal? I will feed your boy's toes to the piranhas and force you to find the arapaima for me!'

Boy did not want the piranhas to have his toes. He clutched his grandfather's shoulder and pressed his other hand to the old man's back, reassuringly. He could feel Grandfather's heart beat dimly, like a muted drum.

The man without a rifle grinned widely and patted his partner on the back. He saluted Grandfather and wiggled his fingers at Boy. 'My friends, you must forgive this one. He is in a great hurry,' the grinning man said.

'So are we,' Grandfather said abruptly. 'We are leaving now.'

'No, no,' declared the grinning man, 'You must not. No one has to lose any toes or anything of that sort. You just help us, okay? Take us to the arapaima and we give you some of the money we make. You and Boy, come work with us. You make some money from all of this, from all this wealth you have stored up here.' He gestured grandly at the water and the trees that surrounded them.

Grandfather shook his grizzled head sadly, resolutely. 'This is my land. My land and Boy's land. Our land. Our animals. Our *fucking* animals.'

Boy knew what was about to happen before it did. He saw the smooth blade end of the paddle and he saw the creek-water reaching welcoming arms out to him. He saw Grandfather arch his back and leap like a wild warrior from centuries ago. He saw the edge of the paddle connect with the head of the gunman. He saw the wood of the paddle's shaft crack into splinters. He saw the blood being swallowed up greedily by the black water. He saw the gun fall into their boat. He knew he should reach for it, but he didn't.

Boy was only a boy. He saw the grinning man, no longer grinning, lunge at Grandfather while his partner groaned in the boat, trying to stem the flow of blood that kept pouring and pouring like the waterfall in the corner of the creek where the arapaima swam. Boy felt his hands reaching for the rifle that lay weakened like a caged animal when tossed aside like that, but he refused to take that kind of power.

Boy jumped, missed his mark and slammed himself on to the men's canoe, upturning it and sending a barrage of cages in the water.

He fell into the cold clutches of the creek, which finally unveiled its secrets to him. He opened his eyes in the golden blackness and saw the thrashing bodies of furry animals flailing madly against the cages as they sank. He saw the birds trying to fly themselves out of traps made of iron and bubbling water. He saw the snakes whipping themselves against the glass, diamond-patterned bodies sinking. The baby jaguar he did not see at all. He only saw death. The creek split itself down the middle for him. He had chosen it, and abandoned Grandfather to the paddle.

He swam and swam, ignoring the kicking legs of the lost souls, moving out of the way of falling iron-cages crashing into the water, knowing that if he wanted to save himself he could not save a single animal.

He felt the waterweeds pulling him down, holding him back, and he felt the black water trying to pry his lips open. Still, he swam and finally raised his head out of the water and clambered on to land, his hands and knees sticking into squelching mud, and little crabs running away from him in fear.

Boy looked around and realized he had swum far enough from the boats and the strange men and Grandfather and the gun and the poor, drowned animals. He could not see them. He wrung the water from his hair and hid himself among the low bushes. He squatted there, shivering, concealed by mud and leaves, without really knowing who he was hiding from. He had left his grandfather alone and the animals were dead.

He waited and waited for Grandfather to come to him, to find him, to forgive him. He was afraid of being alone.

Two gunshots rang out suddenly, bursting the silence like a punctured drum, and slaughtered the paradise that was the creek. Boy looked up as a flock of scarlet ibises shot into the air like a spray of blood, staining the sky.

Georgia and Them There United States

Velma Pollard

 p.213

I

220 Schenectady

Brooklyn New York

April 20, 1953

My dear Sister

I think it is right that I should write you today. I bought my burial spot; or rather paid down on it and have made all plans for my bones to rest right here when my time comes. I went and did that the minute I finished taking the oath to be an American citizen. I bless my luck that I made it. You can't imagine how many unfortunate Jamaicans are here working and hiding with no security to ensure they can stay here and won't suddenly find themselves on Ellis Island one day waiting to be sent back. Thank God I won't ever set eyes on that down-graded place again. I don't know how you stand it. But you always could stand anything. Not me.

Now I think of Balm-in-Gilead with all the darkness and mud, and wonder how I stayed there that long. It is cold here but you don't feel it because there is Central Heating. And it hardly rains. The snow is beautiful when it comes. I hope that one day I will be able to send you the fare for a seventeen-day trip then you will see for yourself. We will go to Coney Island and some of the other wonders of the world.

Kiss the children for me. Poor things. I wish I had money to let them have a future here. But who knows? By the time June is old enough I may be able to sponsor her then she can work and study here. She seems to be fairly bright. Thank God Georgia will escape the Kingston slums. Her visa will come through any time now. It was being held up by this citizenship business. She will learn to type here although she couldn't get a certificate over there. You know the teachers there aren't any good anyway. Stenographers make quite a tidy sum over here.

I must close now. I am celebrating the citizenship with a little party Saturday night. Hope to invite all the cousins.

Be good to your dear self and keep well.

Your sister

Leticia

The letter was lying on the bureau and it was none of my business. Besides, they had always taught me not to read anything not addressed to me. But Aunt Teach was my private and personal study in human psychology. How on earth she could have grown up in the same house as my practical down-to-earth mother I don't know. Here we were, not even aware that we were in misery; and there she was, wasting so much pity on us. Who decides what is meat and what is poison?

Outside, I spread my crocus bag under the sour-sop tree on the slope where the path to our house was almost vertical. The highest spot was my pillow and my body hugged the slope. I clasped my hands under my head and stretched at full bony length, looking up at the sky that was hot and clear with only a stray cloud here and there to remind the world that clouds were possible. I marvelled at the relentless heat I knew was pouring itself a foot or so beyond my shade of sour-sop leaves and the deep cool of my shaded bed. And I marvelled at how the peace of the heat and cool, and the clustered greenery of orange trees as far as eye could see, could mesmerise me. And I knew that the city, my city then, or any future city, could never claim the grass-bound, hill-bound soul of me. I felt a great pity for my aunt; almost as great as the pity she felt for me.

But even more I pitied Georgia who hadn't asked her mother to put her name on any list of children waiting to leave the sun to share their parents' cold ... I thought of her with sympathy but couldn't really guess how truly horrible was the honour her mother and that great accomplice, Uncle Sam, were waiting to inflict upon her. I had missed her – that Georgia.

II

They drove me through the Bronx my first Sunday in New York. I was very very quiet. My friends were very polite. Nobody questioned my silence. They hadn't seen me for a long time. Perhaps my talkative nature had given way to a new sombreness. I was sitting in awesome silence because I beheld an awesome sight. Nothing in my experience had prepared me for the Bronx. Nothing had prepared me for this place people spent whole anxious lifetimes waiting to get visas and letters of invitation to come up to. My imagination had known a Bronx that was clean and beautiful, and far far superior to anything I had ever seen. When Miss

Hannah, the people's warden at church, went up to spend time with her daughter and wrote back a letter to be read to the whole church during 'Notices' time, I was able to read the last line of the return address on the envelope flapping in Parson Brassington's hand: 'Bronx, New York'. And here I was now in the Bronx and in the presence of so much ugliness. All the words that came to me spoke of depression. They were uncomplimentary words that described a place that could not be complimented: burnt out, dirty, dingy, waste. Brooklyn and Harlem wouldn't ever shock me. Not in this way. For I had seen the Bronx first.

III

At noon one ordinary Monday I found my way to the subway station and descended into the bowels of New York to emerge clutching my paper with directions. And quickly, with surprising ease, I found the building where my aunt worked. I asked for Mrs Leticia Grant and heard, 'You Miss Greehnt niece? Go right inside Room Three, sheez waitin fo you.'

And sure she was. Aunt Teach, powdered bright pink, black eyebrows drawn in to make her face look anything but what God intended.

I tower above her and her enthusiastic hug forces me to her head covered with clusters of wig curl. Eventually she surfaces, and putting me away from her, eyes me like the best young Jersey heifer at a country cattle judging contest.

'Well I tell you my June in the US at last (pause). But what happened to your hair? You in this nonsense cutting it off too? I had told my friends expect my niece I should have said my nephew.' (Now, where had I heard that before?)

I smile with the interior confidence that some of the most discerning eyes I know commented on how well that style suited me. Aunt Teach drags me to every last cipher in the office: cool, young men working machines and ageing women like herself, typing. All sixty acknowledging forty; all cheaply overdressed; all happily bewigged.

My sister had told me that in America the wig is the black woman's goodmorning-white-America-how-are-you before coffee, before prayers if any, before good morning to your black mother who sleeps in the bed next to you. But she didn't tell me that the wig could be blonde and she didn't warn me how the wig and the age lines on the neck might contradict each other. These things I had to see for myself.

'So nice to meet you! Delighted. Oh, Mees Greehnt, ain't she cute?'

And me there with my face aching from the permanent thirty-two teeth grin, and by the time they had finished with me, I was wondering which exam I had managed to leave out in the chronicle of achievements Aunt Teach set out … surely I was the brightest thing ever to hit the schools of Jamaica. The co-workers were kind. All of them allowed themselves to look truly impressed.

IV

My second Sunday in God's own country Aunt Teach brought Georgia so they could take me to see Brooklyn and to spend the whole day. I had been apprehensive about her visit; about her wig and her 'bikez' beginning every next sentence and I wondered if the children would be able to keep from laughing and giving me a bad name.

As it was I had no time for all that. Aunt Teach gushed in, predictably, the loveliness of the children, etc. etc. but it was Georgia that held me. She didn't talk much. She only giggled and flicked back the hair of her wig the way white people and horses do. (Her wig was long and straight not short and curly like her mother's.) And while Aunt Teach took off on how I had shamed her before her friends with my baldness, all I could do was stare. I couldn't giggle. I couldn't talk. I just sat. For I was concentrating on Georgia and what Aunt Teach and her visa and Uncle Sam had made of her. She wasn't a person for me. She was just a bewigged, giggling puppet with more make up than anyone should wear this side of the footlights.

Madness takes so many different forms. Aunt Teach had to be most mad to frighten Georgia into this state. She was glad to see me. I know. She was glad, now she had stopped giggling, that I had got a chance at last to visit the great USA. I know. She hoped that I too, wouldn't want to go back to that down-graded place. I know. I appreciated her concern but I appreciated even more the fact that she no longer existed. That there was no Georgia for me to see. That this thing created out of the imagination of my crazy aunt was what I would have to get accustomed to in the name of my cousin who had been simple yes, but not mad until her mother gave her a chance to 'make it' in the US of A.

V

We always envied children in my school who had parents in America. Every time there was a fair or even a film at school they sallied forth in such outstanding splendour that the entire population was filled with envy. There was something really special about American clothes – those that were new, that is, and obviously bought for the wearer as opposed to the anonymous types from

Salvation Army barrels. There was a kind of elegance, a finished look about them that our dressmakers couldn't imitate; at least not the dressmakers we could afford then. And the shoes, with their tiny heels and look of great comfort, as if the wearer would never feel discomfort in them.

We never questioned whether America was a great place to be. It was. Nice clothes were forever coming down and every year somebody had a relative who was going up. And at Christmas there was this endless stream of large cards with powder in their hearts or padded flowers coming from Brooklyn and the Bronx.

I wrote home to my father and begged him not to tell anybody I had gone UP.

Shoes for the Dead

Kei Miller

p.213

He works with quiet and arrogant indifference, the kind you grow to survive a career looked down upon by everyone, that cold exterior which allows a prostitute not to cry any more when, in an aisle in the supermarket, she passes the man she did beastly things to and for the night before. The man is pushing a trolley beside his wife, the one who would shiver at his raw, animal needs, the one whom he loves so much he pays another woman to exorcise his demons through. The prostitute is doing something human now, buying milk and lettuce, and not even looking for a hello, or a profession of friendship, or anything from those eyes, so cold and lifeless as they look straight past her. She's learnt to stop crying now, and she looks at him with arrogant indifference, the same kind which Philip has as he applies the final touch of make-up on a corpse, pushes it back in the freezer and goes out to the front desk because the wind chimes by the door – their music so hefted with death that they never sound exactly like other chimes – have just announced the arrival of a customer.

'May I help you?' asks the mortician with the distinguished subservience of a butler.

The woman doesn't answer at once. There is something in servitude which lulls a master and prolongs commands. She is nearing fifty and the roots of her shoulder-length hair are their natural grey, which makes Philip guess correctly that she is debating the too-bright red and the too-straight chemicals and is approaching a style which reflects her age. The woman takes off her shades with a slight flick of the head, which makes her hair ripple. Putting them in her handbag, she speaks at last with a smile.

'Yes, how you doing? I've come to pay a bill and I hear there's some other things I might have to get for the body.'

There is no grief in her voice; she speaks with the efficiency of one who has expected death and had budgeted two weeks' vacation for when it happened. Her accent is layered with all the places she's been and lived till it's no accent at all, and Philip can barely distinguish the Jamaican which lies beneath it.

'What's the name?' The undertaker reaches below the counter for his thick hard-covered book of records. He doesn't look as he reaches; his is the reckless efficiency which knows that everything is where it should be.

'James Morrison,' she says, and after a while adds, 'He was really old.' But Philip knows that already from her voice without grief.

With what would have been almost a flourish, had it been less formal, less staccato, Philip puts his glasses on his nose and opens the book, turns the pages slowly and then, reaching the last page of entries, runs his thumb down until he finds the name Morrison, James. He could have done it quicker, but there is dignity in a slowness which doesn't waste anybody's time, anyway.

'And he'll be here until Saturday?'

'Yes. It's a morning funeral.'

'And we shall do the work on Mr Morrison. Make-up, clothes …'

'Yes, yes. Of course.' The woman laughs.

'And a hearse will come for him.'

'Yes.'

'All right,' Philip drawls, taking up his calculator, 'that should be' – punching in the digits – 'yes, one thousand nine hundred dollars.'

The woman's face falls. Then she remembers that prices are different in Jamaica, and after she makes the conversion she realizes it's quite cheap. She laughs to herself and stores the experience, the way we collect anecdotes to tell our friends. She giggles and Philip is unsure what she finds funny. She counts out the cash from her wallet and gives it to him.

'You'll need to get me the things by Thursday. Powder, his suit and …' he pauses and inspects her for the first time consciously. Her clothes and her manner suggest she is educated, he decides at last. Not one to value superstition over plain and common decency. '… and shoes,' he finally adds.

He is pleased that she nods readily to this and smiles, taking his hand, shaking it and looking into his face. 'Thank you so much, sir. You don't know how much you've made this whole thing easier for us all.' He's sure it isn't that much, because of her voice.

Though she has looked into his face, she won't remember it, Philip thinks. There is something too congruous between his appearance and his profession; a stereotype with his lankiness, his straight posture, his hairline receded to the middle of his head then stopped sharply like a razor, the rest of his hair neat and thin and low and grey. His appearance is so expected that it cannot imprint itself upon someone's mind, like Ms Kansas and Ms New York and Ms Delaware from last year's beauty contest.

******

When the woman reaches the family house where everyone is staying, she has two anecdotes to share about her trip to the morgue. She waits till she's settled into shorts and a T-shirt and has towelled off her make-up, put on a shelf all the layers of accents from all the places she's been and lived, the layers which stifle the Jamaican accent below. When she sits down to the meal of curried chicken and potato and yam and boiled green bananas, she tells them first of the one thousand nine hundred dollars and how her heart got cold around the edges. And they all laugh dutifully. Then, she adds, 'But stop! Den you nuh hear de real story yet!' and she tells them about the mortician who told her to buy powder, and a suit; she pauses before the punch line to make sure everyone is listening, and to deliver it with sufficient drama – 'and shoes!!'

'But see-ya!' one of her sisters exclaims, before clapping her hands and laughing.

'Yes me dear,' continues the woman, 'shoes! Me just smile and nod and walk out. I buy de powder and I buy de suit. And is blue, 'cause you know how Dada did like blue suit. But kill me dead if me go buy him a pair of shoes!'

'Dat's right!' declares another sister.

'Nobody not looking 'pon him foot in de coffin,' and then she adds the more important reason, 'and Dada walk around enough when him did alive, me nuh want him walk nuh more, now dat him dead!'

With another burst of laughter, and another round of affirmations, the family agrees that the woman with the layers of accents, and the shoulder-length hair with nappy grey roots, is wise not to buy shoes.

******

Philip hears the door chimes on Wednesday morning, the ones that don't sound like other chimes because something about these mourn, like the hollow wailing of pipes. The man at the door has a package, a final wooden house about the size of a grown man. The undertaker signs for it, and on it is a simple note: *The things are inside.* There is no name attached to this message, and in his heart Philip curses the arrogance of a customer who thinks she is the only one who is to send him a coffin and things.

But he only curses inside, so his dignity remains intact until the delivery man and his underclass staff of haulers are gone. Only then does a small amount of the dignity erode. Philip knows this is from the woman with the too-straight, too-red hair. He lifts open the lid of the mahogany box, and sees a smart blue suit, folded neatly with a white shirt and a blue tie. And on top he sees a bottle of baby powder … not the kind he likes, because he prefers a brand only sold in a pharmacy below Half Way Tree which softens death, instead of making it so harsh and ghostly like all the other brands. But he doesn't care about the powder, because he's reasoned long ago that death isn't supposed to be soft. He takes out the suit and throws it in a chair, and throws the powder there too.

There is nothing else in the coffin. He gropes around the crevices of the white satin, but gives up soon, because that is no place shoes could hide. And he curses now, inside, but it shows in his flared nostrils, in his stern eyes; it shows.

He tries to convince himself that this is nothing to get angry over: the indecency, the wanton superstition of the woman and her family. He has seen it once too often, and there were people who asked him to do worse. Some families not only refused to buy shoes, but insisted that he puts pins in the dead one's feet to prevent them from walking again. It happened often enough for his quiet and arrogant indifference not to fall to pieces when he heard it. The people asked him with no shame in their voices, no awkwardness in their eyes. They asked him for the service as if it were a natural thing, and that he should be schooled in the practice. And after so many years Philip has never been able to bring himself to pierce the dead. He lets the woman a half-mile down the road do it, and pays her a small sum. The woman lives in a house between large warehouses, which seems to draw all the shadows to it; a house with flags mounted all around. But when she leaves the house in her red turban she seems to take the shadows with her. She was happy to pierce feet – and dolls – with pins. And Philip couldn't watch after the first time, because she dipped the pins in olive oil sprinkled with black ashes before she stuck them in, and she hummed so low and loud that it rattled the old man. But the woman with the nappy grey roots hasn't asked Philip to pin her Dada down, she just hasn't bought shoes, and the old undertaker decides the gross indecency is nothing to get angry over.

He walks over to his safe. It is behind a not-done-too-well print of the Mona Lisa in the front of his establishment (he prefers establishment to shop, because there is something wrong in the notion of selling for the dead). The safe is unnecessary. There is nothing of value to outsiders in it, other than money whose amount doesn't warrant the effort of breaking in. But Philip values the contents; both the money and a letter for when he's gone. It's not a will, just instructions for his burial arrangements, because he wants that to go well, having seen so many go wrong in his time. In the letter he says he only wants his body viewed for half an hour, because more than that and those who have sharp noses start to smell death, and then decay. After half an hour the coffin is to be locked forever, and the pastor's words are to be short but powerful like poetry, so he only wants Rev E V Grant from Westmoreland to do it, even though he doesn't know the man personally, but he's seen him do funerals, and he is good. In the letter he asks his wife to wear black lace over her head because that looks so proper and respectable on a weeping widow. But most importantly, in the letter, he says he wants a black suit, and a bow tie, and his hat; and he wants shoes. Black English leather, the kind you can shine so bright it glares; the kind with a line of pin-sized holes which run around the whole shoe and meet at the front in a heart shape. That's what he wants most of all, and no expense is to be spared. None.

Philip locks the safe after he's retrieved two hundred dollars and walks out the store not checking anything, with that kind of reckless efficiency that knows everything is where it should be. He only puts up the misleading 'Be back in 15 minutes' sign and pulls the door closed. He hums a song he's learnt to hum to the tune of the door chimes. He thinks they're the liveliest things in his store. The only thing that doesn't have death lingering on it.

He walks down the avenue passing other houses, and warehouses which throw their oppressive shadows on a flagged house perched between them. He passes women who in the early evening wear loose jeans and buttoned up shirts, and do human things … but the fall of night will see them metamorphose into bright colours and tight clothes. Philip looks past them and through them with cold lifeless eyes of no recognition, and they do the same, because they've learnt not to cry.

He walks until he comes to a woman who sells shoes and slippers that he can get for two hundred dollars or less. He realizes he didn't check the size of Morrison, James's, feet, but then he hardly does these days because he's a good estimator. So he asks for a good sturdy pair of English loafers in size eleven.

The woman searches. 'We only got ten an' a half sir,' she says, pushing the shoes to him, hoping to still make a sale. 'I guess that will have to do,' he accepts, handing her the two hundred dollars, and then waiting expectantly until she reluctantly gives him twenty dollars change.

******

The funeral for Morrison, James, came and went peacefully. Peaceful because no one opened the lower lid of the casket and brought him a complaint about the shoes; not like the time in 1968 when a pallbearer with arms weak from alcohol, which was supposed to be a balm for his grief, let go of his burden and the casket tilted and stood vertical and the lid flew open and the dead body came out, and people weren't as scared because the dead body seemed to be standing for a few seconds as they were because he was standing in shoes. The family had cussed Philip bitterly for the whole affair and demanded a refund, using him as a scapegoat for the whole disaster, as if it was the shoes that caused the grieving son to get drunk and drop the coffin.

But the woman who is approaching a style more reflective of her age never comes back to his establishment. He figures she's picked up her layers of accents off the shelf and gone back to that land far away from Jamaica where she lives.

******

Philip settles down in the armchair in the backroom of the parlour to have his lunch. He reaches over to a table close by and pours himself a cup of lukewarm tea. Then, a sound. Philip stops fixing his tea. There are footsteps in the front of the parlour: odd, because the chimes by the door have not announced anyone's arrival; and then, not so odd to Philip by now.

He continues to pour his tea and then stirs it.

The footsteps don't plod. They are quick and hesitant to the floor, like how a man walks in shoes a half size too small. Philip smiles, pleased with his generosity. It's common decency, he thinks to himself. Every man deserves shoes.

The quick hesitant steps of English loafers a half size too small enter his parlour, and blend well with the clip-clops of boots, and the squeesh-squeaks of slippers, and the tap-taps of church shoes. The sounds are not the kind which death can linger on; they are the sound of death itself.

Philip sips his tea, reflecting on many things at once. But foremost he reasons that there is always good company in his parlour, and he thinks again, with renewed conviction, and finally whispers it aloud, 'Every man deserves shoes.'

The Girl Who Can

Ama Ata Aidoo

p.213

They say that I was born in Hasodzi; and it is a very big village in the central region of our country, Ghana. They also say that when all of Africa is not choking under a drought, Hasodzi lies in a very fertile lowland in a district known for its good soil. Maybe that is why any time I don't finish eating my food, Nana says, 'You Adjoa, you don't know what life is about … you don't know what problems there are in this life …'

As far as I could see, there was only one problem. And it had nothing to do with what I knew Nana considered as 'problems', or what Maami thinks of as 'the problem'. Maami is my mother. Nana is my mother's mother. And they say I am seven years old. And my problem is that at this seven years of age, there are things I can think in my head, but which, maybe, I do not have the proper language to speak them out with. And that, I think, is a very serious problem because it is always difficult to decide whether to keep quiet and not say any of the things that come into my head, or say them and get laughed at. Not that it is easy to get any grown-up to listen to you, even when you decide to take the risk and say something serious to them.

Take Nana. First, I have to struggle to catch her attention. Then I tell her something I had taken a long time to figure out. And then you know what always happens? She would at once stop whatever she is doing and, mouth open, stare at me for a very long time. Then, bending and turning her head slightly, so that one ear comes down towards me, she'll say in *that* voice: 'Adjoa, you say what?' After I have repeated whatever I had said, she would either, still in that voice, ask me 'never, never, but NEVER to repeat THAT', or she would immediately burst out laughing. She would laugh and laugh and laugh, until tears run down her cheeks and she would stop whatever she is doing and wipe away the tears with the hanging edges of her cloth. And she would continue laughing until she is completely tired. But then, as soon as another person comes by, just to make sure she doesn't forget whatever it was I had said, she would repeat it to her. And then, of course, there would be two old people laughing and screaming with tears running down their faces. Sometimes this show continues until there are three, four or even more of such laughing and screaming tear-faced grown-ups. And all that performance for whatever I'd said? I find something quite confusing in all this. That is, no one ever explains to me why sometimes I shouldn't repeat some things I say; while at other times, some other things I say would not only be all right, but would be considered so funny they would be repeated so many times for so many people's enjoyment. You see how neither way of hearing me out can encourage me to express my thoughts too often?

Like all this business to do with my legs. I have always wanted to tell them not to worry. I mean Nana and my mother. It did not have to be an issue for my two favourite people to fight over. I didn't want to be told not to repeat it or for it to be considered so funny that anyone would laugh at me until they cried. After all, they were my legs … When I think back on it now, those two, Nana and my mother must have been discussing my legs from the day I was born. What I am sure of is that when I came out of the land of sweet, soft silence into the world of noise and comprehension, the first topic I met was my legs.

That discussion was repeated very regularly.

Nana: 'Ah, ah, you know, Kaya, I thank my God that your very first child is female. But Kaya, I am not sure about her legs. Hm … hm … hm …'

And Nana would shake her head.

Maami: 'Mother, why are you always complaining about Adjoa's legs? If you ask me …'

Nana: 'They are too thin. And I am not asking you!'

Nana has many voices. There is a special one she uses to shut everyone up.

'Some people have no legs at all,' my mother would try again with all her small courage.

'But Adjoa has legs,' Nana would insist; 'except that they are too thin. And also too long for a woman. Kaya, listen. Once in a while, but only once in a very long while, somebody decides – nature, a child's spirit mother, an accident happens, and somebody gets born without arms, or legs, or both sets of limbs. And then let me touch wood; it is a sad business. And you know, such things are not for talking about everyday. But if any female child decides to come into this world with legs, then they might as well be legs.'

'What kind of legs?' And always at that point, I knew from her voice that my mother was weeping inside. Nana never heard such inside weeping. Not that it would have stopped Nana even if she had heard it. Which always surprised me. Because, about almost everything else apart from my legs, Nana is such a good grown-up. In any case, what do I know about good grown-ups and bad grown-ups? How could Nana be a good grown-up when she carried on so about my legs? All I want to say is that I really liked Nana except for that.

Nana: 'As I keep saying, if any woman decides to come into this world with her two legs, then she should select legs that have meat on them: with good calves. Because you are sure such legs would support solid hips. And a woman must have solid hips to be able to have children.'

'Oh, Mother.' That's how my mother would answer. Very, very quietly. And the discussion would end or they would move on to something else.

Sometimes, Nana would pull in something about my father:

How, 'Looking at such a man, we have to be humble and admit that after all, God's children are many …'

How, 'After one's only daughter had insisted on marrying a man like that, you still have to thank your God that the biggest problem you got later was having a granddaughter with spindly legs that are too long for a woman, and too thin to be of any use.'

The way she always added that bit about my father under her breath, she probably thought I didn't hear it. But I always heard it. Plus, that is what always shut my mother up for good, so that even if I had not actually heard the words, once my mother looked like even her little courage was finished, I could always guess what Nana had added to the argument.

'Legs that have meat on them with good calves to support solid hips … to be able to have children.'

So I wished that one day I would see, for myself, the legs of any woman who had had children. But in our village, that is not easy. The older women wear long wrap-arounds all the time. Perhaps if they let me go bathe in the river in the evening, I could have checked. But I never had the chance. It took a lot of begging just to get my mother and Nana to let me go splash around in the shallow end of the river with my friends, who were other little girls like me. For proper baths, we used the small bathhouse behind our hut. Therefore, the only naked female legs I have ever really seen are those of other little girls like me, or older girls in the school. And those of my mother and Nana: two pairs of legs which must surely belong to the approved kind; because Nana gave birth to my mother and my mother gave birth to me. In my eyes, all my friends have got legs that look like legs, but whether the legs have got meat on them to support the kind of hips that … that I don't know.

******

According to the older boys and girls, the distance between our little village and the small town is about five kilometres. I don't know what five kilometres mean. They always complain about how long it is to walk to school and back. But to me, we live in our village, and walking those kilometres didn't matter. School is nice.

School is another thing Nana and my mother discussed often and appeared to have different ideas about. Nana thought it would be a waste of time. I never understood what she meant. My mother seemed to know – and disagreed. She kept telling Nana that she – that is, my mother – felt she was locked into some kind of darkness because she didn't go to school. So that if I, her daughter, could learn to write and read my own name and a little besides – perhaps be able to calculate some things on paper – that would be good. I could always marry later and maybe …

Nana would just laugh. 'Ah, maybe with legs like hers, she might as well go to school.'

Running with our classmates on our small sports field and winning first place each time never seemed to me to be anything about which to tell anyone at home. This time it was different. I don't know how the teachers decided to let me run for the junior section of our school in the district games. But they did.

When I went home to tell my mother and Nana, they had not believed it at first. So Nana had taken it upon herself to go and 'ask into it properly'. She came home to tell my mother that it was really true. I was one of my school's runners.

'Is that so?' exclaimed my mother. I know her. Her mouth moved as though she was going to tell Nana, that, after all, there was a secret about me she couldn't be expected to share with anyone. But then Nana herself looked so pleased, out of surprise, my mother shut her mouth up. In any case, since the first time they heard the news, I have often caught Nana staring at my legs with a strange look on her face, but still pretending like she was not looking. All this week, she has been washing my school uniform herself. That is a big surprise. And she didn't stop at that, she even went to Mr Mensah's house and borrowed his charcoal pressing iron. Each time she came back home with it and ironed and ironed and ironed the uniform, until, if I had been the uniform, I would have said aloud that I had had enough.

Wearing my school uniform this week has been very nice. At the parade, on the first afternoon, its sheen caught the rays of the sun and shone brighter than anybody else's uniform. I'm sure Nana saw that too, and must have liked it. Yes, she has been coming into town with us every afternoon of this district sports week. Each afternoon, she has pulled one set of fresh old cloth from the big brass bowl to wear. And those old clothes are always so stiffly starched, you can hear the cloth creak when she passes by. But she walks way behind us schoolchildren. As though she was on her own way to some place else.

Yes, I have won every race I ran for my school, and I have won the cup for the best all-round junior athlete. Yes, Nana said that she didn't care if such things are not done. She would do it. You know what she did? She carried the gleaming cup on her back. Like they do with babies, and other very precious things. And this time, not taking the trouble to walk by herself.

When we arrived in our village, she entered our compound to show the cup to my mother before going to give it back to the Headmaster.

Oh, grown-ups are so strange. Nana is right now carrying me on her knee, and crying softly. Muttering, muttering, muttering that: '*saa*, thin legs can also be useful … thin legs can also be useful …' that 'even though some legs don't have much meat on them, to carry hips … they can run. Thin legs can run … then who knows? …'

I don't know too much about such things. But that's how I was feeling and thinking all along. That surely, one should be able to do other things with legs as well as have them because they can support hips that make babies. Except that I was afraid of saying that sort of thing aloud. Because someone would have told me never, never, but NEVER to repeat such words. Or else, they would have laughed so much at what I'd said, they would have cried.

It's much better this way. To have acted it out to show them, although I could not have planned it.

As for my mother, she has been speechless as usual.

The Pain Tree

Olive Senior

p.214

I

The person who took care of me as a child was a woman named Larissa. The moment I arrived home, I had a vision of her, instead of my mother, standing by the front steps waiting to greet me with a gift in her hand. It startled me; though she no longer worked for my family, and it had been many years since I'd thought of her, it seemed so real. Suddenly I was a child again, so palpable was her presence. What I'd remembered were the good times we'd had together; it made me feel sad and I didn't know why. I felt cheated of the gift she hadn't delivered, though I knew that to be absurd. Larissa was a poor woman, with nothing to give.

My mother loved to say I was coming home to possess my inheritance. She wrote it like that in her letters. She also told people I'd chosen to study archaeology because I'd been born in a house with seventeenth-century foundations. Yes, I would say to myself, built of the finest cut stone, the mortar hard as iron because it was sweetened with molasses and slave blood. My mother would have been extremely mortified if she'd heard me say that aloud. For us, the past was a condensed version.

I didn't want to possess anything.

When my parents sent me to boarding school in England at the age of ten, I had happily gone, and managed to stay away for fifteen years. But coming home now seemed the right thing since my father died and my mother was left alone. I was their only child.

II

I had never given much thought to the life I was born into, and duty was something new to me. For the first few weeks after my return I fell into whatever my mother had planned for me, trying to get my bearings, but I had no real sense of connecting with anyone or anything, life here seemed so untouched by the changes in the world. My mother kept talking of what a grand opportunity I had for building up the estate to the grandeur it once had, but all I could think of was how much there was I had to break down. I was already feeling suffocated, only now realizing how often in my childhood I had escaped to Larissa.

'Is anyone living in Larissa's old room?' I asked my mother at breakfast one day.

'Of course not, dear. None of these girls want live-in jobs anymore. They're all day workers. Just wait till this country gets the so-called Independence they're all clamouring for. Then there'll be nobody to work for us at all.'

She said this with such petulance that I almost laughed. I looked hard at her, at her impeccably made-up face, even at breakfast, her polished nails and her hair. 'Well-preserved' is the way one would have described her. I though irreverently that that is perhaps why I had studied archaeology. My mother, the well-preserved. Carefully layered. The way she had always looked. The way she would look in her grave. I saw nothing of myself in her, in this house, in this life. But then, I saw nothing of myself anywhere.

III

One day I left the house and walked down the slope to the old slave barracks hidden behind the trees.

In my childhood, the barracks were used for storage, except for a few rooms that housed the people who worked in the great house. As I neared, I could see the buildings were abandoned, maidenhair fern and wild fig sprouting from every crack, the roof beginning to cave in.

I had no difficulty identifying Larissa's from the long line of doors. I threw open the window as soon as I entered the room, but the light that streamed in barely penetrated the dust and cobweb, so I went outside and broke off a tree branch and used it to brush some away.

The old iron bed was still there – without a mattress – as well as the washstand, the small table and battered wooden chair. I sat on the chair, as I often did when I was a child, and looked keenly at the walls, which were completely covered with pages and pictures cut out of newspapers and magazines and pasted down, all now faded and peeling. This is a part of me, I thought with surprise, for I recognized many of the pictures as those I had helped Larissa to cut out. I got the feeling nothing new had been added since I left.

I used to help Larissa make the paste from cassava starch, but the job of sticking the pictures to the wall was hers alone. I brought the newspapers and magazines my parents were done with, and we looked at the pictures together and argued. I liked scenes of far-off lands and old buildings best while her favourites were the Holy Family, the British Royal Family and beautiful clothes. But, as time went on, headlines, scenes, whole pages about the War in Europe took over, and Larissa wanted me to read all the news to her before she fell to with scissors and paste. With the rapidly changing events, even Jesus got pasted over.

The newspaper pages had looked so fresh when we put them up, the ink so black and startling, headlines imposing on the room names and images that were heavy and ponderous like tolling bells: Dun-kirk, Stalin-grad, Roose-velt, Church-ill. And the most important one, the one facing Larissa's bed with the caption above it saying, 'The Contingent Embarking'. Larissa and I had spent countless hours searching that picture in vain; trying to find – among the hundreds of young men on the deck of the ship, to decipher from the black dots composing the picture – the faces of her two sons.

It was I, then about eight years old, who had signed for and brought the telegram to Larissa.

The moment she saw what was in my hand she said, 'Wait, make me sit down,' even though she was already sitting on the steps outside the barracks. She got up and slowly walked into her room, took off her apron, straightened her cap, sat on the bed and smoothed down her dress, her back straight. I stood in the doorway and read the message. Her youngest son was on a ship that went down. I remember being struck by the phrase, 'All hands'.

I never met Larissa's sons; they were raised by her mother someplace else, but she talked of them constantly – especially her youngest, whose name was Zebedee. When the war came, both Moses and Zebedee, like ten thousand other young men, had rushed off to join the Contingents. So far as I know, Moses was never heard from again, even after the war ended.

I can still see myself reading to Larissa about the loss of Zebedee Breeze. 'All hands. All hands,' kept echoing in my head.

Larissa didn't cry. She sat, staring silently at the pictures that covered the walls to a significant depth; the layers represented not just the many years of her own occupancy, but those of the nameless other women who had passed through that room.

I went to sit very close beside her on the bed. She put her arm around me. We sat like that for a long time. I wanted to speak, but my mouth felt very dry. I could hardly get the words out. 'He, Zebedee, was a hero,' was all I could think of saying.

Larissa hugged me tightly with both hands, then pulled away and resumed staring at the wall. She did it with such intensity, it was as if she expected all the images to fly together and coalesce, finally, into one grand design, to signify something meaningful.

'Zebedee Breeze,' I said to myself, over and over, and his name was like a light wind passing. How could he have drowned?

After a while, Larissa got up and washed her face, straightened her clothes, and walked with me back to the house to resume her duties. My parents must have spoken to her, but she took no time off. I didn't see her cry that day or any other. She never mentioned her sons.

And something comes to me now that would never have occurred to me then: how when the son of one of my parent's friends had died, his mother had been treated so tenderly by everyone, the drama of his illness and death freely shared, the funeral a community event. That mother had worn full black for a year to underline her grief and cried often into her white lace handkerchief, which made us all want to cry with her.

Women like Larissa, pulled far from their homes and families by the promise of work, were not expected to grieve; their sorrow, like their true selves, remained muted and hidden. Alone in countless little rooms like the one in which I was sitting, they had papered over the layers, smoothed down the edges, till the flat and unreflective surface mirrored the selves they showed to us, the people who employed them.

Was that why we had come to believe that people like Larissa, people who were not us, had no feelings?

I was suddenly flooded with the shame of a memory that I had long hidden from myself: when I was going off to England, I had left without saying goodbye to Larissa, closest companion for my first ten years.

I can see it now. Me: the child with boundless energy, raring to go. Larissa calmly grooming me, retying my ribbons, straightening my socks, spinning me around to check that my slip didn't show. Was it just my imagination that she was doing it more slowly than usual? The trunks and suitcases were stowed. My parents were already seated in the car. I was about to get in when Larissa said, 'Wait! I forget. I have something for you.' And she rushed off.

I stood for a moment or two. No one was hurrying me. But with a child's impatience, I couldn't wait. I got into the car and the driver shut the door.

'Tell Larissa "bye",' I shouted out the window to no one in particular.

'Wait! She coming,' one of the workers called out, for quite a group had gathered to see us off. But the driver had put the car in gear and we were moving. I didn't even look back.

I had planned to write to Larissa, but never did. For a few years I sent her my love via letters to my mother and received hers in return, but even that trickled away. I never for one moment wondered what it was she had wanted to give me and turned back for. I had completely forgotten about it, until now.

The thought came, unbidden, that only those who are born rich can afford the luxury of not wanting to own anything. We can try it on as a way of avoiding complicity. But in my heart of hearts I know my inheritance already possesses me.

What Larissa wanted more than anything was the one thing a poor woman could never afford: beautiful clothes.

Sometimes when she and I came to paste new pictures on the wall, we went a little bit crazy and ripped at torn edges with glee, digging deep down into the layers and pulling up old pages that had stuck together, revealing earlier times and treasures.

'Look, Larissa,' I would cry, and read aloud. '"Full white underskirts with nineteen-inch flounce carrying three insertions of Real Linen Torchon lace three inches wide." Three inches, Larissa! "Edging at foot to match. Only ten shillings and sixpence."'

'Oh Lord,' Larissa would say and clap her hands. 'Just the thing for me!'

After our laughter subsided, Larissa would carefully lay down her new pictures to cover over what we had ripped up. She did it slowly and carefully but sometimes her hands would pause, as if her thoughts were already travelling.

Now I felt shame, not just for the way I had treated Larissa, but for a whole way of life I had inherited. People who mattered, we believed, resided in the great house. It was we who made history, a series of events unfolding with each generation. And yet, I realized now, it was in this room, Larissa's, that I had first learnt that history is not dates or abstraction but a space where memory becomes layered and textured. What is real is what you carry around inside of you.

IV

Meeting the past like this in Larissa's room, I began to feel almost faint, as if the walls were crawling in towards me, the layers of fractured images thickening, shrinking the space, absorbing the light coming through the window and from the open door until I felt I was inside a tomb surrounded by hieroglyphics: images of war and the crucified Christ, princesses and movie stars, cowboys and curly haired children, pampered cats and dogs, lions and zebras in zoos, long-haired girls strutting the latest fashions, ads for beauty creams, toothpaste and motor cars. Images of people who were never like the people who had occupied this room.

What had these pictures meant to them, the women who had lived here? What were they like, really, these women who were such close witnesses to our lives? Women who were here one day then going – gone, like Larissa. Leaving no forwarding address because we had never asked.

V

Larissa's room with its silent layers of sorrow so humbly borne suffocated me. I had this urge to strip the walls, tear the layers apart. I felt such rage, I rose and put both hands against the wall facing me and I pushed, wanting to send it tumbling, all of it. Such rage that my hands battered at the walls. War! I couldn't stop, couldn't stop my fingers digging into the layers of paper, gouging and ripping. This is where these women buried their rage. Here! I sent huge sheets flying. Here! Half a wall of paper down in one big clump. Over there! Digging down now, struggling with layers of centuries, almost falling over as the big pieces came away in my hands. I couldn't stop scratching at the fragments left behind, wanting to destroy it all, till my nails were broken to the quick and bleeding.

VI

I came to my senses in that dust-laden room, sobbing loudly and holding clumps of rotting old paper in my hand, fragments flying about, clinging to my hair and clothing, sticking to my nose, my mouth, clogging my throat. I coughed and sneezed and spun around, shaking my hair like a mad dog, setting the fragments spinning, joining the dust motes floating in the sunlight streaming in.

What a mess I was.

Ashamed, I summoned up the nerve to look at my handiwork. There were places that could never be stripped, the layers so old they were forever bonded to the walls. In some parts I had managed to strip the walls down to reveal dark ugly stains from centuries of glue and printer's ink and whatever else can stain. The walls were an abstract collage now. No single recognizable image was left. Without meaning to, I had erased the previous occupants.

I felt sick at my behaviour, as if I had committed a desecration. Larissa's room. I had no right.

But the longer I sat in the room, the more I realized it was giving off no disturbing emanations. What I had done had neither added to nor diminished it. The rage had not been the women's but mine. In the wider scheme of things, it was a gesture without meaning. The women like Larissa would always be one step ahead, rooms like this serving only as temporary refuge. They knew, from the history of their mothers and their mothers before them, that they would always move on. To other rooms elsewhere. To raise for a while children not their own who – like their own – would repay them with indifference, ingratitude, or death.

I thought I was taking possession, but the room had already been condemned.

I got up and leaned out the window and was surprised at how fresh and clean the air felt. I offered up my face, my hair, my arms to the wind that was blowing lightly and I closed my eyes so it would wash away the last fragments of paper and cobweb. O Zebedee Breeze! The name of Larissa's son had seemed so magical to me as a child I had often whispered it to myself, and as I whispered it now, it conjured up the long-forgotten image of Larissa and the pain tree.

VII

A few days after I had brought the news of Zebedee's death to Larissa, I saw her walking back and forth in the yard, searching the ground. Finally, she bent and picked something up. Then she took up a stone and walked a little way into the bushes. I was so curious I followed her, but something told me not to reveal myself.

She stopped when she reached the cedar tree, and I watched as she stood for a good while with her head bent close to the tree and her lips moving as if she were praying. Then she pounded the trunk of the tree with the stone, threw the stone down, and strode off without looking back. When I went and examined the tree, I saw that she had hammered in a nail. I was even more astonished to notice there were many nails hammered right into the trunk.

At first, I sensed that this was something so private I should keep quiet about it. But I couldn't help it, and one day I asked Larissa why she had put the nail into the tree.

'Don't is the pain tree?' she asked in a surprised voice, as if that was something everyone knew.

'What do you mean by "pain tree"?'

'Eh, where you come from, girl?' Larissa exclaimed. 'Don't is the tree you give your pain to?'

I must have looked puzzled still, for she took the trouble to explain. 'Let us say, Lorraine, I feel a heavy burden, too heavy for me to bear, if I give the nail to the tree and ask it to take my burden from me, is so it go. Then I get relief.'

'So you put all those nails in the tree?' I asked, for I could not imagine one person having so much pain.

She looked embarrassed then she said, 'Not all of them. I find some when I come here. That's how I know is a pain tree.'

'You mean, other people do this?'

'Of course,' she said. 'Plenty people do it.' Then she paused and said, almost to herself, 'What else to do?'

After that, whenever I remembered, I would go and look at the tree, but I never detected new nails. Perhaps if I had been older and wiser I would have interpreted this differently, but at the time I took it to mean that Larissa felt no more pain.

Once or twice, when I was particularly unhappy, I had myself gone to the tree to try and drive a nail in. But I did so without conviction and the magic didn't work for me, the nails bent and never went in properly and I ended up throwing both nail and stone away in disgust.

'Maybe people like you don't need the pain tree,' Larissa said after my third try.

It was the only time I ever felt uncomfortable with her.

VIII

Leaving Larissa's room, I deliberately left the door and window wide open for the breeze to blow through. I went outside and stood on the steps of the barracks to get my bearings, for the landscape had vastly changed. Then I waded into the bushes to look for a cedar. I had decided to try and find the pain tree.

It took me a while. At first I couldn't believe I had found the right tree, for what had been a sapling was now of massive growth, its trunk straight and tall, its canopy high in the air.

I didn't expect to see any nail marks, but I knew they were there. I walked around the tree, looking up until finally, with the sun striking at the right angle – and, yes, it might have been my imagination – I caught a glint of something metallic, and what looked like pockmarks high up on the trunk.

Standing there, gazing upwards, it came to me why Larissa and all those women had kept on giving the tree their pain, like prayers. Because they knew no matter what else happened in their lives, the tree would keep on bearing them up, higher and higher, year after year.

I had the uncomfortable feeling that I should be grieving not for them, but for myself. People like me would always inherit the land, but they were the ones who already possessed the Earth.

Before I went back to the house, I spent a long time searching the ground for a nail. When I found one, I picked up a stone. I went and stood close to the tree and whispered to it, and then I carefully positioned the nail and pounded it with the stone. It went straight in.

Mint Tea

Christine Craig

p.214

The dress was pink, a very fashionable sort of dusty rose, like fading petals, and Mother had lent her her pearl ear-rings. She could see them gleaming softly when she turned her head and peered into the dim reflection of the mirror. Late afternoon sun fell through the jalousie windows and left gold bars on the wooden floor. Annie hurried in then stepped slowly over them, her shiny patent pumps made her feet look very small, very neat. They stood together, the sisters, looking into the mirror and they smiled slightly into each other's eyes. Florence moved to the door and looked out past the verandah where Father was standing with the horse and buggy, and she caught her breath slightly at the sight of them. Father, so tall and handsome in his dark suit, the brown gleam of the horse and beyond them the mountains. A bird was singing somewhere and Father bent, picked a rose and placed it carefully in his lapel. That bush by the front steps, how it bloomed, always covered in small, fragrant red roses.

The Town Hall had been decorated with palm fronds and hibiscus flowers and they sat in the front row, very important, very grown up. One of the singers, a tall, thin fair man with a moustache, sang all the love songs to Annie, and Florence saw Annie's dark, almond-shaped eyes turned up to him under the perfect wings of her eyebrows. Afterwards, Father bustled them away before 'that city man' could make their acquaintance, hurried them into the buggy and they drove off, up the hilly road. So many bright stars and she and Annie sang one of the songs:

'I'll remember you, always

with a love that's true, always.'

Florence shook her head slightly, as if to dust off the fine powder of memories that seemed increasingly to settle around her mind. It was all so long ago, she thought, yet often her childhood seemed more real, more vivid than this pale, creased up thing that was retirement. Each day so similar, each day so quiet without the regular sound of the school bell signalling a gush of noise as the children streamed out of class.

There was a knock at the gate. Startled, Florence looked out and saw a young woman standing there.

'Please mam, I looking a job as a live-in helper.'

It was mid-afternoon and very hot. The girl looked weary and her dress had dark, wet stains spreading out from her armpits.

'I don't need anyone,' said Florence.

'Please mam,' the girl called quickly. 'I could have a drink of water?'

Florence got her some water and motioned for her to push the gate and come in. The girl came in and stood by the front steps holding a small, brown vinyl bag. The sun was so hot she began to feel confused and when Florence gave her the water, she drank it too quickly and felt slightly sick so that she leaned for a moment against the verandah wall.

'Child, are you ill?'

'No mam. I been walking since morning looking a job.'

'Come, sit on the verandah for a while.'

Esmie walked up the two steps to the verandah and sat on a wooden slatted chair.

'Where are you from?'

'I name Esmie Grant and I grow at Haven Home and I am eighteen years of age.'

Florence gazed at the girl, an awkward, bony sort of body and a face without expression. Her hair was plaited neatly in two sections, a schoolgirl hairstyle, but there was something old, tired looking about her eyes.

'Well,' said Florence firmly, 'you must go back to the Home now, it will soon be dark.'

'I can't go back mam. I am eighteen and I have to leave.'

'You left the Home with no job and no place to go?'

'I don't have no family mam. I have to get a job.'

'What kind of work can you do Esmie?'

'Well mam, my head wasn't so good wid de books but I used to mind de smaller children.'

Florence felt a wave of anger, how could the Home just put her out, no arrangements made for her at all. No wonder so many of these girls ended up on the streets.

'Have you eaten anything since morning?'

'No mam.'

Florence fixed some sandwiches and lemonade, gave them to Esmie and then went inside to call the Home. The Matron confirmed that she had left there that day, that she was a decent girl but had no special skills.

'But how on earth,' Florence asked angrily, 'can you put the girl out and she knows no one, has no place to go?'

'Rules are rules,' Matron replied huffily. The place was already overcrowded, every day there were little ones coming in, and they didn't have staff enough as it was to look after the babies. There was no one to be out finding jobs for the big girls. They would just have to get out there and stand on their own two feet.

Florence brought the conversation to a close and hung up. She hated volubility and she hated complainers and Matron was afflicted with both ailments. Florence returned to the verandah and looked at Esmie.

'Esmie, my name is Miss Gates. I am a retired teacher and I do not have a job for you, but I have a little room at the back and you can stay there for a day or two while you look for a job. But remember that it's only for a short time. The Lord helps those that help themselves so you must do your best to find a job.'

'Yes mam. Thank you mam.' Esmie smiled shyly and Florence saw that her face, rescued briefly by the smile, was pretty.

'And I'm telling you straight,' Florence added, 'keep your mind on sensible things, don't let me see you getting in with any foolish boys.'

Esmie shook her head wearily.

Florence set her to clean out the little room which hadn't been used for years. There was a bed, an old dressing table and the naked light bulb illuminated unkindly the drabness of it. But Florence fetched some curtains, an old blue bedspread and a lace-edged doily for the dressing table so that it looked quite habitable when they were finished. As Esmie unpacked her bag, Florence turned away saddened by the sight. Two dresses, two sets of underwear and a tin of lavender talc. Florence added some toilet articles and a Bible and so Esmie was set up in a corner of Miss Gates' life.

Esmie was neat, tidy, dutiful but she had no skills for job-hunting. Florence was horrified to discover that she could barely read and write and she would only respond to direct questions. 'An underdeveloped soul,' she thought sadly and set herself diligently to Esmie's instruction. But in spite of Florence's considerable experience as a teacher, Esmie proved an unresponsive pupil. Florence encouraged her to read the newspaper and listen to the radio but Esmie seemed to have no real interest in any particular subject, she had no particular liking for one thing or dislike for another. She did as she was told. 'Institution life,' thought Florence and she tried to get her to make simple decisions. Should they have chicken or beef for dinner, eggs or porridge for breakfast.

The weeks passed. Since her retirement, since so many of her friends had long since died, Florence had a dread of becoming a lonely, muddled old woman. She established a very stable routine for herself, one that kept mind and body active. She kept her house tidy, she gardened, she read and she went to church on Sunday. But recently, she had found herself sitting somewhere, perhaps with some mending on her lap, caught up in vivid memories of the past. The early morning smell of the mountains mixed with the light and birds singing. They came over her in a wave, so fresh that she would tilt her face up absorbing the smell of moist leaves and opening flowers and then the sound of Mother in the kitchen grinding coffee beans and she would wait for that smell to form itself, to come slipping out to make the signal that woke up the rest of the house. Mother and Father, Annie, beautiful Annie. They were all dead now and sometimes she felt that she had lived too long and it was time that she too moved on to another life. But here she was with a stranger for company.

Sometimes she grew irritated with Esmie, she was never going to find a job and move on and she didn't want the responsibility of this girl who seemed to progress so very slowly. At other times she was overwhelmed with pity for her, never having had her own parents, her own home.

One Sunday she persuaded Esmie to go to church with her. Esmie sat quiet until the first hymn and then she opened her mouth and a voice so beautiful poured out that Florence found her own strong contralto dropping to a whisper to listen to the effortless, golden soprano pouring out beside her. Esmie's eyes were half-closed, her face expressionless, the voice just rose and streamed out of her body and Esmie seemed quite unaware of it.

After church Florence suggested that she should join the choir.

'No mam,' said Esmie.

Florence was stunned.

'But Esmie, you have been blessed with a beautiful voice, it's a God-given talent. You should join the choir and develop your voice.'

Esmie looked away. She was disinterested in the conversation, unmoved by the compliment.

'I going to change my frock mam and start the dinner,' Esmie said, moving away quickly.

'For heaven's sake, Esmie, stop calling me "mam",' Florence said wearily.

The next day, Florence sent for the piano tuner. He spent hours with his tuning forks and his notes played over and over again. Esmie gave him tea and ignored him but the noise made Florence irritable, she went out for a walk and found herself looking at things in shops. It seemed to her that the shops were full of ugly, badly made things from places like Taiwan and Hong Kong. She decided to buy Esmie a dress but the prices were way above the few notes tucked into her handbag. She returned home hot, tired and bad-tempered. The piano tuner charged an exorbitant fee for his services and left. She drew the curtains in her bedroom and lay down. She was hot, her feet were swollen and her thoughts raced about, disjointed. Her heart was beating too quickly, she must calm herself, breathe in slowly, out slowly …

It was growing dark and Esmie did not know what to fix for supper. Miss Gates never lay down like that, in the day. She went to the bedroom door.

'You sick mam, Miss Gates?' she asked. 'You want I should fix you some mint tea?'

'Yes, thank you, Esmie,' she said, pleased that Esmie had taken the initiative in this one, small act.

Revived by the tea, she found a box of old music sheets and began haltingly at first, then the notes seemed to flow back into her fingers, and she gathered up confidence and launched out fully. Esmie sat on the verandah waiting patiently for Miss Gates to stop playing and tell her what to fix for supper. But Miss Gates flowed on and finally Esmie fixed herself a sandwich and went to her room. She was later summoned and when she went, sleepily, to the living room she was startled by the old lady's face, the excitement there, her eyes sparkled and her close-cropped white hair seemed to crackle around her head. She gave her some sheets of music.

'It's the twenty-third Psalm, you know the words already. I'm going to play the music and you listen and follow the words on the song sheet.'

Esmie took the paper and listened as Miss Gates played and sang in her slightly raspy old contralto voice.

'Now ready? I'm going to start again and you sing it with me.'

Miss Gates played and Esmie sang. She grasped the music immediately and once more the effortless, true voice flowed out.

When it was finished Miss Gates looked at her, still with that sparkle and energy about her.

'Wonderful, Esmie. Just truly wonderful. We will practise a few more times and then you will sing in church on Sunday.'

'No mam,' said Esmie.

Miss Gates flew into a terrible temper. 'Don't you dare tell me "no". So foolish. Why ever not? I can't understand you at all.'

Esmie said nothing but she began to feel a bit anxious, she did not want Miss Gates to get upset. She did not want her to get sick. Miss Gates closed the piano lid and paced up and down in front of the immobile Esmie.

'I have been a teacher all my life. Some were bright, some were not, but they all left my class with something, some sense of themselves, some spark of ambition. Are you listening? I pick up the newspaper every day and see this one or that one, doing well, doing something with their lives. And you, with this great, natural talent, you have no ambition. For the life of me I can't understand it.'

'Please Miss Gates,' Esmie said softly, 'please don't tek on so.'

Florence stopped pacing. She felt dreadfully tired. They locked up the house and went to their rooms. The next day she spent most of the day in her room and she would not eat. Esmie did not know what to do. She knew there was a niece who talked on the telephone sometimes with Miss Gates, but Esmie did not know her name or phone number. If anything happened to the old lady she would not know what to do.

The next day Miss Gates did not even get dressed. She accepted a cup of tea and stayed in bed. There was no washing to do, the house was tidy and Esmie did not know what to do. She knew she must do something. Finally she presented herself at the door.

'Miss Gates, mam.'

'Yes, Esmie?'

Esmie was shocked by the voice, by the face that turned towards her. She looked so old, so small and old.

'Mam, I should get a doctor? What I should do mam?'

Miss Gates turned her head away and did not reply.

Esmie went away. She was frightened now, she was trembling and she felt cold. It was always hot in the Home. There were so many girls. Sometimes she would wake up at night and feel glad that she was awake in the cool and quiet of the night. She went to her room and picked up the Bible Miss Gates had given her. She held it in her hands, not reading it, just feeling the soft, worn leather cover and the slight weight of it in her hands. She liked having her own room there. Miss Gates put up white net curtains and she liked to wake up in the mornings and see them moving slightly, they looked so light as if they were not quite real. Juliet was her friend at the Home but when Juliet was fourteen a lady came from England and said that she was Juliet's aunt, she cried, standing there by Juliet's bed. She had a big bosom and she cried and her bosom heaved up and down. She took Juliet away to live with her. Esmie thought of Miss Gates lying in her room looking so sad and old, she did not want her to go away like Juliet. Then she remembered that she had been pleased when she gave her mint tea. She would make her some tea. She quickly picked some mint and hurried to the kitchen. The mint tea would make the old lady feel better and things would be as they were before. She did not want things to change. She was cold and trembling, she must make the tea quickly, it would make the old lady well again. She reached for a cup and it fell, smashed to bits on the floor. She fell to the floor, picked up a piece of the cup and started to weep.

Florence heard the noise and then silence.

'Esmie, what's that?' There was no reply.

She got up slowly, wearily pulled on a dressing gown and made her way to the kitchen. Esmie was sitting on the floor, blood dripped from her hand, very dark against the pale tiles of the kitchen floor.

'But child, what's wrong? Get up and let me have a look at that hand.'

Esmie sat, crumpled up. She made no sound but tears streamed from her eyes which were wide open, staring.

'Esmie, get up this minute. Get off that floor.'

Esmie stared straight ahead of her.

'Mama, mama.' Her voice was that of a very small child. Then the voice became adult, a soft, crooning voice.

'Mama soon come back baby. I going to church. I going to sing a lovely song for my baby. See your Daddy come to stay wid you. I soon come back.'

Esmie stopped crying, her eyes stared straight in front of her, she was absolutely still, in shock.

Florence stood, leaning against the kitchen counter, her breathing uneven, loud in the still room. Finally she helped Esmie up, bandaged her hand and put her to lie on the sofa.

'What happened, Esmie? What happened to your Mama?'

Esmie's voice was flat and toneless. 'De house catch on fire. Me Daddy give me to somebody an tried to put out de fire. Mama was coming back from church and she see, she run to save me but she an him dead in de fire. I don't know why dem never leave me in dere too. I don't know why.'

'Esmie, how old were you when that happened?'

'I was very small. I never realise it before. I used to have bad dreams.' For a moment she looked hopefully at Miss Gates. 'Maybe is me mixing up de dreams.'

They sat in silence for a long while. The afternoon sun fell through the window in a bright, slatted pattern. It reminded Florence of something. She must remember. Yes, the afternoon that they went to the concert. How excited they were, how grown-up to be going out with Father and how the city man stared and sang love songs to Annie. The next year, she went away to teacher's college and Annie ran away with an American who was studying something in the hills. He was a geologist, that was it. He was an atheist, he did not believe in marriage and Father was set against the friendship, besides he was a big, grown man and Annie was only seventeen. But after that everything was troubled and her memories stopped there. There were earlier ones, of them wading in the river, of Mother teaching them to sing and play the piano, of Father setting off for work, so neat and correct, to run the Farmers' Credit Union in the nearby town. But somehow, after that evening at the concert she found she had to choose her memories more carefully. Her adult life had been full, busy, yet she had screened them out, too many were better left unexamined. Esmie stirred on the sofa and a cushion fell to the floor. Florence picked it up and settled it behind her head.

The light changed and Florence went out on the verandah to see the last of the sunset. A bird was singing and she looked around slowly, searching through the small garden, but it was hidden somewhere and she couldn't see it. Only the sound came, pure, unhesitant as the afternoon faded and the evening asserted itself darkly around her.

To Da-Duh, in Memoriam

Paule Marshall

p.215

'… Oh Nana! all of you is not involved in this evil business Death, Nor all of us in Life.'

– From 'At My Grandmother's Grave' by Lebert Bethune

I did not see her at first I remember. For not only was it dark inside the crowded disembarkation shed in spite of the daylight flooding in from outside, but standing there waiting for her with my mother and sister I was still somewhat blinded from the sheen of tropical sunlight on the water of the bay which we had just crossed in the landing boat, leaving behind us the ship that had brought us from New York lying in the offing. Besides, being only nine years of age at the time and knowing nothing of islands I was busy attending to the alien sights and sounds of Barbados, the unfamiliar smells.

I did not see her, but I was alerted to her approach by my mother's hand which suddenly tightened around mine, and looking up I traced her gaze through the gloom in the shed until I finally made out the small, purposeful, painfully erect figure of the old woman headed our way.

Her face was drowned in the shadow of an ugly rolled-brim brown felt hat, but the details of her slight body and of the struggle taking place within it were clear enough – an intense, unrelenting struggle between her back which was beginning to bend ever so slightly under the weight of her eighty odd years and the rest of her which sought to deny those years and hold that back straight, keep it in line. Moving swiftly towards us (so swiftly it seemed she did not intend stopping when she reached us but would sweep past us out the doorway which opened onto the sea and like Christ walk upon the water!), she was caught between the sunlight at the end of the building and the darkness inside – and for a moment she appeared to contain them both: the light in the long severe old-fashioned white dress she wore which brought the sense of a past that was still alive into our bustling present and in the snatch of white at her eye; the darkness in her black high-top shoes and in her face which was visible now that she was closer.

It was as stark and fleshless as a death mask, that face. The maggots might have already done their work, leaving only the framework of bone beneath the ruined skin and deep wells at the temple and jaw. But her eyes were alive, unnervingly, for one so old, with a sharp light that flicked out of the dim clouded depths like a lizard's tongue to snap up all in her view. Those eyes betrayed a child's curiosity about the world, and I wondered vaguely seeing them, and seeing the way the bodice of her ancient dress had collapsed in on her flat chest (what had happened to her breasts?), whether she might not be some kind of child at the same time that she was a woman, with fourteen children, my mother included, to prove it. Perhaps she was both, both child and woman, darkness and light, past and present, life and death – all the opposites contained and reconciled in her.

'My Da-duh,' my mother said formally and stepped forward. The name sounded like thunder fading softly in the distance.

'Child,' Da-duh said, and her tone, her quick scrutiny of my mother, the brief embrace in which they appeared to shy from each other rather than touch, wiped out the fifteen years my mother had been away and restored the old relationship. My mother, who was such a formidable figure in my eyes, had suddenly with a word been reduced to my status.

'Yes, God is good,' Da-duh said with a nod that was like a tic. 'He has spared me to see my child again.'

We were led forward then, apologetically because not only did Da-duh prefer boys but she also liked her grandchildren to be 'white', that is, fair-skinned; and we had, I was to discover, a number of cousins, the outside children of white estate managers and the like, who qualified. We, though, were as black as she.

My sister being the oldest was presented first. 'This one takes after the father,' my mother said and waited to be reproved.

Frowning, Da-duh tilted my sister's face towards the light. But her frown soon gave way to a grudging smile, for my sister with her large mild eyes and little broad winged nose, with our father's high-cheeked Barbadian cast to her face, was pretty.

'She's goin' be lucky,' Da-duh said and patted her once on the cheek. 'Any girl-child that takes after the father does be lucky.'

She turned then to me. But oddly enough she did not touch me. Instead leaning close, she peered hard at me, and then quickly drew back. I thought I saw her hand start up as though to shield her eyes. It was almost as if she saw not only me, a thin truculent child who it was said took after no one but myself, but something in me which for some reason she found disturbing, even threatening. We looked silently at each other for a long time there in the noisy shed, our gaze locked. She was the first to look away.

'But Adry,' she said to my mother and her laugh was cracked, thin, apprehensive. 'Where did you get this one here with this fierce look?'

'We don't know where she came out of, my Da-duh,' my mother said, laughing also. Even I smiled to myself. After all I had won the encounter. Da-duh had recognised my small strength – and this was all I ever asked of the adults in my life then.

'Come, soul,' Da-duh said and took my hand. 'You must be one of those New York terrors you hear so much about.'

She led us, me at her side and my sister and mother behind, out of the shed into the sunlight that was like a bright driving summer rain and over to a group of people clustered beside a decrepit lorry. They were our relatives, most of them from St Andrews although Da-duh herself lived in St Thomas, the women wearing bright print dresses, the colours vivid against their darkness, the men rusty black suits that encased them like straitjackets. Da-duh, holding fast to my hand, became my anchor as they circled round us like a nervous sea, exclaiming, touching us with their calloused hands, embracing us shyly. They laughed in awed bursts: 'But look Adry got big-big children!', 'And see the nice things they wearing, wrist watch and all!', 'I tell you, Adry has done all right for sheself in New York …'

Da-duh, ashamed at their wonder, embarrassed for them, admonished them the while. 'But oh Christ,' she said, 'why you all got to get on like you never saw people from "Away" before? You would think New York is the only place in the world to hear wunna. That's why I don't like to go anyplace with you St Andrews people, you know. You all ain't been colonised.'

We were in the back of the lorry finally, packed in among the barrels of ham, flour, cornmeal and rice and the trunks of clothes that my mother had brought as gifts. We made our way slowly through Bridgetown's clogged streets, part of a funeral procession of cars and open-sided buses, bicycles and donkey carts. The dim little limestone shops and offices along the way marched with us, at the same mournful pace, towards the same grave ceremony – as did the people, the women balancing huge baskets on top their heads as if they were no more than hats they wore to shade them from the sun. Looking over the edge of the lorry I watched as their feet slurred the dust. I listened, and their voices, raw and loud and dissonant in the heat, seemed to be grappling with each other high overhead.

Da-duh sat on a trunk in our midst, a monarch amid her court. She still held my hand, but it was different now. I had suddenly become her anchor, for I felt her fear of the lorry with its asthmatic motor (a fear and distrust, I later learned, she held of all machines) beating like a pulse in her rough palm.

As soon as we left Bridgetown behind though, she relaxed, and while the others around us talked she gazed at the canes standing tall on either side of the winding marl road. 'C'dear,' she said softly to herself after a time. 'The canes this side are pretty enough.'

They were too much for me. I thought of them as giant weeds that had overrun the island, leaving scarcely any room for the small tottering houses of sunbleached pine we passed or the people, dark streaks as our lorry hurtled by. I suddenly feared that we were journeying, unaware that we were, towards some dangerous place where the canes, grown as high and thick as a forest, would close in on us and run us through with their stiletto blades. I longed then for the familiar: for the street in Brooklyn where I lived, for my father who had refused to accompany us ('Blowing out good money on foolishness,' he had said of the trip), for a game of tag with my friends under the chestnut tree outside our aging brownstone house.

'Yes, but wait till you see St Thomas canes,' Da-duh was saying to me. 'They's canes father, bo.' She gave a proud arrogant nod. 'Tomorrow, God willing, I goin't take you out in the ground and show them to you.'

True to her word Da-Duh took me with her the following day out into the ground. It was a fairly large plot adjoining her weathered board and shingle house and consisting of a small orchard, a good-sized canepiece and behind the canes, where the land sloped abruptly down, a gully. She had purchased it with Panama money sent her by her eldest son, my uncle Joseph, who had died working on the canal. We entered the ground along a trail no wider than her body and as devious and complex as her reasons for showing me her land. Da-duh strode briskly ahead, her slight form filled out this morning by the layers of sacking petticoats she wore under her working dress to protect her against the damp. A fresh white cloth, elaborately arranged around her head, added to her height, and lent her a vain, almost roguish air.

Her pace slowed once we reached the orchard, and glancing back at me occasionally over her shoulder, she pointed out the various trees.

'This here is a breadfruit,' she said. 'That one yonder is a papaw. Here's a guava. This is a mango. I know you don't have anything like these in New York. Here's a sugar apple (the fruit looked more like artichokes than apples to me). This one bears limes …' She went on for some time, intoning the names of the trees as though they were those of her gods. Finally, turning to me, she said, 'I know you don't have anything this nice where you come from.' Then, as I hesitated: 'I said I know you don't have anything this nice where you come from …'

'No,' I said and my world did seem suddenly lacking.

Da-duh nodded and passed on. The orchard ended and we were on the narrow cart road that led through the canepiece, the canes clashing like swords above my cowering head. Again she turned and her thin muscular arms spread wide, her dim gaze embracing the small field of canes, she said – and her voice almost broke under the weight of her pride – 'Tell me, have you got anything like these in that place where you were born?'

'No.'

'I din' think so. I bet you don't even know that these canes here and the sugar you eat is one and the same thing. That they does throw the canes into some damn machine at the factory and squeeze out all the little life in them to make sugar for you all so in New York to eat. I bet you don't know that.'

'I've got two cavities and I'm not allowed to eat a lot of sugar.'

But Da-duh didn't hear me. She had turned with an inexplicably angry motion and was making her way rapidly out of the canes and down the slope at the edge of the field which led to the gully below. Following her apprehensively down the incline amid a stand of banana plants whose leaves flapped like elephants' ears in the wind, I found myself in the middle of a small tropical wood – a place dense and damp and gloomy and tremulous with the fitful play of light and shadow as the leaves high above moved against the sun that was almost hidden from view. It was a violent place, the tangled foliage fighting each other for a chance at the sunlight, the branches of the trees locked in what seemed like an immemorial struggle, one both necessary and inevitable. But despite the violence, it was pleasant, almost peaceful in the gully, and beneath the thick undergrowth the earth smelled like spring.

This time Da-duh didn't even bother to ask her usual question, but simply turned and waited for me to speak.

'No,' I said, my head bowed. 'We don't have anything like this in New York.'

'Ah,' she cried, her triumph complete. 'I din' think so. Why, I've heard that's a place where you can walk till you near drop and never see a tree.'

'We've got a chestnut tree in front of our house,' I said.

'Does it bear?' She waited. 'I ask you, does it bear?'

'Not any more,' I muttered. 'It used to, but not any more.'

She gave the nod that was like a nervous twitch. 'You see,' she said. 'Nothing can bear there.' Then, secure behind her scorn, she added, 'But tell me, what's this snow like that you hear so much about?'

Looking up, I studied her closely, sensing my chance, and then I told her, describing at length and with as much drama as I could summon not only what snow in the city was like, but what it would be like here, in her perennial summer kingdom.

'… And you see all these trees you got here,' I said. 'Well, they'd be bare. No leaves, no fruit, nothing. They'd be covered in snow. You see your canes. They'd be buried under tons of snow. The snow would be higher than your head, higher than your house, and you wouldn't be able to come down into this here gully because it would be snowed under …'

She searched my face for the lie, still scornful but intrigued. 'What a thing, huh?' she said finally, whispering it softly to herself.

'And when it snows you couldn't dress like you are now,' I said. 'Oh no, you'd freeze to death. You'd have to wear a hat and gloves and galoshes and ear muffs so your ears wouldn't freeze and drop off, and a heavy coat. I've got a Shirley Temple coat with fur on the collar. I can dance. You wanna see?'

Before she could answer I began, with a dance called the Truck which was popular back then in the 1930s. My right forefinger waving, I trucked around the nearby trees and around Da-duh's awed and rigid form. After the Truck I did the Suzy-Q, my lean hips swishing, my sneakers sidling zigzag over the ground. 'I can sing,' I said and did so, starting with 'I'm Gonna Sit Right Down and Write Myself a Letter', then without pausing, 'Tea For Two', and ending with 'I Found a Million Dollar Baby in a Five and Ten Cent Store'.

For long moments afterwards Da-duh stared at me as if I were a creature from Mars, an emissary from some world she did not know but which intrigued her and whose power she both felt and feared. Yet something about my performance must have pleased her, because bending down she slowly lifted her long skirt and then, one by one, the layers of petticoats until she came to a drawstring purse dangling at the end of a long strip of cloth tied round her waist. Opening the purse she handed me a penny. 'Here,' she said, half-smiling against her will. 'Take this to buy yourself a sweet at the shop up the road. There's nothing to be done with you, soul.'

From then on, whenever I wasn't taken to visit relatives, I accompanied Da-duh out into the ground, and alone with her amid the canes or down in the gully I told her about New York. It always began with some slighting remark on her part: 'I know they don't have anything this nice where you come from,' or 'Tell me, I hear those foolish people in New York does do such and such ...' But as I answered, recreating my towering world of steel and concrete and machines for her, building the city out of words, I would feel her give way. I came to know the signs of her surrender: the total stiffness that would come over her little hard dry form, the probing gaze that like a surgeon's knife sought to cut through my skull to get at the images there, to see if I were lying; above all, her fear, a fear nameless and profound, the same one I had felt beating in the palm of her hand that day in the lorry.

Over the weeks I told her about refrigerators, radios, gas stoves, elevators, trolley cars, wringer washing machines, movies, airplanes, the cyclone at Coney Island, subways, toasters, electric lights: 'At night, see, all you have to do is flip this little switch on the wall and all the lights in the house go on. Just like that. Like magic. It's like turning on the sun at night.'

'But tell me,' she said to me once with a faint mocking smile, 'do the white people have all these things too or it's only the people looking like us?'

I laughed. 'What d'ya mean,' I said. 'The white people have even better.' Then: 'I beat up a white girl in my class last term.'

'Beating up white people!' Her tone was incredulous.

'How you mean!' I said, using an expression of hers. 'She called me a name.'

For some reason Da-duh could not quite get over this and repeated in the same hushed, shocked voice, 'Beating up white people now! Oh, the lord, the world's changing up so I can scarce recognise it any more.'

One morning toward the end of our stay, Da-duh led me into a part of the gully that we had never visited before, an area darker and more thickly overgrown than the rest, almost impenetrable. There in a small clearing amid the dense bush, she stopped before an incredibly tall royal palm which rose cleanly out of the ground, and drawing the eye up with it, soared high above the trees around it into the sky. It appeared to be touching the blue dome of sky, to be flaunting its dark crown of fronds right in the blinding white face of the late morning sun.

Da-duh watched me a long time before she spoke, and then she said very quietly, 'All right, now, tell me if you've got anything this tall in that place you're from.'

I almost wished, seeing her face, that I could have said no. 'Yes,' I said. 'We've got buildings hundreds of times this tall in New York. There's one called the Empire State building that's the tallest in the world. My class visited it last year and I went all the way to the top. It's got over a hundred floors. I can't describe how tall it is. Wait a minute. What's the name of that hill I went to visit the other day, where they have the police station?'

'You mean Bissex?'

'Yes, Bissex. Well, the Empire State building is way taller than that.'

'You're lying now!' she shouted, trembling with rage. Her hand lifted to strike me.

'No, I'm not,' I said. 'It really is. If you don't believe me I'll send you a picture postcard of it soon as I get back home so you can see for yourself. But it's way taller than Bissex.'

All the fight went out of her at that. The hand poised to strike me fell limp to her side, and as she stared at me, seeing not me but the building that was taller than the highest hill she knew, the small stubborn light in her eyes (it was the same amber as the flame in the kerosene lamp she lit at dusk) began to fail. Finally, with a vague gesture that even in the midst of her defeat still tried to dismiss me and my world, she turned and started back through the gully, walking slowly, her steps groping and uncertain, as if she was suddenly no longer sure of the way, while I followed triumphant yet strangely saddened behind.

The next morning I found her dressed for our morning walk but stretched out on the Berbice chair in the tiny drawing room where she sometimes napped during the afternoon heat, her face turned to the window beside her. She appeared thinner and suddenly indescribably old.

'My Da-duh,' I said.

'Yes, nuh,' she said. Her voice was listless and the face she slowly turned my way was, now that I think back on it, like a Benin mask, the features drawn and almost distorted by an ancient abstract sorrow.

'Don't you feel well?' I asked.

'Girl, I don't know.'

'My Da-duh, I goin' boil you some bush tea,' my aunt, Da-duh's youngest child, who lived with her, called from the shed roof kitchen.

'Who tell you I need bush tea?' she cried, her voice assuming for a moment its old authority. 'You can't even rest nowadays without some malicious person looking for you to be dead. Come, girl.' She motioned me to a place beside her on the old-fashioned lounge chair. 'Give us a tune.'

I sang for her until breakfast at eleven, all my brash irreverent Tin Pan Alley songs, and then just before noon we went out into the ground. But it was a short, dispirited walk. Da-duh didn't even notice that the mangoes were beginning to ripen and would have to be picked before the village boys got to them. And when she paused occasionally and looked out across the canes or up at her trees it wasn't as if she were seeing them but something else. Some huge, monolithic shape had imposed itself, it seemed, between her and the land, obstructing her vision. Returning to the house, she slept the entire afternoon on the Berbice chair.

She remained like this until we left, languishing away the mornings on the chair at the window gazing out at the land as if it were already doomed; then, at noon, taking the brief stroll with me through the ground during which she seldom spoke, and afterwards returning home to sleep till almost dusk sometimes.

On the day of our departure she put on the austere, ankle-length white dress, the black shoes and brown felt hat (her town clothes she called them), but she did not go with us to town. She saw us off on the road outside her house and in the midst of my mother's tearful protracted farewell, she leaned down and whispered in my ear, 'Girl, you're not to forget now to send me the picture of that building, you hear.'

By the time I mailed her the large coloured picture postcard of the Empire State building she was dead. She died during the famous '37 strike which began shortly after we left. On the day of her death England sent planes flying low over the island in a show of force – so low, according to my aunt's letter, that the downdraft from them shook the ripened mangoes from the trees in Da-duh's orchard. Frightened, everyone in the village fled into the canes. Except Da-duh. She remained in the house at the window so my aunt said, watching as the planes came swooping and screaming like monstrous birds down over the village, over her house, rattling her trees and flattening the young canes in her field. It must have seemed to her lying there that they did not intend pulling out of their dive, but like the hardback beetles which hurled themselves with suicidal force against the walls of the house at night, those menacing silver shapes would hurl themselves in an ecstasy of self-immolation onto the land, destroying it utterly.

When the planes finally left and the villagers returned they found her dead on the Berbice chair at the window.

She died and I lived, but always, to this day even, within the shadow of her death. For a brief period after I was grown I went to live alone, like one doing penance, in a loft above a noisy factory in downtown New York and there painted seas of sugarcane and huge swirling Van Gogh suns and palm trees striding like brightly-plumed Watussi across a tropical landscape, while the thunderous tread of the machines downstairs jarred the floor beneath my easel, mocking my efforts.

Savi's Trial

Hazel Simmons-McDonald

p.215

I

'I'm Savitree. Please have a seat. How can I help?'

'How can I help you?' I repeated louder because he was standing there staring at me as though he was in some sort of trance. Mr Blenman, a senior partner in the firm, had insisted that I see this Mr Gervais Singh, even though I had reminded him that I would be away on holiday and did not want to take on any new assignments. I had been clearing my desk and looking forward to starting my holiday the following day. I held out my hand.

'Oh, sorry,' Mr Singh said. He shook my hand hastily and lowered himself to the edge of the chair, leaning forward and plunking his elbows on my desk, seeming unable to shift his gaze from my face. 'Sorry, I didn't mean to stare.'

'That's OK.' He seemed agitated and I tried to put him at ease. 'What can I do for you?'

'I don't know how to begin but I need some legal advice.' He shook his head as though trying to deny something or get rid of a memory. 'This has been a horrible day. I got a call from the hospital to say that my mother had been admitted. When I got there she was in the Intensive Care Unit with a tube coming out of her mouth and an intravenous hook up. The doctor said she had ingested something that made her violently ill. My father had called the paramedics because she had been vomiting blood. I thought this was related to her cancer but the doctor said he thought she had ingested poison. They will let us know tomorrow whether they have to do surgery because of possible damage to her stomach.'

'This must be distressing for you and your father; but how can I help?'

'I'm worried. He couldn't stop crying and kept saying "It's my fault, it's my fault" over and over. The paramedics said his behaviour was unusual and they mentioned having to report it. If they do, I expect the police may want to question my father at some point. Earlier this year, my mother was diagnosed with cancer and she has refused conventional treatment. She has been taking some herbal concoctions but they have never made her ill. She's lost a lot of weight and she told us to let her be. She said if this is how she is meant to die that's how she'll die. It's been tough watching her get weaker but she's strong minded.'

I wasn't sure why he thought it necessary to give me all these details.

'So what's the problem with your father?' I probably sounded a bit irritated because he glanced at me and quickly looked away.

'We thought that perhaps a certain combination of the herbs might have caused the problem or that my mother used too much of one thing or combined some in error. But the doctors ruled that out. They said they found a trace of poison in the tests they ran and that may be responsible.' He shook his head again. 'She's in a bad way but I'm hoping she'll pull through.'

'So, the herbs were tainted with poison … by mistake?'

'No. My father told me that he and my mother had discussed her situation and she told him she didn't want to get to a stage where she was totally useless in a bed, wasting away. He said they agreed that he would help her to take something that would let her go quickly and painlessly. She's suffered a lot from the cancer already – it was at an advanced stage when she was diagnosed.' He paused and glanced at me again then he continued when I was silent. 'At first he said he wasn't sure what happened. Then he said he had slipped a couple drops of something into her tea to ease her pain, but she had just a sip before she started to be sick. The cup was still full almost to the brim when I checked at home before coming here. Perhaps she got ill from an accumulation of other things she's been eating – the bitter cassava or the brown rice?' He was talking softly, to himself. He looked up at me and said. 'I don't know.' He pressed his knuckles into his eyes, sighed then went on. 'He said he told the paramedics he put something in her tea and I guess that raised a red flag. I'm worried, that's why I've come.' His voice cracked. 'You know what will happen if my mother dies.'

'Yes, that's tough.'

'My father loves my mother. He could only have done something if she wanted him to do it and if he thought it would help. I'm not even sure that he put anything in the tea apart from the saccharine drops she uses or if he put in anything at all. Maybe he just said that.'

'Could be. But you don't know what happened, so if I were you I wouldn't jump to the conclusion that he and your mother had tried euthanasia. I know it's an offence here, but there's nothing concrete to suggest …'

'I know, I know, but I'm worried and I need to talk with someone legal.' He paused briefly then continued. 'All this unfolded this morning and I'm not sure what the paramedics …' He stopped abruptly and looked up at me. 'I threw out the cup of tea when I went home.'

'Where is your father now?'

'He's at the hospital, sitting with my mother in the ICU. He says he won't leave until she can speak to him but that may not happen for a while. I'll go there later and take him home. Can you speak with him?'

'Do you have any idea what might have been in the tea?'

'No. I don't. It didn't smell funny or anything. I don't even believe he put anything in. Maybe the saccharine drops which she uses every day. He's forgetting things these days. It may have been the saccharine.'

'So now we won't know because you threw out the tea.'

'Yes, and I washed up.'

'Do you have siblings?'

'No, I'm an only child. I had a sister who died soon after birth. My parents live in Belvedere, in the country; it's an easy drive but my father will stay with me tonight. I can bring him in the morning if you wish.'

'I won't be in tomorrow. Was there anyone else in the house when this happened?'

'No. Someone usually goes in to help during the day, but she wasn't there when this happened.'

'OK, I'll speak with your father if you think it will help, but it's too late now and I'm away on holiday from tomorrow. I'll have to let Mr Blenman know about this. If nothing happens while I'm away, I can meet with your father when I get back. I'll need some contact information.'

He handed me a card from a small case he pulled from his pocket. 'Call me any time,' he said. 'And thank you.' He held on to my hand a little longer than I thought necessary. I walked to the door and opened it.

'I wouldn't worry too much at this stage. Just think about helping your mother at this point.'

'Thanks a heap. I appreciate this,' he said as he reached out and placed his hand over mine on the door knob. He was clearly grateful. I pulled my hand away gently and closed the door.

II

As I expected, nothing happened while I was away but I followed up on my promise to meet with Mr Singh. I called Gervais Singh to get an update on his mother's condition and to arrange an interview with his father.

'We could meet over dinner,' he said. 'Is this evening OK?'

'That's fine. How about Carib Spice? Or perhaps Chinese Specialties if you prefer that. They're both centrally located and close enough.'

'Carib Spice is fine. See you at 6:30?'

He was waiting on the sidewalk when I got there.

'Something about you …' He smiled as he opened the door. 'I think my mother will like you instantly.' The smell of fried onions and baked bread filled the room. We found a table for two in an alcove.

'Then I must meet her,' I said, shrugging off my jacket. I thought it time that a case should be made for female lawyers to vary their wardrobe in court. The heat could be unbearable.

'I'm going to the hospital to see her after dinner. Would you like to come with me? My father will be there so you may have a chance to speak with him.'

'Has he said anything more?'

'No. Every now and then he repeats that it's his fault and he holds her hand and whispers in her ear. I can't always hear what he says but I've picked up the odd words "forgive" and "pain". The doctors say she is pulling out of this. We expect the best.'

'Good, then. What she has to say will help.' I hardly noticed what I ate as I listened attentively to the snatches of his life's story he shared.

'I got a scholarship to go to university. At first, my mother didn't want me to leave home. She was overprotective and she would often say she didn't want to lose me. I couldn't understand this but my father said it was because my sister had died as a baby and I was all they had. Eventually I persuaded her that I would be fine staying in the students' residence and I promised to return to visit during every holiday.' I thought him intense, the way he leaned forward, looking directly into my eyes as he spoke. That was slightly disturbing but at the same time, engaging. By the time we walked out of the restaurant we were laughing and sharing quips like good friends.

Mr Singh had his back to the door when we entered the room. He was leaning forward and speaking softly to his wife who was looking up at him but obviously couldn't speak because a tube hung from the corner of her mouth and disappeared under the bed. Gervais cleared his throat and Mr Singh turned around.

'Eh eh, is you son; I glad to see you.' Gervais walked over to the bed and touched his mother's hand.

'How you feeling, Ma?' She looked up at him and blinked slowly once.

'You see? She getting better. She know is you. Who you bring?' He peered at me over Gervais's shoulder.

'This is Miss King, Pa. She is the lawyer I told you about.'

He leaned forward, squinting, and extended his hand. 'Nice to meet you, Miss.' He clasped my hand, peering at me through narrowed eyes.

'Miss King is the lawyer I asked to come and speak with you just in case.'

'Yes, yes. You want to sit, Miss?' He motioned me to the chair next to the bed where he had been sitting.

'How Ma doing?'

'Doctor say she doing well. He say the tubes will come out tomorrow.'

'Perhaps it's better for us to speak outside the room,' I said.

'Good idea,' Gervais said. He leaned forward and touched his mother's hand gently. She turned her head and looked at me where I sat close to her bed. She blinked twice, and her gaze shifted quickly from my face to her son's face, then to Mr Singh's. There was a gurgling sound in her throat as though she wanted to cough or speak. Mr Singh rushed towards the door, saying 'I go call the nurse.' Gervais leaned over his mother.

'Is all right, Ma. Is all right,' he whispered.

'Please wait outside.' The nurse brushed past and bent over Mrs Singh. We stood in the corridor beside the door of the room. Mr Singh kept looking into the room through the square aperture in the door where a pane of glass must have been at one time.

'I don know what happen to Minna,' he muttered. 'Look, Nurse coming.' He moved away from the door.

'She's OK,' the nurse said. 'Her blood pressure is slightly elevated and her pulse rate is a tad too fast but she's OK. Perhaps it's better if we limit the number of visitors this evening.'

'You stay, Pa. I'll walk Miss King to the car park. I'll come back to take you home, and we can go to her office tomorrow morning.' He turned to me. 'Is that OK with you, Savi?'

'That's fine,' I said, noting that he had dropped the Miss King and used the diminutive form of my name. Mr Singh pushed the door open to go back into the room.

'Nice to meet you, Miss King. We will talk tomorrow.'

'Ma looked really agitated in there,' Gervais said. 'At what time tomorrow would you like to meet?' he asked. I found my car keys and unlocked the door.

'I have an appointment at three so if we meet just before noon, that will give us some time to get your father's story.' He leaned forward, kissed my cheek and before I could say anything he opened the door quickly.

'See you tomorrow then.' I drove off feeling somewhat confused but strangely not offended and thinking that it was perhaps a proper culmination to the evening. I felt a level of comfort with him that was unusual for new acquaintances.

III

I met with Mr King and Gervais as we had arranged, but he wasn't much help because he couldn't remember if he had put anything in his wife's tea. He was stressed and this made him distracted and confused. We bought lunch in the hospital cafeteria and sat outside under a flowering flamboyant tree.

Mr Singh placed a cold trembling hand on mine. I tried to reassure him. 'Don't worry, Mr Singh. I'm sure things will work out fine. If the police find some reason to pursue this, I will defend you.'

He looked at me and said, 'You remind me of how Minna did look when we marry.'

Gervais chuckled. 'That's a good omen, then,' he said.

Mr Singh looked at me across the table. He covered his eyes with his hands and sighed deeply.

'It's going to be OK, Pa,' Gervais said. 'Not to worry.'

'Is Minna I worrying 'bout, Vais. She suffer so much already, first with the baby girl and always tinking 'bout what happen to she. Then she get de cancer and that put suffering pon suffering.'

'What did happen to her, Pa? Why is Ma blaming herself?'

'We ain know wha happen to de chile, Vais. Is lose we lose she. She disappear from de cradle one morning jus' so. Is you one dat left.'

Gervais seemed stunned. 'Why you never tell me that before, Pa?'

'Minna say it better if you don know. She say if we tell you, you will have a weight to carry and she din want you grow up wid anyting so on your mind. You and de lil girl was twins, Vais.'

Gervais stared at his father, then he looked at me, his mouth open. This information given in a casual way by Mr Singh clearly troubled him. Mr Singh continued as though eager to unburden himself of a weight he had carried for too long. 'I 'member de morning clear like was yesterday. Minna did go down by de jetty to buy fish and I was in de back garden. You an you sister was in de big wicker basket we keep you in when we was outside. I hear Dulcie call out as she passin to go to work. She use to hail Minna to give she de latest gossip. I tell she Minna out and I roun de back. She say she will pass back later and I hear de gate close. I go roun de corner to pick some coreilli for Minna to cook. I wasn gone long den I hear Minna cry out. "Raffie," she shout, "Where de baby? Where de lil girl?" When I look was only you in de basket, Vais. I run out, go up and down de road, I ask Miss Hettie by de corner if she see somebody pass wif a baby or a bundle. She say she ain't see nuffing. It don have nobody else in de street. I go back in de house and Minna bawlin.'

'But Pa, you didn't go to the police?'

'Vais, children – girl children was disappearin in de place dat time. It was like a malady. One story was bout a father dey say trow way he girl chile in de river because him did want a boy. Up de road from where we was living, Vashti lil girl disappear and dey say is Vashti husband do something wid she. Ah was fraid to go to de police. Dey would say is me do something with de chile. Whole week I look for she. When we don find she we pack up and go back to Belvedere. Minna never get over it. I sure is dat give she de cancer.'

I thought about his account of the disappearance of the child and the reason he gave for not telling Gervais the truth before. I knew I would have to speak with Mrs Singh not just about her illness but about the information Mr Singh had just given. I wondered why Mr Singh chose this moment to tell his son about this event that had happened long ago. He seemed to remember the details well. Gervais said he was forgetful. I wondered what he was thinking about his father's revelation and I asked him as he walked me to my car. He was silent for a long while then he said:

'The thought that I have a sister, a twin who is possibly alive somewhere fills me with anxiety and longing at the same time. My mother was probably right because if I'd known before now, I would have started a search a long time ago. When this is all over I'll do just that.'

He held my arm as he opened the door and helped me in. 'Shall we meet later? Dinner, perhaps?'

'Perhaps we shouldn't. I need to maintain professional distance in the event that there is a case and I have to defend your father.'

'You just said it. It's my father you'd be defending, not me. That shouldn't matter, should it?'

I put the key in the ignition and started the car.

'It shouldn't in theory, but I think it best for us to be cautious. We'll see how things work out after that.'

'Just so you know, I plan to be around – and not as a client. I hope you will let me.' He leaned through the window, kissed my cheek, turned abruptly and walked away. I needed to clear my head, to restore equilibrium to the situation and my own feelings which were drawn towards this stranger. I drove in the direction of my parents' house.

IV

'You look tired, Savi. What's up?'

'It's a situation with a client – I should say possible client. There aren't any charges but the son came to see me. I haven't been able to pin down the full story yet. The father is distracted by his wife's illness and he hasn't been able to say definitively what – if anything – he put in her tea. The tests showed a trace of poison although the son said he doesn't believe his father would have done anything to hurt his mother. He thinks he put the usual saccharine in her tea.'

My father looked at me over the rim of his glasses, one eyebrow raised quizzically. 'I'm sure you'll be able to handle it, if it gets to trial, Savi. I have confidence in my girl.' He was a retired judge and he always made my cases seem simpler than I imagined them.

'I'm hoping it won't get to that but I'd like to have an opportunity to speak with Mrs Singh; that's the wife. She's recovering from the effects of what may be poisoned tea. Their son, Gervais, is rather nice but he's too close to the situation to be objective. There isn't any need to pursue this now, but I told Gervais I would meet his parents and help with advice.'

'Hmm … do I sense a particular interest?' He folded the newspaper and looked at me directly, one eyebrow still raised.

'We've had some meetings, dinner, lunch and I enjoy his company. There's an openness about him that I like. I think you'd like him and he's the sort of person Mama would have liked too. I miss her, mostly at times like this you know.'

'Me too, but you must be comforted in knowing that her leaving us meant freedom from pain. You were her sunlight and she spoiled you.'

'Hah! I'm no worse off for that, am I?' I went over and sat beside him on the sofa. 'Something Mr Singh said today nags me. He said his son's twin disappeared when they were small. He seems to think that Mrs Singh's illness is a result of her anguish over the loss of the girl. She was never able to get over it. He told Gervais about it today and it was the first time Gervais had heard that story. Until now he believed his sister had died from some illness in infancy. I don't know why he chose to tell this story out of the blue.' I felt my father's arm stiffen slightly under my touch.

'Yes, that's odd.'

'Dad …' I waited a long while before I could ask him what I wanted to know.

'What is it?'

'I know I was adopted …' my voice trailed off.

'Yes, Savi, you were; but you're our very own. We loved you from the moment we saw you. Your mother was devastated when we discovered she could not have a baby so we decided to adopt. The agency did not have small babies at the time, mostly older children and your mother wanted a baby. Our helper told us of two women who were about to put their babies up for adoption and we agreed to take you in as a foster child first. We made the arrangements and she brought you to us one day. You stole our hearts there and then.'

'Which woman, Dad? Do you know which woman I came from?'

'No. Our helper offered to arrange a meeting, but your mother preferred not to meet the woman to avoid complications. I wanted your mother to be happy and went along with her decision.'

'Can we find the helper?'

'Savi, she died years ago. I'm not even sure of the name of the person involved. I can't recall.'

'What if it was the Singhs?' I had always thought that I would be able to trace my birth parents if I chose to, but until this moment I had not wanted to do so.

'Savi, I'm sorry. I should have followed this in the official way. We were just so happy to have you. I never imagined this could become complicated.'

'What was the name of the baby she brought? I could ask the Singhs the name of the little girl they lost and that would let us know.'

'We didn't have a name and your mother didn't want to know. She only wanted to receive you and to go through the motions of having a baby as though she had given birth to it. So we selected your name that same day then went through the process of baptism and so on. Where did the Singhs live?'

'In Belvedere.'

'Well I'm sure the possibility of any link with the Singhs is remote because our helper never moved from this community. I wouldn't give it another thought.'

I remembered after I left that Gervais had said they moved to Belvedere after the child went missing. The idea that there might be even the remotest possibility of a link with the Singhs bothered me.

V

It was a week before I could bring myself to face Gervais and his father again. I resolutely refused to pick up the phone on the many occasions he called and I never returned the calls. One afternoon I finally decided to go to the hospital unannounced to speak with Mr Singh and, hopefully, Mrs Singh. I pushed open the door to the room. Mrs Singh was sitting up against a bank of pillows, looking frail. Mr Singh was sitting on one side of the bed and Gervais was standing on the other side. Both had their backs to the door and each one was affectionately holding a hand of Mrs Singh and leaning towards her as she seemed to be saying something to them through laboured breathing. Mrs Singh looked towards the door when I walked in. Her eyes opened wide, her lips moved and Gervais turned sharply towards me. He came quickly to my side.

'Savi, where have you been? I've been calling you all week. My mother wanted to see you. Now she has fluid on her lungs and she can hardly breathe.' His father's voice from the bedside interrupted.

'Call the nurse, Vais, call the nurse.'

I walked over to the bedside. Mrs Singh looked up at me, smiled, said something as she stretched her arm towards me and tried to raise her body from the pillows that propped her up. I couldn't make out what she said as her breathing became more laboured.

'Vais, call the doctor, call the doctor.' Mr Singh was beside himself. The nurse came in and shooed us out of the room. The doctor pushed past us as we made our way out. Mr Singh walked around in the same small circle, wringing his hands while Gervais leaned against the wall chewing his bottom lip and glancing at me occasionally. There was nothing I could say to them in this moment, but the look on Mrs Singh's face when she saw me troubled me and I knew it would haunt me for a long time. The doctor came out and shook his head.

'I'm sorry,' he said. 'She's gone.'

A thin wail escaped Mr Singh's lips as he ran past the doctor into the room. Gervais stood still against the wall, his head bent. I felt an indescribable sadness for him, for his father and for the feeling of loss that began from the moment Mrs Singh reached out to me. My thoughts raced as I walked to the car park. I sensed an ordeal ahead and I could not shake the growing feeling of apprehension that sometimes gripped me when I entered the courtroom for a trial.

Mom Luby and the Social Worker

Kristin Hunter

p.216 Puddin' and I been livin' with Mom Luby three years, ever since our mother died. We like it fine. But when Mom Luby took us down to the Welfare, we thought our happy days were over and our troubles about to begin.

'Chirren,' she said that day, 'I got to get some of this State Aid so I can give you everything you need. Shoes for you, Elijah, and dresses for Puddin' now she's startin' school. And lunch money and carfare and stuff like that. But the only way I can get it is to say I'm your mother. So don't mess up my lie.'

Mom Luby is old as Santa Claus, maybe older, with hair like white cotton and false teeth that hurt so much she takes them out and gums her food. But she's strong as a young woman and twice as proud. Much too proud to say she's our grandmother, which is something the Welfare people might believe.

So we went down there scared that morning, Puddin' holding tight onto both our hands. But we was lucky. The lady behind the desk didn't even look at us, and we got out of that gloomy old State Building safe and free. Man! Was I glad to get back to Division Street where people don't ask questions about your business.

When we got home, a whole bunch of people was waiting for Mom to let them in the speakeasy she runs in the back room. Jake was there, and Sissiemae, and Bobo and Walter and Lucas and Mose and Zerline. They are regular customers who come every evening to drink the corn liquor Mom gets from down South and eat the food she fixes, gumbo and chicken wings and ribs and potato salad and greens.

Bobo picked Puddin' up to see how much she weighed (a lot), until she hollered to be let down. Jake gave me a quarter to take his shoes down to Gumby's Fantastic Shoe Shine Parlor and get them shined and keep the change. We let the people in the front door and through the red curtain that divides the front room from the back. Soon they were settled around the big old round table with a half-gallon jar of corn. Then Sissiemae and Lucas wanted chicken wings, and I had to collect the money while Mom heated them up on the stove. There was so much to do, I didn't pay no attention to the tapping on the front door.

But then it came again, louder, like a woodpecker working on a tree.

'Elijah,' Mom says, run see who it is trying to chip a hole in that door. If it be the police, tell them I'll see them Saturday.'

But it wasn't the cops, who come around every Saturday night to get their money and drink some of Mom's corn and put their big black shoes up on the table. It was a little brownskin lady with straightened hair and glasses and black high-top shoes. She carried a big leather envelope and was dressed all in dark blue.

'Good afternoon,' she says. 'I am Miss Rushmore of the Department of Child Welfare, Bureau of Family Assistance. Is Mrs Luby at home?'

'I am she,' says Mom. 'Never been nobody else. Come in, honey, and set yourself down. Take off them shoes, they do look like real corn-crushers to me.'

'No thank you,' says Miss Rushmore. She sits on the edge of one of Mom's chairs and starts pulling papers out of the envelope. 'This must be Elijah.'

'Yes ma'am,' I say.

'And where is Arlethia?'

'Taking her nap,' says Mom, with a swat of the broom at the middle of the curtain, which Puddin' was peeking through. She's five and fat, and she loves to hang around grownups. Especially when they eating.

Mom hit the curtain with the broom again, and Puddin' ran off. The lady didn't even notice. She was too busy peeking under the lids of the pots on the stove.

'Salt pork and lima beans,' she says. 'Hardly a proper diet for growing children.'

'Well,' says Mom, 'when I get me some of this State Aid, maybe I can afford to get them canned vegetables and box cereal. Meanwhile you welcome to what we have.'

The lady acted like she didn't hear that. She just wrinkled up her nose like she smelled something bad.

'First,' she says, 'we must have a little talk about your budget. Do you understand the importance of financial planning?'

'Man arranges and God changes,' says Mom. 'When I got it, I spends it, when I don't, I do without.'

'That,' says the lady, 'is precisely the attitude I am here to correct.' She pulls out a big yellow sheet of paper. 'Now this is our Family Budget Work Sheet. What is your rent?'

'I ain't paid it in so long I forgot,' Mom says. Which set me in a fit because everybody but this dumb lady knows Mom owns the house. Behind her back Mom gave me a whack that stopped my giggles.

The lady sighed. 'We'll get to the budget later,' she says. 'First, there are some questions you left blank today. How old were you when Elijah was born?'

'Thirty-two,' says Mom.

'And he is now thirteen, which would make you forty-five,' says the lady.

'Thirty-eight,' says Mom without batting an eye.

'I'll put down forty-five,' says the lady, giving Mom a funny look. 'No doubt your hard life has aged you beyond your years. Now, who is the father, and where is he?'

'Lemme see,' says Mom, twisting a piece of her hair. 'I ain't seen Mr Luby since 1942. He was a railroad man, you see, and one time he just took a train out of here and never rode back.'

'1942,' Miss Rushmore wrote on the paper. And then she said, 'But that's impossible!'

'The dear Lord do teach us,' says Mom, 'that nothing in life is impossible if we just believe enough.'

'Hey, Mom, we're out of corn!' cries Lucas from the back room.

Miss Rushmore looked very upset. 'Why,' she says, 'you've got a man in there.'

'Sure do sound like it, don't it?' Mom says. 'Sure do. You got one too, honey?'

'That's my business,' says the lady.

'I was just trying to be sociable,' says Mom pleasantly. 'You sure do seem interested in mine.'

I ran back there and fetched another mason jar of corn from the shed kitchen. I told Lucas and Bobo and them to be quiet. Which wasn't going to be easy, cause them folks get good and loud when they get in a card game. I also dragged Puddin' away from the potato salad bowl, where she had stuck both her hands, and brought her in the front room with me. She was bawling. The lady gave her a weak smile.

'Now,' Mom says. 'About these shoes and school clothes.'

'I am not sure,' Miss Rushmore says, 'that you can get them. There is something wrong in this house that I have not yet put my finger on. But this is what you do. First you fill out Form 905, which you get at the Bureau of Family Assistance, room 1203. Then you call the Division of Child Welfare and make an appointment with Mr Jenkins. He will give you Form 202 to fill out. Then you go to the fifth floor, third corridor on the left, turn right, go in the second door. You stand at the first desk and fill out Form 23-B, Requisition for Clothing Allowance. You take *that* to Building Three, room 508, third floor, second door, fourth desk and then –'

'Lord,' Mom says, 'by the time we get clothes for these chirren, they will have done outgrowed them.'

'I don't make the rules,' the lady says.

'Well, honey,' says Mom, 'I ain't got time to do all that, not right now. Tonight I got to go deliver a baby. Then I got to visit a sick old lady and work on her with some herbs. Then I got to go down to the courthouse and get a young man out of jail. He's not a bad boy, he's just been keepin' bad company. *Then* I got to preach a funeral.'

The lady looked at Mom like she was seeing a spirit risen from the dead. 'But you can't do those things!' she says.

But I happen to know Mom Luby *can*. She's a midwife and a herb doctor and an ordained minister of the Gospel, besides running a place to eat and drink after hours. And she wouldn't need Welfare for us if people would only pay her sometimes.

Mom says, 'Honey, just come along and watch me.'

She picked up her old shopping bag full of herbs and stuff. Miss Rushmore picked up her case and followed her like somebody in a trance. Mom has that effect on people sometimes.

They were gone about two hours, and me and Puddin' had a good time eating and joking and looking into everybody's card hands.

I was surprised to see Mom bring Miss Rushmore straight into the back room when they got back. She sat her down at the table and poured her a drink of corn. To tell the truth, that lady looked like she needed it. Her glasses was crooked, and her shoes were untied, and her hair had come loose from its pins. She looked kind of pretty, but lost.

'Mrs Luby,' she said after a swallow of corn, 'you don't need my help.'

'Ain't it the truth,' says Mom.

'I came here to help you solve your problems. But now I don't know where to begin.'

'What problems?' Mom asks.

'You are raising these children in an unhealthy atmosphere. I am not even sure they are yours. And you are practising law, medicine, and the ministry without a licence. I simply can't understand it.'

'Can't understand what, honey?'

The lady sighed. 'How you got more done in two hours than I ever get done in two years.'

'You folks oughta put me on the payroll,' says Mom with a chuckle.

'We can't,' says Miss Rushmore. 'You're not qualified.'

Lucas started laughing, and Bobo joined in, and then we all laughed, Mose and Zerline and Jake and Sissiemae and Puddin' and me. We laughed so hard we rocked the room and shook the house and laughed that social worker right out the door.

'She got a point though,' Mom says after we finished laughing. 'You need an education to fill out forty pieces of paper for one pair of shoes. Never you mind, chirren. We'll make out fine, like we always done. Cut the cards, Bobo. Walter, deal.'

Berry

Langston Hughes

p.216

When the boy arrived on the four o'clock train, lo and behold, he turned out to be coloured! Mrs Osborn saw him the minute he got out of the station wagon, but certainly there was nothing to be done about it that night – with no trains back to the city before morning – so she set him to washing dishes. Lord knows there were a plenty. The Scandinavian kitchen boy had left right after breakfast, giving no notice, leaving her and the cook to do everything. Her wire to the employment office in Jersey City brought results – but dark ones. The card said his name was Milberry Jones.

Well, where was he to sleep? Heretofore, the kitchen boy and the handy-man gardener-chauffeur shared the same quarters. But Mrs Osborn had no idea how the handy-man might like Negroes. Help were so touchy, and it was hard keeping good servants in the country. So right after dinner, leaving Milberry with his arms in the dish water, Mrs Osborn made a bee line across the side lawn for Dr Renfield's cottage.

She heard the kids laughing and playing on the big screened-in front porch of the sanatorium. She heard one of the nurses say to a child, 'Behave, Billy!' as she went across the yard under the pine and maple trees. Mrs Osborn hoped Dr Renfield would be on his porch. She hated to knock at the door and perhaps be faced with his wife. The gossip among the nurses and help at Dr Renfield's Summer Home for Crippled Children had it that Mrs Osborn was in love with Dr Renfield, that she just worshipped him, that she followed him with her eyes every chance she got – and not only with her eyes.

Of course, there wasn't a word of truth in it, Mrs Osborn said to herself, admitting at the same time that that Martha Renfield, his wife, was certainly not good enough for the Doctor. Anyway tonight, she was not bound on any frivolous errand toward the Doctor's cottage. She had to see him about this Negro in their midst. At least, they'd have to keep him there overnight, or until they got somebody else to help in the kitchen. However, he looked like a decent boy.

Dr Renfield was not at home. His wife came to the door, spoke most coldly, and said that she presumed, as usual, the Doctor would make his rounds of the Home at eight. She hoped Mrs Osborn could wait until then to see him.

'Good evening!'

Mrs Osborn went back across the dusk-dark yard. She heard the surf rushing at the beach below, and saw the new young moon rising. She thought maybe the Doctor was walking along the sea in the twilight alone. Ah, Dr Renfield, Dr Ren …

When he made the usual rounds at eight he came, for a moment, by Mrs Osborn's little office where the housekeeper held forth over her linens and her accounts. He turned his young but bearded face toward Mrs Osborn, cast his great dark eyes upon her, and said, 'I hear you've asked to see me?'

'Yes, indeed, Dr Renfield,' Mrs Osborn bubbled and gurgled. 'We have a problem on our hands. You know the kitchen man left this morning so I sent a wire to the High Class Help Agency in the city for somebody right away by the four o'clock train – and they sent us a Negro! He seems to be a nice boy, and all that, but I just don't know how he would fit in our Home. Now what do you think?'

The Doctor looked at her with great seriousness. He thought. Then he answered with a question, 'Do the other servants mind?'

'Well, I can't say they do. They got along all right tonight during dinner. But the problem is, where would he sleep?'

'Oh, yes,' said Dr Renfield, pursing his lips.

And whether we should plan to keep him all summer, or just till we get someone else?'

'I see,' said Dr Renfield.

And again he thought. 'You say he can do the work? … How about the attic in this building? It's not in use … And by the way, how much did we pay the other fellow?'

'Ten dollars a week,' said Mrs Osborn raising her eyes.

'Well, pay the darkie eight,' said Dr Renfield, 'and keep him.' And for a moment he gazed deep into Mrs Osborn's eyes. 'Goodnight.' Then turned and left her. Left her. Left her. Left her.

So it was that Milberry entered into service at Dr Renfield's Summer Home for Crippled Children.

Milberry was a nice black boy, big, good natured and strong – like what Paul Robeson must have been at twenty. Except that he wasn't educated. He was from Georgia, where they don't have many schools for Negroes. And he hadn't been North long. He was glad to have a job, even if it was at a home for Crippled Children way out in the country on a beach five miles from the nearest railroad. Milberry had been hungry for weeks in Newark and Jersey City. He needed work and food.

And even if he wasn't educated, he had plenty of mother wit and lots of intuition about people and places. It didn't take him long to realise that he was doing far too much work for the Home's eight dollars a week, and that everybody was imposing on him in that taken-for-granted way white folks do with Negro help.

Milberry got up at 5:30 in the mornings, made the fire for the cook, set the water to boiling for the head nurse's coffee, started peeling potatoes, onions, and apples. After breakfast he washed up all the dishes, scoured the pots and pans, scrubbed the floors, and carried in wood for the fireplace in the front room (which really wasn't his job at all, but the handy-man's who had put it off on Milberry). The waitresses, too, got in the habit of asking him to polish their silver, and ice their water. And Mrs Osborn always had something extra that needed to be done (not kitchen-boy work), a cellar to be cleaned out, or the linen in her closet reshelved, or the dining-room windows washed. Milberry knew they took him for a work horse, a fool – and a nigger. Still he did everything, and didn't look mad – jobs were too hard to get, and he had been hungry too long in town.

'Besides,' Milberry said to himself, 'the ways of white folks, I mean some white folks, is too much for me. I reckon they must be a few good ones, but most of 'em ain't good – leastwise they don't treat me good. And Lawd knows, I ain't never done nothin' to 'em, nothin' a-tall.'

But at the Home it wasn't the work that really troubled him, or the fact that nobody ever said anything about a day off or a little extra pay. No, he'd had many jobs like this one before, where they worked you to death. But what really worried Milberry at this place was that he seemed to sense something wrong – something phoney about the whole house – except the little crippled kids there like himself because they couldn't help it. Maybe it was the lonesomeness of that part of the Jersey coast with its pines and scrubs and sand. But, more nearly, Milberry thought it was that there doctor with the movie beard and the woman's eyes at the head of the home. And it was the cranky nurses always complaining about food and the little brats under them. And the constant talk of who was having an affair with Dr Renfield. And Mrs Osborn's grand manner to everybody but the doctor. And all the white help kicking about their pay, and how far it was from town, and how no-good the doctor was, or the head nurse, or the cook, or Mrs Osborn.

'It's sho a phoney, this here place,' Milberry said to himself. 'Funny how the food ain't nearly so good 'cept when some ma or pa or some chile is visitin' here – then when they gone, it drops right back down again. This here hang-out is jest Doc Renfield's own private gyp game. Po' little children.'

The Negro was right. The Summer Home was run for profits from the care of permanently deformed children of middle-class parents who couldn't afford to pay too much, but who still paid well – too well for what their children got in return. Milberry worked in the kitchen and saw the good cans opened for company, and the cheap cans opened for the kids. Somehow he didn't like such dishonesty. Somehow, he thought he wouldn't even stay there and work if it wasn't for the kids.

For the children grew terribly to like Milberry.

One afternoon, during his short period of rest between meals, he had walked down to the beach where those youngsters who could drag themselves about were playing, and others were sitting in their wheel chairs watching. The sky was only a little cloudy, and the sand was grey. But quite all of a sudden it began to rain. The nurses saw Milberry and called him to help them get the young ones quickly back to the house. Some of the children were too heavy for a nurse to lift easily into a wheel chair. Some couldn't run at all. The handy-man helper wasn't around. So Milberry picked up child after child, sometimes two at once, and carried them up to the broad screened-in porch of the Home like a big gentle horse. The children loved it, riding on his broad back, or riding in his arms in the soft gentle rain.

'Come and play with us sometimes,' one of them called as Milberry left them all on the safe dry porch with their nurses.

'Sure, come back and play,' another said.

So Milberry, the next day, went down to the beach again in the afternoon and played with the crippled children. At first the nurses, Miss Baxter and Mrs Hill, didn't know whether to let him stay or not, but their charges seemed to enjoy it. Then when the time came to go in for rest before dinner, Milberry helped push the wheel chairs, a task which the nurses hated. And he held the hands of those kids with braces and twisted limbs as they hobbled along. He told them stories, and he made up jokes in the sun on the beach. And one rainy afternoon on the porch he sang songs, old southern Negro songs, funny ones that the children loved.

Almost every afternoon then, Milberry came to the beach after the luncheon dishes were done, and he had washed himself – except those afternoons when Mrs Osborn found something else for him to do – vases to be emptied or bath tubs scoured. The children became Milberry's friends. They adored him and he them. They called him Berry. They put their arms about him.

The grown-up white folks only spoke to him when they had some job for him to do, or when they were kidding him about being dark, and talking flat and southern, and mispronouncing words. But the kids didn't care how he talked. They loved his songs and his stories.

And he made up stories out of his own head just for them – po' little crippled-up things that they were – for Berry loved them, too.

So the summer wore on. August came. In September the Home would close. But disaster overtook Milberry before then.

At the end of August a week of rain fell, and the children could not leave the porch. Then, one afternoon, the sun suddenly came out bright and warm. The sea water was blue again and the sand on the beach glistened. Miss Baxter (who by now had got the idea it was part of Milberry's job to help her with the children) went to the kitchen and called him while he was still washing luncheon dishes.

'Berry, we're going to take the children down to the beach. Come on and help us with the chairs as soon as you get through.'

'Yes, m'am,' said Berry.

When he came out on the porch, the kids were all excited about playing in the sun once more. Little hunchbacks jumped and cried and clapped their hands, and little paralytics laughed in their wheel chairs. And some with braces on had already hobbled out the screen door and were gathered on the walk.

'Hello, Berry,' the children called.

'Hey, Berry,' they cried to the black boy.

Berry grinned.

It was a few hundred yards to the beach. On the cement walk, you could push a couple of wheel chairs at a time to the sand's edge. Some of the children propelled their own. Besides the nurses, today the handy-man was helping for the sun might not last long.

'Take me,' a little boy called from his wheel chair, 'Berry, take me.'

'Sho, I will,' the young Negro said gently.

But when Berry started to push the chair down from the porch to the walk, the child, through excess of joy, suddenly leaned forward laughing, and suddenly lost his balance. Berry saw that he was going to fall. To try to catch the boy, the young Negro let the chair go. But quick as a wink, the child had fallen one way onto the lawn, the chair the other onto the cement walk. The back of the chair was broken, snapped off, except for the wicker. The little boy lay squalling on the ground in the grass.

Lord have mercy!

All the nurses came running, the handy-man, and Mrs Osborn, too. Berry picked up the boy, who clung to his neck sobbing, more frightened, it seemed, than hurt.

'Po' little chile,' Berry kept saying. 'Is you hurt much? I's so sorry.'

But the nurses were very angry, for they were responsible. And Mrs Osborn – well, she lit out for Dr Renfield.

The little boy still clung to Berry, and wouldn't let the nurses take him at all. He had stopped crying when Dr Renfield arrived, but was still sniffing. He had his arms tight around the black boy's neck.

'Give that child to me,' Dr Renfield said, his brown beard pointing straight at Berry, his mind visualising irate parents and a big damage suit, and bad publicity for the Home.

But when the Doctor tried to take the child, the little boy wriggled and cried and wouldn't let go of Berry. With what strength he had in his crooked braced limbs, he kicked at the doctor.

'Give me that child!' Dr Renfield shouted at Berry. 'Bring him into my office and lay him down.' He put on his nose glasses. 'You careless black rascal! And you, Miss Baxter –' the Doctor shrivelled her with a look. 'I want to see you.'

In the clinic, it turned out that the child wasn't really hurt, though. His legs had been, from birth, twisted and deformed. Nothing could injure them much further. And fortunately his spine wasn't weak.

But the Doctor kept saying, 'Criminal carelessness! Criminal carelessness!' Mrs Osborn kept agreeing with him. 'Yes, it is! Indeed, it is!' Milberry was to blame.

The black boy felt terrible. But nobody else among the grown-ups seemed to care how he felt. They all said: 'What dumbness! He had let that child fall!'

'Get rid of him,' Dr Renfield said to the housekeeper, 'today. The fool nigger! And deduct ten dollars for that broken chair.'

'We don't pay him but eight,' Mrs Osborn said.

'Well, deduct that,' said the Doctor.

So, without his last week's wages, Milberry went to Jersey City.

The Two Grandmothers

Olive Senior

p.217

I

Mummy, you know what? Grandma Del has baby chickens. Yellow and white ones. She made me hold them. And I help her gather eggs but I don't like to go out the back alone because the turkey gobbler goes gobble! gobble! gobble! after my legs, he scares me, and Mr SonSon next door has baby pigs. I don't like the mother pig though. Grandma lives in this pretty little house with white lace curtains at all the windows, Mummy you must come with me and Daddy next time, and you can peek through the louvres Grandma calls them jalousies isn't that funny and you can see the people passing by. But they can't see you. Mummy why can't we have lace curtains like Grandma Del so we can peek through nobody ever goes by our house except the gardeners and the maids and people begging and Rastas selling brooms? Many many people go by Grandma Del's house they all call out to her and Grandma Del knows everyone. My special friend is Miss Princess the postmistress who plays the organ in church she wears tight shiny dresses and her hair piled *so* on her head and she walks *very slow* and everybody says she is sweet on Mister Blake who is the new teacher and he takes the service in church when Parson doesn't come and then Miss Princess gets so nervous she mixes up all the hymns. Mister Mack came to fix Grandma's roof and Grandma said 'poorman poorman' all the time. Mister Mack's daughters Eulalie and Ermandine are big girls at high school in town though Eulalie fell and they don't know what is to be done. Mummy, why are they so worried that Eulalie fell? She didn't break her leg or anything for she is walking up and down past the house all day long and looks perfectly fine to me.

Mummy, I really like Grandma Del's house it's nice and cosy and dark and cool inside with these lovely big picture frames of her family and Daddy as a baby and Daddy as a little boy and Daddy on the high school football team, they won Manning Cup that year Grandma says, did you know that Mummy? and Daddy at university and a wedding picture of Daddy and you and me as a baby and all the pictures you send Grandma every year but those are the small pictures on the side table with the lovely white lace tablecloth. In the picture frame on the wall there is Great-grandpapa Del with a long beard and whiskers, he is sitting down in a chair and Great-grandmama is standing behind him, and then there is a picture of Grandma herself as a young lady with her hair piled high like Miss Princess and her legs crossed at the ankles she looks so lovely. But you know what, Mummy, I didn't see a picture of Daddy's father and when I asked Grandma she got mad and shooed me away. She got even madder when I asked her to show me her wedding picture. I only wanted to see it.

Mummy, do you know that Grandma sends me to Sunday School? We stay over for big church and I walk home with her and all the people, it's so nice. Only Parson comes to church in a car. Mummy did you go to Sunday School? I go with Joycie a big girl next door and Grandma made me three dresses to wear. She says she cannot imagine how a girl-child (that's me) can leave home with nothing but blue jeans and T-shirts and shorts and not a single church dress. She has this funny sewing machine, not like Aunt Thelma's, she has to use her feet to make it go just like the organ in church Miss Princess pumps away with her feet to make it give out this lovely sound and works so hard you should see her and the first time I went to Grandma's church I was so scared of the bats! The church is full of bats but usually they stay high up in the roof. But as soon as the organ starts playing on Sunday the bats start swooping lower and lower and one swooped so low I nearly died of fright and clutched Grandma Del so tight my hat flew off.

Did I tell you Grandma made me a hat to wear to church with her own two hands? She pulled apart one of her old straw hats, leghorn she said, and made me a little hat that fits just so on my head with a bunch of tiny pink flowers. Grandma didn't send it with me though, or my Sunday dresses, she says she will keep them till I return for she knows that I am growing heathenish in town. When Grandma dresses me up for church I feel so beautiful in my dresses she made with lace and bows and little tucks so beautiful and my hat, I feel so special that my own Grandma made these for me with her own two hands and didn't buy them in a store. Grandma loves to comb my hair she says it's so long and thick and she rubs it with castor oil every night. I hate the smell of castor oil but she says it's the best thing for hair and after a time I even like the smell. Grandma Del says my skin is beautiful like honey and all in all I am a fine brown lady and must make sure to grow as beautiful inside as I am outside but Mummy, how do I go about doing that?

Nights at Grandma's are very funny. Mummy can you imagine there's no TV? And it's very, very dark. No street lights or any lights. We go to bed early and every night Grandma lights the oil lamps and then we blow them out when we are going to bed, you have to take a deep breath, and every morning Grandma checks the oil in the lamps and checks the shades. They have 'Home Sweet Home' written around them. So beautiful. She cleans the shades with newspapers. She says when I come next year I'll be old enough to clean them all by myself. Grandma knows such lovely stories; she tells me stories every night not stories from a book you know, Mummy, the way you read to me, but stories straight from her head. Really! I am going to learn stories from Grandma so when I am a grown lady I will remember all these stories to tell my children. Mummy, do you think I will?

II

Mummy, you know Grandma Elaine is so funny she says I'm not to call her Grandma any more, I'm to call her Towser like everybody else for I'm growing so fast nobody would believe that she could have such a big young lady for a granddaughter. I think it's funny I'm practising calling her Towser though she is still my grandmother. I said to her, 'Grandmother, I mean Towser, Grandma Del introduces me to everyone as her granddaughter she calls me her "little gran".' And Grandma Elaine says, 'Darling, the way your Grandmother Del looks and conducts herself she couldn't be anything but a grandmother and honey she and I are of entirely different generations.'

Grandma Elaine says such funny things sometimes. Like she was dressing to go out last night and she was putting on make up and I said 'Grandma' (she was still Grandma then) I said, 'Grandma, you shouldn't paint your face like that you know, it is written in the Bible that it's a sin. Grandma Del says so and I will never paint my face.' And she said, 'Darling, with all due respect to your paternal grandmother, she's a lovely lady or was when I met her the one and only time at the wedding, and she has done one absolutely fantastic thing in her life which is to produce one son your esteemed father, one hunk of a guy, but honey, other than that your Grandmother Del is a country bumpkin of the deepest waters and don't quote her goddam sayings to me.' Mummy, you know Grandma Elaine *swears* like that all the time? I said, 'Grandma you mustn't swear and take the name of the Lord in vain.' And she said, 'Honeychile with all due respect to the grey hairs of your old grandmother and the first class brainwashing your daddy is allowing her to give you, I wish my granddaughter would get off my back and leave me to go to Hell in peace.' Can you imagine she said that?

She's really mad that you allow me to spend time with Grandma Del. She says, 'Honey, I really don't know what your mother thinks she is doing making you spend so much time down there in the deepest darkest country. I really must take you in hand. It's embarrassing to hear some of the things you come out with sometimes. Your mother would be better advised to send you to Charm School next summer you are never too young to start. Melody-Ann next door went last year and it's done wonders for her, turned her from a tomboy into a real little lady.' (Though, Mummy, I really can't stand Melody-Ann any more, you know.) 'And your mother had better start to do something about your hair from now it's almost as tough as your father's and I warned your mother about it from the very start I said "Honey, love's alright but what about the children's hair?". If you were my child I would cut it right off to get some of the kinks out.' Mummy, you won't cut off my hair, will you? Daddy and Grandma Del like it just the way it is. What does Grandma Elaine mean when she says my hair is tough, Mummy?

Anyway, Mummy, can I tell you a secret? Gran, I mean Towser, told me and says it's a secret but I guess since you are her daughter she won't mind if I tell you. Do you know that Towser has a new boyfriend? He came to pick her up on Saturday night, remember I told you Joyce was staying up with me and we watched TV together while Towser went out? That's the time she was painting her face and she put on her fabulous silver evening dress, you know the strapless one and her diamonds with it, the ones her husband after Grandpapa gave her, and I was so proud she was my grandmama she looked wonderful like a million dollars and when I told her so she let me spray some of her perfume on myself before Mister Kincaid came. He is a tall white man and he kissed Towser's hand and then he kissed my hand and he had a drink with Towser and was very nice and they drove off in a big white car like what Uncle Frank drives Mummy, a Benz, and Towser was looking so pleased the whole time, and before Mister Kincaid came she whispered and said her new boyfriend was coming to take her to dinner and he was so nice and handsome and rich. Towser was looking as pleased as Eulalie did when the mail van driver was touching her when they thought nobody was looking but I was peeking through the louvres at Grandma Del's and I saw them.

But Mummy, I don't know why Towser wants me to spend more time with her for she is never there when I go; always rushing off to the gym and the pool and dinners and cocktails or else she is on the phone. I love Towser so much though, she hugs me a lot and says things that make me laugh and she gives me wonderful presents. Do you know she made Joyce bake a chocolate cake for me? And my new bracelet is so lovely. It's my birthstone you know, Mummy. You know what, Grandma Elaine, I mean Towser, says she is going to talk to you about taking me to see my cousins Jason and Maureen in Clearwater when she goes to do her Christmas shopping in Miami. Oh Mummy, can I go? You know all the girls in my class have been to Miami and you've never taken me. Mum, can we go to Disneyworld soon? I'm so ashamed everyone in school has been to Disneyworld and I haven't gone yet. When Towser goes out Joyce and I sit in the den and watch TV the whole time, except I usually fall asleep during the late show but Joyce watching everything until TV signs off, and next morning when she is making me breakfast she tells me all the parts that I missed. Mummy, can't we get a video? Everyone in my class has a video she says she is getting Mister Kincaid to give her one as a present. Towser is so much fun. Except, Mummy, what does she have against my hair? And my skin? She always seems angry about it and Joyce says Grandma is sorry I came out dark because she is almost a white lady and I am really dark. But Mummy, what is wrong with that? When I hold my hand next to Joyce my skin is not as dark as hers or Grandma Del's or Daddy's even. Is dark really bad, Mummy?

III

Mummy, did you know that a whistling woman and a crowing hen are an abomination to the Lord? That's what Grandma Del told me and Pearlie when Pearlie was teaching me to whistle. Don't tell Grandma but I *can* whistle. Want to hear me? – ! – ! – ! Ha ha. Mummy, can you whistle? Pearlie is my best friend in the country, she lives near to Grandma in this tiny house, so many of them and all the children sleep together in one room on the floor and Mummy, you know what? Pearlie has only one pair of shoes and one good dress and her school uniform though she hardly goes to school and some old things she wears around the house that have holes in them. Can you imagine? And you should see her little brothers! Half the time they are wearing no clothes at all. Mummy, can you send Pearlie some of my dresses and some of my toys but not my Barbie doll? She doesn't have any toys at all, not a single one.

And Pearlie is just a little older than me and she has to look after her little brothers when her mummy goes to work. She has to feed them and bathe them and change them and while she is changing the baby's nappies her little brothers get into so much trouble. And when they break things when her mother comes home she beats Pearlie. Poor Pearlie! She can balance a pan of water on her head no hands you know. I wish I could do that. She goes to the standpipe for water and carries the pan on her head without spilling a drop. Sometimes I go with her; I borrow a pan and though it's smaller than Pearlie's I always end up spilling the water all over me and the pan gets heavier and heavier till I can hardly bear it before we get to Pearlie's house. Pearlie can wash clothes too. I mean real clothes, not dolly clothes. Really. Her baby brother's nappies and things and she cooks dinner for them but the way they eat is really funny. They don't have a real kitchen or anything. She has three big rocks in the fireplace and she catches up a fire when she is ready and she has to fan it and fan it with an old basket top and there is a lot of smoke. It makes me sneeze. Then when the fire is going she puts on a big pot of water and when it is boiling she peels things and throws them in the water to cook – yams and cocos and green bananas and that's what they eat, no meat or rice or salad or anything. Pearlie uses a sharp knife just like a big person and she peels the bananas ever so fast, she makes three cuts and goes zip! zip! with her fingers and the banana is out if its skin and into the pot. She says you must never put bananas and yams to boil in cold water for they will get drunk and never cook. Did you know that?

Once I helped her to rub up the flour dumplings but my dumplings came out so soft Pearlie said they were like fla-fla and she won't let me help her make dumplings again. Pearlie has to do all these things and we only get to play in the evenings when her mother comes home and you can imagine, Mummy, Pearlie has never seen TV? And she has never been to the movies. Never. Mummy, do you think Pearlie could come and live with us? I could take her to the movies though I don't know who would look after her baby brothers when her mother goes to work. You know Pearlie doesn't have a father? She doesn't know where he is. I'd die without my Daddy. Grandma Del says I'm to be careful and not spend so much time with Pearlie for Pearlie is beginning to back-chat and is getting very force-ripe. Mummy, what is force-ripe?

Sometimes I play with Eulalie's baby. His name is Oral and he is fat and happy and I help to change his nappy. He likes me a lot and claps his hands when he sees me and he has two teeth already. He likes to grab hold of my hair and we have a hard time getting him to let go. Mummy why can't I have a baby brother to play with all the time? Eulalie and Ermandine love to comb my hair and play with it they say I am lucky to have tall hair but Grandma Del doesn't like Eulalie and Ermandine any more. She says they are a disgraceful Jezebel-lot and dry-eye and bring down shame on their father and mother who try so hard with them. Sometimes my Grandma talks like that and I really don't understand and when I ask her to explain she says, 'Cockroach nuh bizniz inna fowl roos,' and she acts real mad as if I did something wrong and I don't know why she is so vexed sometimes and quarrels with everyone even me. She scares me when she is vexed.

You know when Grandma Del is really happy? When she is baking cakes and making pimento liqueur and orange marmalade and guava jelly. Oh, she sings and gets Emmanuel to make up a big fire out in the yard and they put on this big big pot and we peel and we peel guava – hundreds of them. When we make stewed guavas she gives me a little spoon so I can help to scoop out the seeds and I have to be real careful to do it properly and not break the shells. Mummy, right here you have this little glass jar full of stewed guavas from Grandma Del that I helped to make. Grandma gets so happy to see her kitchen full of these lovely glass jars full of marmalade and guava jelly. But you know what? Grandma just makes it and then she gives it all away. Isn't that funny? And one time she baked a wedding cake and decorated it too – three cakes in different sizes she made and then she put them one on top of the other. Grandma is so clever. She allowed me to help her stir the cake mix in the bowl but it was so heavy I could barely move the spoon. When it was all finished she let me use my fingers to lick out the mixing bowls. Yum Yum. Why don't you bake cakes so I can lick out the bowls, Mummy?

This time I found that I had grown so much I couldn't get into the church dresses Grandma made for me last time. So she made me some new dresses and she says she will give the old ones to Pearlie. Mummy can you believe that everyone in church remembered me? And they said: 'WAT-A-WAY-YU-GROW' and 'HOW-IS-YU-DAADIE?' and 'HOW-IS-YU-MAAMIE?' till I was tired. Mummy, that is the way they talk, you know, just like Richie and the gardener next door. 'WAT-A-WAY-YU-GROW.' They don't speak properly the way we do, you know. Mummy, Eulalie and Ermandine don't go to church or school any more and Ermandine says when I come back next year she will have a little baby for me to play with too and Eulalie says *she* will have a new little baby.

IV

Mummy, you know what the girls in school say? They say I am the prettiest girl in school and I can be Miss Jamaica. When I'm big I'll go to the gym like you so I can keep my figure and I must take care of my skin for even though I have excellent skin, Towser says, I must always care for it. Towser spends hours before the mirror every morning caring for her skin and her new boyfriend Mister Samuels is always telling her how beautiful she looks. Towser really loves that. Mister Samuels is taking her to Mexico for the long Easter weekend and Towser is going to Miami to buy a whole new wardrobe for the trip. She says she is going to bring me all the new movies for the video. Mummy, when I am old like Grandma will men tell me I'm beautiful too? Can I have my hair relaxed as soon as I am twelve as you promised? Will you allow me to enter Miss Jamaica when I am old enough? You know Jason likes me a lot but he's my cousin so he doesn't count. Mom, am I going to Clearwater again this Christmas to spend time with Jason and Maureen? Maureen is always fighting with me you know but Jason says she's jealous because she isn't pretty like me, she's fat and she has to wear braces on her teeth. Will I ever have to wear braces? Mom, when I go to Miami can I get a training bra? All the girls in my class are wearing them and a make up starter kit? Mom, when are we going to get a Dish?

V

Mom, do I have to go to Grandma Del's again? It's so boring. There's nothing to do and nobody to talk to and I'm ashamed when my friends ask me where I'm going for the holidays and I have to tell them only to my old grandmother in the country. You know Gina is going to Europe and Melody-Ann is spending all of her holidays in California and Jean-Ann is going to her aunt in Trinidad? Mom, even though Grandma Del has electricity now she has only a small black and white TV, and I end up missing everything for she doesn't want me to watch the late show even on weekends, and Grandma's house is so small and crowded and dark and she goes around turning off lights and at nights Grandma smells because she is always rubbing herself with liniment for her arthritis and it's true Grandma is in terrible pain sometimes. Mummy, what is going to happen to Grandma when she is real old? She's all alone there.

She got mad at me when I told her I didn't want to rub castor oil on my hair anymore because I was having it conditioned and the castor oil smells so awful. And on Sundays Grandma still wants me to go to church with her. It's so boring. We have to *walk* to church and back. It's *miles* in the hot sun. I can't walk on the gravel road in my heels. If a parent passed and saw me there among all the country bumpkins I would die and Grandma says I am far too young to be wearing heels even little ones and I tell Grandma I'm not young any more. I'll be entering high school next term and everybody is wearing heels. She criticises everything I do as if I am still a baby and she doesn't like me wearing lip gloss or blusher though I tell her you allow me to wear them. And Grandma still wants me to come and greet all her friends, it's so boring as soon as somebody comes to the house she calls me and I have to drop whatever I am doing, even watching TV, and I have to say hello to all these stupid people. It's so boring Mom you wouldn't believe it, there's nobody but black people where Grandma lives and they don't know anything, they ask such silly questions. And they are dirty. You know this girl Pearlie I used to play with when I was little she is so awful-looking, going on the road with her clothes all torn up and you should see her little brothers always dirty and in rags with their noses running. I can't stand to have them around me and Pearlie and everybody is always begging me for clothes and things and I can't stand it so I don't even bother to go outside the house half the time. When anybody comes I can see them through the louvres and I just pretend I am not there or I am sleeping. And everybody is just having babies without being married like Pearlie's mother and they are not ashamed. The worst ones are those two sisters Eulalie and Ermandine, you can't imagine how many children they have between them a new one every year and Grandma says not a man to mind them.

But Mummy, something terrible happened. That Eulalie and I got into an argument. She's so ignorant and I told her it was a disgrace to have babies without being married and she said, 'Who says?' and I said, 'Everybody. My Mummy and Grandma Elaine and Grandma Del for a start.' And she said, 'Grandma Del? Yes? You ever hear that she that is without sin must cast the first stone?' And I said, 'What do you mean?' And she said, 'Ask your Grannie Del Miss High-And-Mighty since her son turn big-shot and all. And her who his father? And why she never turn teacher? And why her daddy almost turn her out of the house and never speak to her for five years? And why they take so long to let her into Mothers'

Union?' And Eulalie wouldn't tell me anymore and they were so awful to me, they started singing, 'Before A married an' go hug up mango tree, A wi' live so. Me one.' You know that song, Mummy? I went home to ask Grandma Del what Eulalie meant but Mummy when I got home it was just weird I got so scared that I got this terrible pain in my tummy, my tummy hurt so much I couldn't ask Grandma Del anything and then when I felt better, I couldn't bring myself to say anything for I'm scared Grandma Del will get mad. But Mummy, do you think Grandma Del had Daddy without getting married? Is that what Eulalie meant? Mummy, wouldn't that make Daddy a bastard?

VI

Mummy, please don't send me to stay with Auntie Rita in Clearwater again. Ever. Nothing, Mummy … It's that Maureen. She doesn't like me.

Mummy, am I really a nigger? That's what Maureen said when we were playing one day and she got mad at me and she said, 'You're only a goddam nigger you don't know any better. Auntie Evie married a big black man and you're his child and you're not fit to play with me.' Mummy, I gave her such a box that she fell and I didn't care. I cried and cried and though Auntie Rita spanked Maureen afterwards and sent her to bed without any supper, I couldn't eat my supper for I had this pain in my tummy, such a terrible pain and Uncle Rob came into the bedroom and held my hand and said that Maureen was a naughty girl and he was ashamed of her and *he* thought I was a very beautiful, lovely girl …

But Mummy, how can I be beautiful? My skin is so dark, darker than yours and Maureen's and Jason's and Auntie Rita's. And my hair is so coarse, not like yours or Maureen's but then Maureen's father is white. Is that why Maureen called me a nigger? I hate Maureen. She is fat and ugly and still wearing braces …

******

Mummy, why can't I have straight hair like Maureen? I'm so ashamed of my hair. I simply can't go back to Clearwater.

VII

Mom, I don't care what Dad says I can't go to stay with Grandma Del this summer because the Charm Course is for three weeks and then remember Towser is taking me to Ochi for three weeks in her new cottage. Do you think Towser is going to marry Mr Blake? Then I am going with you to Atlanta. You promised. So I really don't have any time to spend with Grandma this summer. And next holidays remember you said I can go to Venezuela on the school trip?

I don't know what Dad is on about because if he feels so strongly why doesn't he go and spend time with his mother? Only that's a laugh because Daddy doesn't have time for anybody any more, I mean is there ever a time nowadays when he is at home? I know Grandma Del is getting old and she is all alone but she won't miss me, she quarrels with me all the time I am there. Mom, I just can't fit her in and that is that.

O.K. You know what? I have an idea. Why don't we just take a quick run down to see Grandma this Sunday and then we won't have to worry about her again till next year? Daddy can take us and we can leave here real early in the morning though I don't know how I am going to get up early after Melody-Ann's birthday party Saturday night, but we don't have to stay long with Grandma Del. We can leave there right after lunch so we will be back home in time to watch *Dallas*. Eh, Mom?

What is a short story?

The term 'short story' is used to describe a literary form that is a short prose narrative or short prose fiction. It is different from an anecdote, which usually narrates a single incident in a simple, unelaborated way. It is also different from a novel in that it is much shorter and more concentrated. However, we use some common terms to talk about both a novel and a short story. Like a novel, a short story has:

- a plot, which is the pattern that the writer uses to organise the events or action of the story, and which has a beginning, a middle and an end; the plot may be humorous (comic) or sad (tragic), or it may be romantic or satirical (it may combine all of these)

- characters, or people who take part in the action

- a setting, or the place and the time that the action happens

- a point of view, or the perspective from which the author narrates the events and describes the characters

- style, which is the way the author uses language to shape the story

- a theme, which is the unifying idea that holds the story together; we can think of the theme as the author's personal vision, expressed through the use of the elements of fiction (i.e. plot, character, setting, point of view and style).

A good short story, whether it is written in the mode of realism, fantasy or naturalism (see 'Glossary of terms') appeals to the readers not only because it uses the elements of fiction to create a unified narrative, but also because it touches us emotionally and intellectually. A good short story sparks our imagination and presents us with a condensed vision of life that engages our thoughts and feelings.

What should we look for in reading a short story?

Above everything else, we should read stories for the pleasure they can provide. The way in which we approach and respond to a story will determine how much we get out of it. When we become involved in reading to the extent that we begin to relate what the author has to say to our own experience, the story becomes more meaningful to us.

So, is there a best way to study a short story? Perhaps not. Each individual has his or her own way of getting at the underlying meaning of a text. However, when we first read a story we want to enjoy it simply by seeing how the events unfold. We want to allow ourselves to feel and to be drawn into the magic that the author weaves for us. Perhaps the best way to do this is to read in a comfortable and relaxed way, and to give the story our full attention from beginning to end. On a second reading, however, we need to be more careful. We want to see what goes into the story to understand how the author develops it, to discern the narrative pattern that the author uses, and so on. When we are reading for these purposes we need to be more objective, and the questions we ask about the story (e.g. How is the plot developed? What is this character like? What motivated this action?) should be more focused and specific because we want to understand how the story is put together.

The following are suggestions for some useful things that you can do as you read a story the second time:

- Underline the parts that you find striking.

- Jot down notes about the parts that you think are interesting and most important, about your impressions of the characters, about the setting, and so on.

- Become engaged with the text by asking yourself questions about the different parts of the story as you go along, and after you have read the story through.

In the next section we describe each of the main elements of fiction and include a few guiding questions to help you to read with a critical perspective.

What makes good fiction?

When we speak about plot, character, setting, point of view, style and theme we are talking about elements of fiction, or the things that contribute to the telling of a good story.

Plot

The plot of a narrative is the set of events that make up the action. It is what happens in a story. There are characters who are 'participants' in the action and they make things happen and things happen to them. The action usually involves a conflict which has to be resolved. The conflicts in short stories can be varied. There are conflicts where the main character has to struggle with forces which may be *internal* (within the character) or *external* (outside the character) or both. The conflicts usually mean that the main character faces opposition of some sort. Very often, the forces against which the main character has to struggle are linked in the story. There is usually a crucial point in a story, where the main character has to face the forces that oppose him or her, and must make a choice which will lead to the working out or resolution of the conflict.

The following are some questions that you can ask yourself to help you understand the plot.

- How are the events presented in the story?

- How is the plot developed? Does the author use a linear (chronological) pattern, where events happen in their natural sequence in time? If the pattern is not linear, what is it like?

- Is flashback (see 'Glossary of terms') one of the techniques used?

- Do any of the early events or incidents prepare the reader for later ones? Do any lead you to anticipate the outcome?

- What is the nature of the conflict? At what point of the story does the climax (see 'Glossary of terms') happen?

- Does the climax bring about a change in character or a change in situation?

Character

This refers to anyone who plays a part in the narrative. Stories are about people, about the things that happen to them, about the things they do, the things that are done to them, and the ways in which they react to situations. The things that the characters say, as well as the things that they do, help us to understand the reasons or motivation for their actions. As you read a story, try to figure out the motivation of the characters as this initiates action. In critical works about literature you may see the terms 'flat', 'round' and 'stereotype' used to describe certain types of characters.

- A *flat* character is one who is simple, one-dimensional and who remains unchanged throughout the course of the narrative.

- A *round* character is complex in mood and motivation, is fully described; that is, he or she is presented in a detailed way, and changes as a result of the situations and events that he or she encounters.

- A *stereotype* is an oversimplified character, one who acts and thinks in a predictable way. A stereotype is usually a stock character (see below).

- A *stock* character is a conventional character who behaves in ways that we can predict, such as the wicked witch in fairy-tale stories.

We refer to the main character of a story as the *protagonist* or hero/heroine. Another character with whom the main character may be in conflict is called the *antagonist*. We expect a character to behave like normal people do; that is, in a believable or plausible way. We also expect a character to behave in ways that are in keeping with the personality that the author has established for that character. For example, in 'The Girl Who Can' the grandmother sets aside her traditional view about the need for a girl to have shapely legs to attract a husband as she witnesses her granddaughter's success on the track. We can understand the change in the grandmother's perspective as she begins to appreciate the girl's athletic prowess. This is presented to the reader as a plausible development for a character who has strong traditional African values and fixed views about the role of women in African culture. The reasons that characters do things must be plausible and consistent with the impressions that we have formed of them. You can ask yourself:

- Are the characters believable?

- How are the characters presented by the author?

- What is the main character like?

- Does the author present fully developed characters or are some of the characters stereotypes?

- What are the conflicts that the main character faces?

- Does this character change as a result of the events that he or she experiences in the story?

- What is the nature of the change? If there is no change, why not?

Setting

This term is normally used to refer to the place and the time in which the action of a story takes place. It is also used to refer to the mood and atmosphere created by the author, and the culture and shared values and beliefs of the characters. In some stories, the author only uses a few details to create a sense of the setting, while in others the full effect of the story depends on the presentation of an increasing amount of descriptive details. The author decides whether the setting is going to play an important part in the story, a decision that usually determines the choice of the setting and the extent to which it is described.

Apart from providing the reader with a sense of where and when the story takes place, the setting can also serve other purposes, such as contributing to the plot. In 'The Creek', for example, it is the creek which is both the setting and the catalyst for the climax of the story. The setting of a story can also underline its theme, as in the case of 'The Pain Tree' in which Larissa's room, with layers of photographs pasted onto the walls, signals the ways in which she – and other servants – dealt with the reality of class distinctions that kept them subordinate, and their hammering of nails into the pain tree nearby signified their way of alleviating the pain of having to endure this situation.

Examples of questions that you can ask about the setting are:

- How important is the setting of the story?

- Does the setting help to develop the plot? How does it do so?

- What does the setting contribute to our understanding of the meaning of the story?

- Does it have any influence on the characters?

Point of view

A story is told by someone, it does not just happen. The author makes a decision about the point of view or perspective from which he or she wants the reader to 'see' the action of the story. In simple terms, point of view has to do with *who tells the story*. In first-person point of view or first-person narration, the narrator uses 'I' or 'we' and is a character in the story. You must not confuse the 'I' who is telling the story with the author. The narrator's voice in this case is different from the author's. In first-person narration the narrator can only know and talk about the things that have been revealed in the story. He or she can reflect on these things and make deductions from them. The perspective is limited in the sense that the narrator cannot describe the thoughts of the other characters. This is the point of view that is used in Carolyn Cole's 'Emma', for example.

With third-person point of view the narrator can be *omniscient*; that is, he or she knows everything that is happening and can describe the thoughts and feelings of all the characters. The narrator can also express his or her views about the characters and evaluate their actions. In this case, the narrator is intrusive. An alternative perspective in third-person point of view is one in which the narrator does not comment on characters or make judgements about the action of the story. In this instance the narrator is not intrusive, and chooses to be impersonal, to show the reader the events and characters without commenting upon them. In third-person point of view the narrator is not involved in the story. The narrator uses 'he', 'she' or 'they' to describe the characters' actions and relates the story from a distance, giving a wide view of events.

First-person point of view lacks this broad perspective, but it can provide the reader with a sense of immediacy when the events are narrated, as though they are taking place at that moment in time. Sometimes the first-person narrator recalls events from the past. Recalling and recounting events from the past is referred to as a *retrospective point of view* and some of the stories in this book which use this are 'Mint Tea', 'It's Cherry Pink and Apple Blossom White' and 'The Day the World Almost Came to an End'.

Sometimes an author tries to get the best of both points of view and chooses to write in the third person, but presents the action through the eyes of a character. In this kind of story the author can convey the sense of immediacy that use of the first-person point of view allows, but he or she can also look at the main character from a distance and interpret and evaluate that character's actions, thoughts and feelings.

You can ask yourself:

- Does the point of view that is used help the author to expose the theme? If so, how?

- To what extent is the narrator a reliable witness to events?

- Would the choice of a different point of view change the story significantly?

Style

In simple terms, style refers to the way in which authors express themselves. It refers to the way in which an author uses language, vocabulary and imagery; it refers to the way he or she organises the events of the story, and the way in which the action of the story is paced. The author makes conscious choices about these things, and as readers we become uncomfortable when the style does not suit the subject matter. This is particularly important in first-person narration, where the language used must be appropriate for the character who uses it. For example, the language used by the narrator in 'The Man of the House' is appropriate for a young boy. In 'Shabine', on the other hand, although the story is about a boy's observations, the point of view is retrospective. Here, the language that the narrator uses is appropriate for an adult who is an intellectual and who is reflecting on another person from his boyhood.

Authors use dialogue for several purposes, one of which is to reveal character. Because of this, the language that an author chooses to let his or her characters use is important. When an author uses dialect (regional variations of a language) and idiom (the way different people use language) in a creative way it makes the language and the characters real for us. This is the case in 'The Boy Who Loved Ice Cream' and 'The Man of the House' among other stories in this collection. The author's choice of descriptive details, the imagery and the appeal to our senses through the use of language make the scenes and characters in the story come alive.

Questions that you can ask about style are:

- Does the author use figurative language (see 'Glossary of terms') in telling this story, or is the language literal (plain)?

- If figurative language is used, what is its effect?

- Does the author use dialogue to advance the action of the story? If dialect is used, what is its effect?

- What examples of figurative language are most striking in the story?

- Why are they striking? How do they contribute to the meaning and theme of the story?

Theme

The theme is the central idea or meaning that an author develops and explores through the action and the imagery (see 'Glossary of terms') of a story. The ways in which the author chooses to expose the theme are called *thematic devices.* All the elements of fiction contribute to the exploration of the theme. In trying to understand the theme of a story it is useful to explore the outcome of the conflict and the change that has taken place in the main character.

Sometimes the title of the story can give the reader a clue as to what the theme is. However, the theme is more than just a topic of the story; it is more than a statement of the subject matter.

Try to understand the theme by asking:

- What is the theme of the story?

- Does the title provide a clue to what the theme is?

- Is there only one theme or are there several themes?

- Does the author suggest the theme through the imagery that he or she uses in the story?

Notes and questions

p.1
Raymond's Run

Toni Cade Bambara was born in 1939 in New York. She is an African-American novelist and short-story writer of what she calls 'straight-up fiction', which seems to mean fiction that does not owe anything to autobiographical or biographical facts, or to incidents that actually occurred (to the best of her knowledge). She uses this phrase at the end of her preface to *Gorilla, My Love* (1972). In the preface she asserts that she does not write 'autobiographical fiction' or fiction that uses 'bits and snatches of real events and real people'. In *Gorilla, My Love* Bambara displays a highly sensitive ear for the rhythms and nuances of black speech.

- What is it about the narrator's language that makes her come alive in our imagination?

- How much does she reveal of her own personality, even as she sketches other people for us?

- How does the story's resolution suggest the idea of growth?

p.8
Blackout

Roger Mais (1905–1955) is best known for his novels *The Hills Were Joyful Together*, *Brother Man* and *Black Lightning*, in which he compellingly depicts the lives and problems of working-class Jamaicans in urban and rural settings. His short stories often venture beyond these experiences into the existence of characters who have to deal with issues other than those of survival, but no less urgent.

This story narrates a brief encounter between two people from diametrically opposed worlds, a moment when each has to acknowledge and communicate with the other against the background of a blackout made necessary by a distant world war that would change their lives and the worlds they came from. Their conversation represents a small area of light in the darkness that normally prevents a white American woman and a black Jamaican man from really seeing each other. Yet the story insists on the irony that is implicit in the idea that these two are just a man and a woman, especially since this is happening on a West Indian island that is still a colony.

- What effect does Mais achieve by giving us access to the woman's consciousness, but not the man's?

- How does the story ensure that our sense of the man changes over the course of the encounter?

- Does the final paragraph of the story alter our understanding of what this encounter means?

p.12

Shabine

Hazel Simmons-McDonald is a St Lucian writer of poetry and fiction, and also a senior academic who recently retired as Principal of the Open Campus of the University of the West Indies.

This story, which comes from the collection *Shabine and Other Stories*, brings together a man's intense awareness of the present and his acutely felt sense of the past, both focused on the compelling figure of a woman who seems to embody the racial and class tensions of her society. It is these tensions that have created an unbridgeable gulf between the unnamed man and the woman who has always fascinated him. His fascination, then, and now, is no way lessened by his regret about what might have happened between them but did not.

- How does the story succeed in making us share the man's fascination with Justine?

- Discuss the author's use of the paradise plum in her control of the story's plot and its mood.

- What impressions do you form of the man from whose perspective the story is told?

- What does this story suggest about race and class relations in the society in which it is set?

p.16

Blood Brothers

John Wickham was born and educated in Barbados, the setting of many of the stories that have established him as one of the best practitioners of the craft in the Caribbean. He has been Editor of *BIM*, the literary journal, and literary editor of *The Nation* newspaper.

This story comes from *Discoveries*, his third collection. It evokes the love–hate relationship between twin brothers from the perspective of the less confident sibling, culminating with a moment of resolution which changes both brothers and redefines their relationship. Note how carefully Wickham establishes the contrasts between the twins and leads us into the setting of the closing scene.

- Discuss the range of meanings implied in the story's title, and show how they relate to its content.

- How does Wickham use details to establish the differences between the brothers?

- The twins are 13 years old. Is their age at all significant in the resolution of the story?

Buried with Science

John T. Gilmore is a Barbadian academic and writer who is currently a professor of Caribbean Studies at the University of Warwick in the UK, having earlier lectured at the Cave Hill campus of the University of the West Indies. He has always been deeply interested in the history, heritage and lore of his native Barbados. *Buried with Science* is the title story of Gilmore's collection of short fiction in which he celebrates this history and lore.

- How do you respond to the rum-shop conversation that leads to Wilbert's conviction that there was treasure to be found in the old tomb?

- What is it that leads the young men to attempt a second raid on the tomb, although they found no treasure the first time?

- What do they find when they open the small coffin? Explain how it would have got there and why.

- What treasure do the boys get at the end of the story?

Emma

Carolyn Cole is a playwright who resides in New York City, USA. In this story she presents the complexity of adult relationships through the perspective of an innocent child who, like her friend and playmate, is fascinated by the adult world. Their pretend play is patterned on the actions and behaviour of the adults, especially that of Emma, the narrator's mother.

- The events of the story are filtered through the consciousness of the child narrator. What effects does the author achieve by using this technique?

- Discuss how the author's choice of point of view contributes to the creation of empathy in the story.

- From the children's perspective everything is a game. Discuss the author's use of this motif in the story.

- Contrast the characters of Mrs Robinson and Emma.

- Would you consider Emma to be a tragic figure? Why or why not?

Two Boys Named Basil

This story by Mark McWatt is part of a collection entitled *Suspended Sentences: Fictions of Atonement* in which the author uses as a framing device the concept of a group of students having to write stories for a collection as a penalty for having done something wrong. 'Hilary Augusta Sutton' is the persona of one such storyteller. The story 'she' creates is about the extraordinary relationship between two boys of the same age, both named Basil, whose lives become intertwined after they first meet each other as 10 year olds. The friendship that develops is a deeply symbiotic one in which the two seem to be parts of a single whole, as necessary to each other as they are competitive. It ends only when one of them disappears during a school outing. The narrative culminates with the present-day acceptance by the survivor of the continuing presence of his friend in his life.

- How does the author establish the complementary nature of the relationship between the two boys?

- Identify and discuss the significance of three incidents which are pivotal in the development of their linked lives.

- Comment on the effectiveness of the closing section of the story.

 p.53

Victory and the Blight

Earl Lovelace is a celebrated Trinidadian novelist, perhaps best known for his novel *The Dragon Can't Dance*. He has also published short stories and plays. This story appears in the collection *A Brief Conversion and Other Stories*.

- Tell in your own words what Victory was afraid of when he saw Brown and the stranger enter the barbershop to play draughts at the beginning of the story.

- As the story progresses, what other interests and activities of Victory emerge? And how are these connected to his barbershop?

- Describe the change that occurs, over the course of the story, in Victory's attitude towards Ross, the newcomer. What brings about this change?

- At the end of the story, when Ross sits in the barber chair and asks for a haircut, what does this mean to Victory? And in what way does the end of the story comment on the story's title?

p.61

Child of Darkening Humour

Noel D. Williams is a Guyanese writer of short fiction who won gold and silver medals for stories he submitted to the Jamaica Annual Literary Competition. This story is one for which he won a gold medal in 1973. Through focusing on the life of one family, in a middle-class suburb of Jamaica, the story portrays the class and, to a lesser extent, the racial tensions that exist in the society. The story also depicts

Jamaica in a state of political and social fragility, together with the uncertainty of its citizens during this transitional period. The author carefully unfolds the tapestry of Jamaica's social fabric through the characters who visit Gran's home and through the perspective of Gran herself and of her grandson, Morgan.

- Study the characters who visit the Segree household and discuss what each one reveals about the society in which they live.

- Consider the title of the story and discuss its relevance and significance to the theme or themes of the story.

- Discuss the roles of Gran and Morgan in the story.

The Man of the House

As in most of Frank O'Connor's other work, the rhythm of the language in 'The Man of the House' is unmistakably Irish. O'Connor believed that a story should have the sound of a person speaking, and he captures the natural tones of the Irish accent in his dialogue. In this story O'Connor presents a moving account of a young boy's attempt to cope with the household chores and at the same time care for his sick mother. The boy's inability to resist the temptation of drinking his mother's medicine and his ensuing anguish is recounted with compassion and a touch of humour. This story reflects the sympathy that O'Connor often exhibits towards his characters.

- How does the narrative point of view affect the presentation of events in this story?

- Discuss the relevance and appropriateness of the title in relation to the subject matter and main theme of the story.

The Day the World Almost Came to an End

In this story Pearl Crayton (born in 1932) presents a compelling account of the terror experienced by a 12-year-old girl at the prospect of the world coming to an end. At the same time, Crayton's presentation of the naïveté and gullibility of the main character is conveyed with a touch of humour. The narrative point of view is retrospective, recalling events in the past, and this allows Crayton to reflect and comment on the childhood incident with the tolerance of an adult.

- Discuss Crayton's handling of the narrative point of view and characterisation in this story.

- Discuss the ways in which Crayton conveys the tension between the gullibility and the terror of the young protagonist.

It's Cherry Pink and Apple Blossom White

Barbara Jenkins was born in Trinidad. She studied at the University College of Wales, Aberystwyth and at the University of Wales, Cardiff. She began writing short fiction in 2008 and her stories have twice won the Commonwealth Short Story Prize for the Caribbean region as well as other prizes. She has published her work in several journals and a collection *Sic Transit Wagon* from which this story comes.

- What are some of the themes explored in this story?

- How does the author reveal the development of the main character?

- Compare the relationships in the narrator's family and those of the family of the shop owners where she lived for a while. What do we learn of the narrator's reactions to her experiences in these families?

- What techniques does the author use to establish a sense of the world of the child narrator?

The Boy Who Loved Ice Cream

Olive Senior was born in Jamaica in 1941. She studied journalism at universities in the UK and Canada. When she returned to Jamaica she worked in a few jobs in her field before joining *The Institute of Jamaica*, as editor of the *Jamaica Journal*. In 1967 she won the Commonwealth Prize for her first collection of stories, *Summer Lightning*. She has also published several collections of poems. Senior now lives in Toronto, Canada, but travels widely all over the world, giving lectures and conducting workshops.

This story, from *Summer Lightning*, reveals Senior's understanding of rural Jamaica and her sensitivity to the circumstances of the rural poor and the concerns of the young people in that setting. In a tightly structured tale that takes as its central focus a young boy's desire to taste ice cream, Senior weaves several thematic strands that explore the tensions and concerns of rural life in Jamaica.

- Examine the author's use of dialect in the story and discuss its effectiveness.

- What are some of the themes that Senior explores in this story? How does she control the development of these themes?

- Discuss the character of Papa in the story.

Uncle Umberto's Slippers

This story, from Mark McWatt's collection *Suspended Sentences: Fictions of Atonement*, is narrated from the point of view of a young boy who reveals events in the life of the Callistro family of which he is a member. The author allows us to learn about the mysterious events surrounding Uncle Umberto's encounters with a lady in blue through the perspective of Uncle Umberto himself, and the subsequent disappearance of his slippers through Aunt Teresa, Umberto's wife.

- Why does the narrator describe the making of the slippers in such detail?

- What is the effect of the shifting of perspective from the boy to Uncle Umberto and Aunt Teresa for the 'magical' sequences of the story?

- What do you make of the magical sequences? Do they help us to understand Uncle Umberto better?

- Discuss the characters in the story. What do we learn about the personalities of Uncle Umberto and the narrator?

- What do you think happened to the slippers after Aunt Teresa found them? When you consider the magical elements in the story, how do you think the mysterious disappearance might be explained?

- What do you think might account for the worn nature of the slippers at the end (well after Uncle Umberto had died) when Aunt Teresa found them?

The Creek

Subraj Singh is Guyanese and a recent graduate of the University of Guyana. He has written a collection of short stories entitled *Rebelle*, which won the Guyana prize for the Best First Book of Fiction in 2015.

- In what ways is the setting of the story important in the development of the events in the plot?

- What is the nature of the conflict in the story?

- Contrast the character of the grandfather with that of the poachers.

- How does the narrative point of view affect the events of the story?

- Discuss the ending of the story. What do you think happened? Imagine a scene after Boy hears the gunshots. Describe what happens.

Georgia and Them There United States

Velma Pollard is a Jamaican poet and writer of short fiction who has published widely in both genres. This story from the collection *Karl and Other Stories* offers an unusual perspective on the Caribbean dream of migration to the USA. Beginning with the memory of a letter that complacently celebrates the fulfilment of that dream, the narrator creates a sense of herself as committed to the pleasures of her island home, even though (unlike her cousin) she is qualified for seeking the opportunities of 'over there'. This commitment is affirmed when she does visit the USA, and has her worst fears confirmed about what it demands of the West Indian migrant: she sees what it has done to her cousin, Georgia. Yet the story ends ambiguously; despite her distaste, she has had to become a migrant herself.

- How does the story evoke the West Indian's attempts to adapt to life in the USA?

- Describe the personality of the narrator, as revealed in her recounting of events.

- What is the effect of the letter with which the story begins?

Shoes for the Dead

Kei Miller was born and grew up in Kingston, Jamaica. He attended the University of the West Indies, where he began his career as a writer. He later studied in England and completed a Ph.D. in English Literature at the University of Glasgow. Since 2006 he has published several books of poetry and fiction which have won him important literary prizes, including the Forward Prize for *The Cartographer Tries to Map a Way to Zion* (2014). This story, 'Shoes for the Dead', is from his first published collection of stories, *Fear of Stones and Other Stories*.

- Explain why the woman – and the entire family of the deceased – is uneasy with the notion of buying shoes for the corpse to wear in the coffin. Is it simply a matter of expense?

- Note the irony of people being afraid to put shoes on the dead while at the same time showing no grief or sorrow at the relative's passing.

- Discuss the attitude and actions of Philip, the undertaker. To what extent are these explained by what happens in the final section of the story?

The Girl Who Can

Ama Ata Aidoo was born in 1942 in Ghana. She studied creative writing at Stanford University in California and she has worked as a lecturer at a number of universities in Ghana, other parts of Africa and the United States. She has published several collections of short fiction.

- In this story the author presents the complex world of the adult through the eyes of the young protagonist. What does she achieve through this?

- Discuss the characters of the grandmother and the mother. What do we learn about the personality of Adjoa?

- In what way or ways is the title significant to the development of the plot?

 p.138

The Pain Tree

Olive Senior was born in Jamaica in 1941. She studied journalism at universities in the UK and Canada. When she returned to Jamaica she worked in a few jobs in her field before joining *The Institute of Jamaica*, as editor of the *Jamaica Journal*. In 1967 she won the Commonwealth Prize for her first collection of stories, *Summer Lightning*. She has also published several collections of poems. Senior now lives in Toronto, Canada, but travels widely all over the world, giving lectures and conducting workshops.

'The Pain Tree' is the title story from her most recent collection. It is a story about a young woman who returns to Jamaica after studying abroad, remembering her life of privilege in the past and the various levels of social class in her youth – as she thinks about her former nursemaid and revisits the now abandoned room in the maid's quarters, where she used to spend time talking to her and pasting pictures on her wall.

- What emotions does this story evoke in the reader? Whom do you identify with more closely, Larissa or the voice that tells the story?

- Why does the narrator get angry and destroy the pictures on the walls? With whom is she angry?

- Why does the narrator pound a nail into the pain tree at the end of the story? What does this tell us about her relationship with her country, with the maid and with her past?

 p.147

Mint Tea

Christine Craig is a Jamaican who has published children's fiction, a range of non-fiction material on feminist and health topics, as well as the poetry and short stories for which she is best known. 'Mint Tea' is the title story of her first volume of short stories. It is centred on the relationship that develops between an uncommunicative and passive young woman and an ageing retired teacher who is increasingly being beset by memories, even as she continues to live an active life. From their differing positions, these two women must come to terms not only with each other, but also with their own past.

- How does the title image become significant in the action of the story?

- What part do social and class differences play in the relationship between the women?

- Discuss the significance of music and singing in the action of the story.

p.156

To Da-Duh, in Memoriam

This autobiographical story by the Caribbean-American novelist Paule Marshall (born in 1929) explores the experience of acknowledging a cultural heritage that is formed from different and irreconcilable parts. The encounter between the nine-year-old city-dweller who lives in America and her West Indian grandmother begins a difficult but necessary relationship. Both of them need to learn how to expand their imagination to understand each other's worlds. Each needs to learn how to love the other if they are to gain a fuller understanding of their mutual culture. The grandmother is forced by her granddaughter to acknowledge the modern world and its technology and ways of life. However, she cannot accept its authority or incorporate it into her world. She confronts the planes, acknowledges their power, and chooses to die. The story is as much about the granddaughter, who also comes to acknowledge that her heritage includes the world of her grandmother's island as well as the world of the city. Marshall's concern with the significance of the past and the need for respecting ancestors is balanced by the delicacy and care with which she evokes the consciousness of her young main character. The story becomes an elegy, lamenting the death of a system of values as much as the death of an individual.

- Identify and discuss one moment in the story when the relationship between granddaughter and grandmother changes.

- What is the effect on the reader of the description of the grandmother's death following the appearance of the planes?

- How does the use of physical description contribute to the unfolding of the story?

p.166

Savi's Trial

Hazel Simmons-McDonald is a St Lucian writer of poetry and fiction, and also a senior academic who recently retired as Principal of the Open Campus of the University of the West Indies.

'Savi's Trial' is about a young lady lawyer who undertakes to defend the father of a young man who comes to engage her services on his behalf. The father is charged with deliberately causing his wife's death in order to end her suffering from the cancer that afflicts her. The story, however, is soon complicated by the young man's amorous interest in the lawyer and by what the father reveals about the young man's sister who supposedly died when they were both babies.

- The reader's interest in the attempted mercy-killing of the old man's wife is quickly superseded by other interests and concerns in the story. What are these?

- Explain what happens in section IV of the story – Savi's conversation with her father. How does this advance the story and pave the way for the final brief section?

- What do you think is meant by the final sentence of the story? Does the 'ordeal', in your opinion, have to do with the trial for mercy-killing, or the relationship between Savi and Gervais – or something else?

Mom Luby and the Social Worker

Kristin Hunter (born 1931 in Philadelphia) began her writing career at age 14 as a columnist for *The Pittsburg Courier*. She has written books for young people and also adult novels. This story, which comes from her first book of short fiction, *Guests in the Promised Land*, has appeared in anthologies such as *The Unforgetting Heart*, a collection of stories by African American writers. In this story, Hunter uses humour and satire as forms of social commentary on the welfare system in the United States.

- How does the author use (a) humour and (b) satire to comment on the welfare system? What is the nature of the irony in the story?

- The social worker represents the bureaucracy of the welfare system. How is that system presented and what are Mom Luby's reactions to it?

- Discuss the character of Mom Luby and Hunter's treatment of this character.

- Discuss the effectiveness of the narrative point of view used by the author in the story.

Berry

From the 1920s until his death in 1967, Langston Hughes was one of the leading African-American writers, using every genre of writing to convey in accessible and memorable images the different facets of the experience of being black in America. Best known as a poet, Hughes published several volumes of short stories, the finest of which was *The Ways of White Folks*, from which this story is taken.

'Berry' is a straightforward narrative that recounts the process by which a black man becomes indispensable to a Home for Crippled Children and is inevitably made the scapegoat when an accident occurs. The story presents racism and stereotyping as lived experience, utilising several perspectives, including that of the black man, whose viewpoint is the only trustworthy one. The ugly assumptions of racism are set off against the authentic affection which this man arouses in the children, whose physical disabilities are the counterpart of the social disability of being black.

- In what sense can this story be said to be about the difference between reality and appearance?

- How does the author prepare us for the climactic event of the accident and the subsequent dismissal of Berry?

- How does the story represent the relationships that white people have with one another?

- What does the author do to establish Berry as morally superior to those who perceive him as naturally inferior to them?

The Two Grandmothers

p.189

Olive Senior was born in Jamaica in 1941. She studied journalism at universities in the UK and Canada. When she returned to Jamaica she worked in a few jobs in her field before joining *The Institute of Jamaica*, as editor of the *Jamaica Journal*. In 1967 she won the Commonwealth Prize for her first collection of stories, *Summer Lightning*. She has also published several collections of poems. Senior now lives in Toronto, Canada, but travels widely all over the world, giving lectures and conducting workshops.

This story from her second collection displays her characteristic sensitivity to the awareness and preoccupations of the young, and her ability to re-create the world as it is seen by them.

- How does the main character's view of her two grandmothers and their different worlds reveal her own increasing preoccupations?

- What are the social issues raised by her changing view of the world?

- How does Senior control our response to the main character and make us change our opinion of her as the story progresses?

Glossary of terms

action Events that take place in the story or that make up the plot. This includes the things that the characters do, and also the things that are done to them. Although there may be other minor plots (or subplots) in a story there is usually only one central action.

anecdote A short, simple, sometimes humorous narration of an incident. Some stories use one or more anecdotes to develop character or to advance the plot.

antagonist The opposite of protagonist (the hero/heroine). The antagonist is usually a character who opposes the protagonist. The conflict between the protagonist and antagonist forms the basis of the plot or the action of the story.

anticlimax A resolution of the plot that is disappointing and unexpected. It can happen where we expect the climax to happen, or sometimes after the climax. An anticlimax is usually considered to reflect weak writing, but sometimes an author may use it deliberately to underscore a particular view of life, for example, as futile or boring.

atmosphere The mood that the author creates through the use of language to describe the setting. Usually the atmosphere leads the reader to develop expectations about the course of events in the story. It is important in establishing the tone of the story.

character Any person who takes part in a story (see pages 201–2).

climax The high point, or the turning point in a story. Usually the part of the story in which the most important event takes place. After the climax the plot is usually resolved. The events leading up to the climax are referred to as the *rising action,* those after the climax are referred to as the *falling action* and lead the reader to the eventual resolution or outcome of the plot.

complication The development of conflict either between characters or between a character and his or her situation. The plot advances through the complication. The reader expects that the conflict that has been introduced will lead to a climax and eventual resolution. Suspense is built up through the complication.

conflict The opposition that the main character or protagonist faces from another character (in this case the antagonist), from the events that take place, from the situations in the story or from the protagonist's own personality or temperament.

crisis The turning point in the story; that is, the climax.

denouement Borrowed from French and translated literally means 'the untying of a knot'. It refers to the conclusion of the plot in which the author presents the resolution or the outcome of the story.

dialogue The words spoken by the characters in the story or their conversations with each other make up the dialogue of a story. Dialogue serves several purposes in a narrative. It can advance the plot to its climax and eventual resolution. It can also reveal the personalities of the characters, thereby helping the reader to form impressions of them.

diction The author's choice and arrangement of words in the narrative. This is an important aspect of style and will determine the effect that the story has on the reader.

didactic When a story or some other literary work is used to teach a lesson or present a moral, it is referred to as being didactic.

distance Used to indicate how far the author or narrator is removed from the events, actions and characters in a narrative. If a narrator is aloof from the events that are presented, he or she is distant.

dramatic irony A situation in a narrative or other literary work in which the author and the reader or audience share knowledge of which a character is unaware.

episode A specific and brief incident that is narrated in its entirety and at once. A story may contain one episode. A story may also contain a series of episodes that are held together by a common setting and character (or characters), and that develop towards one climax and resolution. This kind of story is usually referred to as episodic.

exposition When authors present background information that the reader needs to know in order to follow the events that take place in a story. Sometimes the background information is concerned with events that happened prior to the ongoing ones in the story.

falling action The events that take place after the climax and in which we see the resolution of the plot.

fantasy A kind of narrative in which the events that are presented could not have happened in real life.

fiction A story in which an author narrates events purely from his or her imagination. The plot, action and characters are all invented by the author. Fiction is the opposite of fact.

figurative language An author's use of words or a group of words in a non-factual or non-literal way to describe events, scenes and characters vividly and to convey the main sensations that the thing described evokes. *Metaphors* and *similes* are figures of speech or examples of figurative language.

first-person narration The telling of a story from the point of view of a person directly involved in the action. The narrator is a character and uses 'I' and 'we'. The reader views the events, action and other characters through the narrator's perspective (see page 203).

flashback When the events of a story are interrupted so that the author can present events that happened before, the author is using a technique that is referred to as flashback.

genre A type of literary work or a way of classifying literature. For example, the short story is a type or genre. Other types are poetry, plays, novel, and so on.

hero/heroine The main character or protagonist of a story. The term 'heroine' has been used traditionally to refer to a main character who is female. However, in recent times the term 'hero' has been more widely used to refer to characters of both genders.

imagery An author tries to convey sensations in a story and usually achieves this through the use of words in a non-factual or literary way. An image will appeal directly to one or more of the five senses – sight, sound, touch, taste or smell.

irony When the reader of a story or an audience at a play becomes aware of something that the characters don't know, we have an instance of *dramatic irony*. *Verbal irony* refers to meanings that for the reader or audience go beyond the factual or literal meanings of the words that are actually used by the character. Irony can be used for comic effect, but it is often tinged with bitterness.

magic realism Used to describe a type of fiction in which realistic details are presented in conjunction with fantastic ones.

metaphor A comparison in which one thing is described in terms of another thing, for example, 'he was a lion in battle' (see also 'simile').

motivation Characters act in response to various forces (internal and/or external) in their lives. The things that force characters to act in the ways that they do is referred to as the motivation for their actions.

naturalism Sometimes referred to as extreme realism. The term is used to describe a work in which the author presents a clinical or scientific view of the world. This view holds that it is human nature and the environment in which we live that make us behave in the way that we do.

pace The rate (how quickly or slowly) at which the action progresses. An author can control the pace of a story by varying the length of words, sentences and paragraphs, or by expanding or compressing incidents in the story.

persona The fictional character or the image that that character presents to the reader.

plot The set of events that make up the action (see pages 200–1).

point of view Who is telling the story (see page 203).

protagonist The hero or main character of a story (see pages 201–2).

realism A story which reflects real-life experience. The author presents events, incidents and episodes that might actually happen in the real world.

resolution The working out of the conflict in a story. The resolution takes place during the events after the climax (the falling action) and the conclusion follows.

rising action All the events, incidents and episodes that contribute to the development of the conflict of the story.

satire A work in which a subject, perhaps a particular person or an aspect of human behaviour, is made to look ridiculous. It is presented in such a way as to make the reader feel scornful, derisive, indignant or contemptuous towards it.

setting The place and time in which the action of a story takes place (see page 202).

simile A comparison between two things. The comparison is usually an example of figurative language, but unlike the metaphor the author uses the words 'like' or 'as' to make the comparison more directly, for example, 'he was *like* a lion in battle'.

style The way in which the author uses language as a form of expression (see page 204).

subplot A minor or secondary plot in a story that may involve minor characters and which may also contribute to the complication of the story. The subplot sometimes serves the function of providing contrast or relief from the tension of the main plot.

suspense When the author keeps the reader in a state of uncertainty about the outcome of the action of a story. The feeling of anxiety that the reader experiences is called suspense.

theme The central idea or meaning in a story (see pages 204–5).

tone The author's attitude towards the characters, the setting, the action and subject matter. The tone is revealed through the words that the author uses.

unity The way in which various parts of a work relate to a central organising principle.

Acknowledgements

Every effort has been made to trace all copyright holders, but if any have been inadvertently overlooked the Publishers will be pleased to make the necessary arrangements at the first opportunity. The Publishers would like to thank the following for permission to reproduce copyright material:

p.1 'Raymond's Run' by Toni Cade Bambara, from GORILLA, MY LOVE. Copyright © 1971 by Toni Cade Bambara. Reprinted with the permission of The Permissions Company, Inc., on behalf of Karma B. Smith/Estate of Toni Cade Bambara; **p.8** 'Blackout' from LISTEN THE WIND AND OTHER STORIES by Roger Mais, published by Longman, 1986. Reprinted with permission of Pearson Education Ltd.(ebook & audio rights © The Estate of Roger Mais); **p.12** 'Shabine' by Hazel Simmons-McDonald from SHABINE AND OTHER STORIES. Copyright © Hazel Simmons-McDonald. Reprinted with the kind permission of the author; **p.16** 'Blood Brothers' from DISCOVERIES: SHORT STORIES by John Wickham, published by Longman; **p.20** 'Buried with Science' by John T. Gilmore from BURIED WITH SCIENCE, published by Dido Press, 2003. Reprinted with the kind permission of the author; **p.27** 'Emma' by Carolyn Cole, first published in BREAKING ICE edited by Terry McMillan, published by Penguin Putnam Inc.; **p.38** 'Two Boys Named Basil' by Mark McWatt from SUSPENDED SENTENCES: FICTIONS OF ATONEMENT. Copyright © Mark McWatt. Reprinted with the kind permission of the author; **p.53** 'Victory and the Blight' by Earl Lovelace from A BRIEF CONVERSION AND OTHER STORIES published by Heinemann, 1988. Reprinted with the kind permission of the author; **p.61** 'Child of Darkening Humour' by Noel D. Williams from 22 JAMAICAN SHORT STORIES published by LMH Publishing Limited. Reprinted with permission of LMH Publishing Ltd, Kingston; **p.71** 'The Man of the House' by Frank O'Connor reprinted by permission of Peters Fraser & Dunlop (www.petersfraserdunlop.com) on behalf of the Estate of Frank O'Connor; **p.80** 'The Day the World Almost Came to an End' by Pearl Crayton from FICTION: THE UNIVERSAL ELEMENTS. Published by Litton Educational Publishing Inc.; **p.86** 'It's Cherry Pink and Apple Blossom White' by Barbara Jenkins from SIC TRANSIT WAGON & OTHER STORIES. Published by Peepal Tree Press. Reprinted by permission of the publishers.; **p.93** 'The Boy Who Loved Ice Cream' by Olive Senior from SUMMER LIGHTNING AND OTHER STORIES published by Longman, 1986. Reprinted with permission of Hodder Education; **p.105** 'Uncle Umberto's Slippers' by Mark McWatt from SUSPENDED SENTENCES: FICTIONS OF ATONEMENT. Copyright © Mark McWatt. Reprinted with the kind permission of the author; **p.117** 'The Creek' by Subraj Singh from REBELLE AND OTHER STORIES. Reprinted with the kind permission of the author; **p.122** 'Georgia and Them There United States' by Velma Pollard, from KARL AND OTHER STORIES © Velma Pollard. Reprinted with the kind permission of the author; **p.127** 'Shoes for the Dead' by Kei Miller from FEAR OF STONES AND OTHER STORIES, published by Carcanet. Reprinted with the kind permission of the author;

p.133 'The Girl Who Can' by Ama Ata Aidoo from OPENING SPACES: CONTEMPORARY AFRICAN WOMEN'S WRITING. Published by Heinemann Educational Books, 1999; **p.138** 'The Pain Tree' by Olive Senior from THE PAIN TREE, published by Peepal Tree Press. Reprinted by permission of the publishers; **p.147** 'Mint Tea' by Christine Craig from MINT TEA AND OTHER STORIES, published by Heinemann. Copyright © Christine Craig. Reprinted with permission of Pearson Education Limited; **p.156** 'To Da-duh, in Memoriam' by Paule Marshall from MERLE AND OTHER STORIES. Copyright © 1983 Paule Marshall; **p.166** 'Savi's Trial' by Hazel Simmons-McDonald. Copyright © Hazel Simmons-McDonald. Reprinted with the kind permission of the author; **p.177** 'Mom Luby and The Social Worker' by Kristin Hunter from GUESTS IN THE PROMISED LAND. Reprinted by permission of Don Congdon Associates, Inc. © 1973 by Kristin Hunter; **p.182** 'Berry' from THE WAYS OF WHITE FOLKS by Langston Hughes, copyright © 1934 by Alfred A. Knopf, a division of Penguin Random House LLC, copyright renewed 1962 by Langston Hughes. Used by permission of Alfred A. Knopf, an imprint of the Knopf Doubleday Publishing Group, a division of Penguin Random House LLC. All rights reserved (ebook & audio rights © The Estate of Langston Hughes); **p.189** 'The Two Grandmothers' by Olive Senior, from THE ARRIVAL OF THE SNAKE WOMAN AND OTHER STORIES published by Longman © Olive Senior. Reprinted with the kind permission of the author.